Of
Liberty

ROYAL INSTITUTE OF PHILOSOPHY LECTURE SERIES: 15
SUPPLEMENT TO *PHILOSOPHY* 1983

EDITED BY:

A. Phillips Griffiths

CAMBRIDGE UNIVERSITY PRESS

CAMBRIDGE
LONDON NEW YORK NEW ROCHELLE
MELBOURNE SYDNEY

Published by the Press Syndicate of the University of Cambridge
The Pitt Building, Trumpington Street, Cambridge CB2 IRP
32 East 57th Street, New York, NY 10022, USA
296 Beaconsfield Parade, Middle Park, Melbourne 3206, Australia

Library of Congress catalogue card number: 83–1895

British Library Cataloguing in Publication Data
Of liberty.—(Royal Institute of
Philosophy Lecture series; 15)
1. Liberty
I. Griffiths, A. Phillips   II. Series
323.44′01   JC585
ISBN 0 521 27415 X

Printed in Great Britain by Adlard & Son Ltd, Bartholomew Press, Dorking

Contents

DEDICATION

IN MEMORIAM J. C. REES

Preface

Mill's *On Liberty* was published in 1859. The Royal Institute of Philosophy lectures delivered in 1980–81 were stimulated by a reconsideration of that work. They all surely show that the problems to which Mill addressed himself are still as taxing today as they were then.

In editing this series it has been borne in on me that a conventional introduction to them would not be appropriate. They are so many and relevant cross-currents that to give a conspectus of *Of Liberty* would require a space as large as the main body of the articles: to which the reader no doubt wishes to hurry on.

One of the lectures, entitled 'Liberty and Justice' was given by J. C. Rees of University College, Swansea. Sadly, he died a few weeks later. We have a manuscript, but the author annotated it in his own hand to the effect that it should not be published without considerable revision. That wish must be respected. This volume is dedicated to his memory.

I would thank Professor H. D. Lewis, Mr Renford Bambrough and Dr Stuart Brown for their help during the lecture sessions. I am also grateful to Dr Benjamin Gibbs for contributing a supererogatory addition to the following contents in the form of a spirited reply to Professor Antony Flew's spirited paper.

A. Phillips Griffiths

Liberty and Authority

D. D. RAPHAEL

Everybody supports freedom—even authoritarians, though what they call freedom looks suspiciously like bondage. Rousseau begins *The Social Contract* with a flourish: 'Man is born free, and everywhere he is in chains.' He ends up by trying to persuade us that the chains, the restraints of law and organized society, are necessary for true freedom. He wants us to believe that true freedom, the freedom essential for human existence, is not the happy-go-lucky freedom of Liberty Hall, do as you like, but the straight and narrow path of duty, of conformity to law. The universal popularity of the idea of freedom does not mean that everybody is really agreed about it. Plato, Rousseau, Hegel and his followers—they all talk of a true or genuine freedom, but they oppose this to Liberty Hall, to doing as you please.

Why so? Not because they are killjoys at heart, but because they think Liberty Hall is dangerous. Democratic freedom, says Plato, is very attractive. Doing what you like, of course that is attractive. At first sight, what could be better? But it cannot last, he says. It soon leads to despotism. Complete freedom soon leads to no freedom at all. Why is that? Because complete freedom for all means the absence of order; the absence of law; anarchy, chaos. When Plato says that this leads to despotism, he does not mean that there is some necessary connection between the two. He has given us his reading of history—that is to say, the history that he knew. It is only *Plato's* reading of the history of his time, and his interpretation is coloured by his initial prejudice against democracy. He disliked democracy for two reasons. First, his family background was aristocratic; and secondly, it was under a democratic regime that Plato's teacher Socrates was unjustly condemned to death. So Plato, in his list of political structures, put democracy near the bottom. Not quite *at* the bottom. That would have been too much for his readers to stomach, or indeed for himself. The place at the bottom was reserved for despotism, dictatorship. Everyone was agreed about that. But Plato put democracy next to the bottom. He also took a pessimistic view of history. The Golden Age was in the past. Every day in every way things were getting worse and worse. So Plato viewed political history as a process of decline from the best, aristocracy, to the worst, despotism. Since democracy was next to the bottom on the list, it was bound to lead to despotism, because the next step down was despotism and because change had to be a step down and not a step up.

It was a metaphysical interpretation of history, then, that led Plato to say that the freedom of democracy would be followed by the bondage of despotism. He *purports* to give an argument,[1] namely that an extreme of one kind always leads to an extreme of the opposite kind, a general proposition which implies that extreme freedom leads to extreme bondage. But he cannot have taken this argument seriously. Or if he did, he must have been very short-sighted in his logic. For if it were true that an extreme of one kind always leads to an extreme of the opposite kind, it would also follow that extreme bondage is succeeded by extreme freedom; it would mean not only that democracy leads to dictatorship but also that dictatorship leads to democracy. History would be a shuttling to and fro between these two, instead of being, as Plato believed, a steady process of decline from utopia to despotism.

Plato's metaphysical interpretation of history as a regress is the converse of the equally metaphysical interpretation placed upon history by Hegel and Marx with their idea of dialectical progress. Marx's interpretation especially is something like a mirror-image of Plato's, the same thing backwards. It is not really the same thing, but sufficiently alike for the comparison to be striking. Marx does not begin with despotism. He begins with 'primitive communism', because he believed, on the evidence of a very little anthropology, that primitive societies have no private property. The *second* stage in the history of society, according to Marx, is one of slavery under a despot. Just why there should be this 'fall' from a primitive paradise to the utmost degradation is left rather obscure. But from the second stage onwards we have Plato's history in reverse. For Plato, the history of society declined from the perfect or 'true' freedom of aristocracy, through timocracy, oligarchy, and democracy, to the perfect slavery of despotism. For Marx, it progressed from the slavery of despotism, through feudalism, capitalism, and socialism, to the perfect freedom of paradise regained in communism once more. At each stage there is a weakening of the bonds of the masses, an increase in relative freedom.

Metaphysical interpretations of history are all very fine, but they rub up against the facts. It is just not true that despotism or tyranny in ancient Greece always followed democracy. As a *generalization*, though by no means a universal rule, it would be more true to say that despotism tended to give way to democracy. Marx's theory of the history of society is more impressive, but it too does not fit the facts very well. His view of primitive society was based on insufficient evidence. The suggestion that universal primitive communism was followed by universal slavery is based on no evidence at all. And as for the later part of his picture, socialist revolutions have occurred in peasant rather than in capitalist societies.

[1] *Republic*, 563A–564A.

The mirror-image resemblance between Marx's theory of history and Plato's does not of course mean that Marx resembled Plato in thinking that democratic freedom is dangerous. On the contrary, Marx regards freedom and democracy as essential features of his ideal communistic society. Yet you do not have to share the aristocratic politics of Plato in order to think that freedom can be dangerous. Some years ago Professor Charles and Mrs Winifred Whiteley of Birmingham University published a little book in which they discussed various aspects of our new permissive society. They were far from being altogether critical, and on the whole they regarded the gains of the permissive society as outweighing the losses. But they did find some losses and dangers, and in one place they produced an interesting variant of Plato's view about the dangers of freedom—though they were, I think, unconscious of its resemblance to Plato's view and they were certainly anti-Platonic in their general political and social ideas. They said that people who are easy-going are easily manipulated by propaganda, and that you need to have firm moral convictions in order to stand up to dictators. As evidence they cited the Jehovah's Witnesses in Nazi Germany, who stood out as strongly as anyone against Hitler's propaganda.[2] The Whiteleys would of course have agreed that firm moral convictions can include a firm conviction of the value of freedom. The danger that they saw does not come from a belief in freedom or from the practice of tolerance based on such a belief, but from the kind of Liberty Hall that rests on no firm convictions at all. All the same, their argument strikes me as shaky. The Jehovah's Witnesses were impervious to Nazi propaganda because they were already imbued with the propaganda of their own mental dictator, Judge Rutherford. We surely want people to have their minds *open* to ideas different from those which they have already accepted.

The thinker who gives us the most vivid picture of Liberty Hall and its dangers is Thomas Hobbes. Hobbes writes of a state of nature in which men are free and equal. Far from its being a state of perfect bliss, as in a Marxist utopia, or even imperfect bliss, as in Plato's idea of democracy, it is a veritable hell. Hobbes's state of nature is an imaginary picture of what life would be like in the absence of organized society. It is not meant as a historical account of primitive man but as a hypothesis of how any group of men would behave were it not for the restraints of law and government. Hobbes takes it for granted that most people are predominantly selfish. They are chiefly out for themselves. This would not matter if a man lived alone. Nobody else would be affected by his selfishness. But if people come into contact with each other, selfishness means that somebody is going to get hurt. For if the supply of desirable things is limited (as it usually is), and if two or more selfish people want a desirable

[2] C. H. and Winifred M. Whiteley, *The Permissive Morality* (Methuen 1964), 94.

thing, there is going to be competition and conflict between them. In the ordinary way one expects considerations of ethics and the rule of law to control the conflict. But if there is no rule of law, Hobbes suggests, ethics will go by the board, there will be general suspicion and distrust, and from time to time there will be punch-ups and worse. The state of nature, says Hobbes, is a state of war. He does not mean that in a state of nature men will be for ever fighting each other. Remember that not so very long ago people talked of a 'cold war' between the Western powers and the Soviet Union. There was no actual fighting, but there was a continual danger of it, and meanwhile there was mutual suspicion and distrust.

Hobbes himself tells us to look, for evidence, at the international scene. States, he says, because of their independence (i.e. their freedom from legal restraint), are in the 'posture of gladiators'. If we doubt whether the same thing would apply to individuals, Hobbes points out to us that, even in an organized society with laws and police, we lock our doors when we go to bed, and in some places we do not venture out alone. This shows the distrust and insecurity which we feel even in organized society. How much worse would it be if there were no system of law, no police force, no government? In a state of nature, says Hobbes, there would be 'continual fear, and danger of violent death; and the life of man, solitary, poor, nasty, brutish, and short'.

So Hobbes gives a pretty bleak interpretation of the dictum that 'man is free by nature'. Complete freedom contradicts itself unless men have nothing to do with each other. To be free is to be able to do as you like. But if you do as you like at all times with no thought of your neighbours, you are likely to prevent them from doing as they like. In Hobbes's state of nature every man has complete freedom in that he may do whatever he likes, unrestrained by law. But there is also a sense in which every man has very little freedom in the state of nature; for if you have to go in continual fear of your neighbours, if your wishes are always liable to be frustrated by the acts and the plots of other men, and in particular if you are always in danger of death, the last thing you want, then you have very little freedom, you have very little real opportunity to do as you like. Complete freedom for all means little effective freedom for anyone.

Obviously, then, freedom must be restrained if it is to be effective. What we should aim at is a maximum amount of freedom that is compatible with similar freedom for other people. This is one of the primary purposes of law. The law prohibits us from doing things which we might want to do, in order that we should not prevent other people from doing what they want to do. We do not get a maximum of effective freedom if people are left to do just as they like. Supporters of anarchism fondly suppose that this is the best way, and that if people are not controlled by law they will co-operate out of brotherly love. It does not happen. No doubt Hobbes exaggerated when he depicted most people as predominantly selfish, but selfishness is prominent enough in human nature to rule out the rosy picture of the anarchists. We must have some control.

On the other hand it will not do to follow Hobbes and have an extreme degree of control by law and government. That will prevent people from encroaching on freedom, but it leaves so little freedom that one might as well be in prison. The aim is a *maximum* of freedom for all. So the extent of legal authority should be kept to the *minimum* that is needed for the protection of liberty. This is the principle of Liberal political philosophy, at least of old-style Liberalism, which confined itself to the one value of liberty.

It is all very well to say that the state should restrict the control of freedom so as to allow the maximum amount of freedom for all. As a principle this sounds fine, but it is so general that it gives no guidance for practice. Is it possible to be more specific?

John Stuart Mill tried to be more specific in his essay *On Liberty*. He tried to draw a line between the proper scope of authority and that of liberty. As a matter of fact, when Mill talked of the scope of authority, he was not thinking simply of the law and the state. He was thinking of social pressure as well. It is difficult enough to suggest a practicable principle for limiting the authority of law, which consists for the most part of a definite set of rules. It is really impossible to suggest a principle for limiting the exercise of social pressure, which is manifested not only in action but also in words, looks, tone of voice, cast of countenance, all sorts of little things often not deliberate at all. Still, let us look at Mill's principle as if it were a proposal for the limits of law. It has been used like that in recent controversy about the scope of the criminal law.

Mill argues that society is entitled to limit a man's freedom in order to prevent him from doing harm to others. If he is going to harm himself, that is his own business, not the business of society. Furthermore, when it comes to control by *law*, Mill makes an additional specification. The law should restrict a man only if he is violating a definite obligation or if his action will harm the definite rights of definite individuals. General harm to society at large, according to Mill, is not a fit subject for legal control, though it can be brought under the control of moral opinion.

The objection has often been made that Mill is unrealistic in drawing a distinction between actions that affect oneself only and actions that affect others. All actions have *some* effect on other people, if only because an effect on oneself will mean a difference in one's future actions that affect other people. For instance, suppose a man is a drunkard. Of course, if he has a wife and family, his action of spending all his money on drink and then getting tight is going to affect them right away. They will not have any money for food or clothing, and they may well have to put up with abuse and even blows from the drunkard. But suppose he has no dependants. Then he harms no one but himself. True for the moment,

5

but not for the future. For if he has no money tomorrow through having spent it all today, or if he ruins his health and cannot work next year, he will go begging of his friends or asking help from a public authority or charitable society, and he will be using resources that could have been spent on more deserving causes.

Mill tries to guard against this objection with his limitation of the principle as applied to the law. He agrees that it is proper to try to get the drunkard to mend his ways by expressing disapproval of him. But it is not proper, Mill says, to control his actions by *law* unless we can see that he is going to violate definite obligations or harm the rights of specified individuals. If the impoverished drunkard steals money to which somebody else has a right, or if he gets drunk in a pub and starts hitting people on the nose, he should be restrained by law; he is violating the rights of definite individuals. But if you say simply that his private binges are going to make him a burden to society one day, that is not enough to justify laws restricting his access to drink. What he does is bad, bad for himself certainly, and probably bad for society in the future. But the harm that he does to himself is his own look-out, and the harm that he may do in an indirect way to society generally does not, in Mill's opinion, outweigh the value of freedom, of leaving people to do as they please. Here it is a question of weighing values against each other, and Mill urges us to consider freedom more important than the prevention of some unspecified harm to society.

Put like that the argument sounds persuasive. Here you have this one individual who chooses to behave in a way that most people would deplore. Well, he *chooses* it. Surely he is entitled to choose what kind of life he is going to live. If it harms him, that is his business. It is better that people should choose for themselves, even if they choose badly, than that they should have their lives run for them by the orders of authority. Is not this the expression of democratic faith? Mill himself uses the argument in that way when he writes about democracy in his essay on *Representative Government*. A man who chooses for himself, even if he chooses badly, acts like a man. One who has his life run for him by authority acts like a sheep. The foolish man may well do harm to society as well as to himself, but if it is just a general risk to society vaguely, if we cannot point to specific harm to the rights of particular individuals, it is not such a great evil and it should be tolerated for the sake of the greater good of freedom.

Yes, it sounds a persuasive case when put like that; the freedom of the isolated individual set against a vague possibility of harm to society generally. But let us change the example and look at things that are more obvious to us than they were to John Stuart Mill a hundred years ago. What about the owner of a factory the furnaces of which belch sulphurous fumes into the atmosphere? What about all the car drivers who pump carbon monoxide into the air of our cities? What about the manufacturers who pour millions of gallons of poisonous effluent into rivers and estuaries? We do not have to think only of private individuals or private companies. What about electricity power stations, publicly owned, that pour smoke into the atmosphere? They keep it pretty clean, as compared, say, with the fumes from the exhaust of a diesel engine that is not well maintained; but still it carries quite a lot of acid into the atmosphere and eventually affects buildings if not the lungs of human beings. What about those local authorities that discharge inadequately treated sewage into rivers or coastal waters? Only rarely can you say of such nuisances that they damage definite rights of specified individuals. Yet there is no doubt that these nuisances do cause harm to society generally. Can we shrug off this harm on the ground that it is vague, that we cannot specify the individuals who will suffer from a particular nuisance? Plainly not.

Perhaps someone will say that the control of these nuisances does not diminish liberty. I think it does. If pollution is to be reduced, there has to be a lot of expensive research; and when the research has come up with recommendations, these usually require expensive new equipment to be added to the factory, motor car, or sewage works. The manufacturer or the car owner who is required to pay for the equipment, and indirectly for the research, thereby has less money to spend on other things. To that extent he is less free to do as he likes. If I have to pay £100 for a device that will reduce the amount of carbon monoxide emitted by my motor car, then I have £100 less to spend as I would choose. The same thing applies not only to the private factory owner but also to the electricity power station and the local authority sewage works. If the electricity board is required to install expensive machinery in its power stations, in order to purify the smoke that comes out of its chimneys, it finds the cost by raising the price of electricity, which means that consumers, members of the public, pay more and so have less money to spend as they please. Similarly the local authority that is required to install a more elaborate sewage plant has to increase the rates in order to pay for it; and if members of the general public have to pay higher rates, they have that much less money to spend as they please.

Oh well, you may say, that is a minor decrease of liberty. A man who can afford to run a car is not badly off. He can have and do quite a lot of the things that he would like. To make him pay another £100 is a small thing. Again, the factory owner is usually a rich man. He is not going to be deprived much of things that he would like to do when he is made to fork out a few hundred thousands for new equipment. Anyway he will get it back by increasing the price of his products. It is just the same as with the electricity board and the local authority. It is the public who pay in the end. And the public have no business to complain. For the legal control serves *their* interest. It is for their sake, and for the sake of their children's children, that they are made to pay up for cleaner air and water.

7

What they lose on the swings they more than gain on the roundabouts. It is better to have clean air and water than to have a little more money to spend on joy-riding or drink.

This reply is irrelevant. It says in the first place that the amount of liberty curtailed is small, and secondly that the loss of liberty is outweighed by the benefit produced. Nobody will deny these two points, but they do not affect the criticism that Mill's principle is unacceptable. Mill does not say that his principle gives the criterion for a *major* interference with liberty. He says it is the criterion for *any* interference with liberty. And again, Mill does not say that liberty may be curtailed for the sake of general benefit to society provided that the social benefit is great enough to outweigh the loss of liberty. He says that general benefit can *never* outweigh a loss of liberty.

Otherwise one could apply the same considerations to Mill's drunkard. One could say that to prevent him from getting drunk is not a large curtailment of his liberty. He is still allowed to drink a moderate amount of alcohol, and after that he can take to lemonade. No doubt he likes whisky better, but he can have some whisky, and lemonade is not so bad. Is his case any different from that of the motorist who is made to stump up £100 and who therefore has to limit his joy-riding a little? He can still do a fair amount of motoring, and after that he can walk. No doubt he prefers to drive, but walking is quite pleasant too. Then again, one can say that the restrictions on the would-be drunkard are outweighed by the benefit that he receives, in health and in pocket, and by the benefit to society, which will not have to support him in his poverty next year.

Mill's principle says quite flatly that liberty may not be curtailed simply in order to prevent harm to society. Yet we should all agree that legislation to prevent pollution is justified for that reason. Such legislation is undoubtedly a curtailment of liberty. Nobody asks us: do you prefer to spend some of your money on paying for cleaner air rather than on more beer and cigarettes? After all, we cannot be at all confident that the majority of people would say yes. Our legislators and, one hopes, the knowledgeable section of the populace, just take it for granted that it is justifiable to pass the legislation for the sake of the public welfare.

So far as Mill's principle is concerned, the point is that freedom is curtailed even though the bad effects of freedom cannot be pinned down as infringing specific rights of specific individuals. The bad effects are harm to society generally. We cannot say who exactly will become ill or have his life shortened as the result of the polluted air. But we know that this is likely to happen to some people some time.

Mill does in fact specify two alternative ways in which a harmful action can come within his principle. Self-regarding action may be restricted, he says, either if it infringes the rights of definite individuals or if it disables the agent from performing a definite public duty that he has. Mill explains the second of these as follows. 'No person ought to be punished simply for being drunk; but a soldier or a policeman should be punished for being drunk on duty.'[3] The point is that the soldier and the policeman will not be able to carry out the duties of their office if they are drunk at the time. This second alternative would not apply to most of the examples I have given. A motorist has a duty to the public to drive with care. Like the policeman and the soldier, he disables himself from carrying out that duty if he drives when drunk. But he does not disable himself by using a vehicle that pollutes the atmosphere. One can hardly say that the private factory owner has any specific duties to the public in his role as manufacturer, unless it be not to deceive the public about the character of the goods he produces. At any rate he does not disable himself from any public duty by having furnaces that pollute the atmosphere. Nor does the electricity board. The board does have a public duty to supply electricity. The smoke from its power stations does not disable the board from carrying out its duty. On the contrary, the board may say, the burning of the furnaces, with the consequent smoke, enables the board to carry out its duty. The local authority and its sewage works can be distinguished from the others. The local authority does have a duty to dispose of sewage without danger to health, and so one can say that if its treatment of the sewage fails to avoid pollution of the local river or coastal waters, the authority is causing danger to health and so violating its duty.

If legislation is passed, requiring motorists, factory owners, and electricity boards to fit anti-pollution devices, *then* all these people will have a definite duty to the public not to pollute the atmosphere. They will have a legal duty because the law requires this of them. But before the law is passed, when there is simply debate on whether the nuisance is great enough to justify legislation, we cannot say that the polluters already have a duty in the sense that Mill gives to the term.

Still, we can modify Mill's principle, taking account of something else that he says in the context. 'Whenever', he says, 'there is a definite damage, or a definite risk of damage, either to an individual or to the public, the case is taken out of the province of liberty, and placed in that of morality or law.'[4] That is a wider formulation, and a more sensible one. There is certainly definite *risk* of damage to the public when motor cars or factory chimneys pollute the atmosphere. The only trouble now is whether this wider formulation can distinguish these cases from that of the drunkard. If a man habitually gets drunk, is there not a definite *risk* of damage to the public, since he is very likely to become a burden on public resources in due course, either through ill-health or through

[3] *On Liberty*, Ch. 4: Everyman edition of J. S. Mill, *Utilitarianism*, etc., 138; Fontana edition, 213.

[4] Ibid.

poverty? Perhaps one might say that the risk is not *definite*, as it is with pollution of the atmosphere. I am not sure that one can draw a firm distinction, but at any rate we shall all agree that it is justifiable to make pollution the subject of legal control.

Mill talks about the freedom of individuals, and I have asked how his principle applies to features of modern technology. His principle looks rather shaky there, if interpreted strictly, but this is *not* because nineteenth-century Liberalism was in favour of economic freedom, *laissez faire*, with no government control of commerce and industry. Some modern legislation that restricts economic freedom would be allowed by Mill's principle. Take, for instance, the requirement that an employer who lays off workpeople must provide them with redundancy payments. That is quite a considerable interference with the freedom of employers, if you contrast it with the old system of allowing the boss to 'hire and fire' just as he pleased. Yet Mill's principle permits this restriction of freedom. For the laying-off of workers does adversely affect the definite rights of definite persons. When Mill speaks of rights he means moral as well as legal rights. He talks of 'certain interests, which, either by express legal provision or by tacit understanding, ought to be considered as rights'.[5] Now the tacit understanding of what ought to be considered as rights is not a static thing. Present-day ideas of human rights include the right to work. Everyone today would agree that unemployment is among the major evils both for society and for the individual. A man who is out of work has lost a vital interest. It is therefore perfectly proper to say that the laying-off of workers does definite harm to the rights of definite individuals. So it is quite justifiable, on Mill's principle, to limit the freedom of employers to dismiss workers.

What about the freedom of workers? Can we justify restrictions on the freedom of workers to strike? If a particular strike is in breach of a contract between employer and worker, then it violates a distinct right of a distinct individual and so comes within the scope of Mill's principle on that ground. What if a strike is not a breach of contract? There is still no doubt that the interests of the employer are harmed, but one can doubt whether his *rights* are violated. The damage to his interests is not a breach of a *legal* right, but one might well say, in terms of Mill's philosophy, that since the interests are vital interests they ought to be considered as moral rights. However that may be, there is certainly a definite risk of damage to the public, much more definite, in fact, than the risk of damage that pollution may cause. So if we are going to adopt the wider interpretation of Mill's principle that will cover legislation against pollution, we must undoubtedly agree that the principle also permits legal restrictions on the right to strike.

So far I have been talking about the question whether Mill can make a real distinction between actions that should be left free because they do not

[5] Ch. 4: Everyman, 132; Fontana, 205.

harm other people and those that may be controlled because of their adverse effects on others. I want now to turn to a different question concerning Mill's principle. Assuming that a distinction can properly be made between actions that affect oneself alone and those that affect other people also, can we agree with Mill that the law should have nothing to do with the first class of actions, those that affect the agent alone? Can we agree that even if a man does himself harm, this is entirely a matter for him; society should not intervene?

This question has come up in recent discussion of actual and possible changes in the law relating to certain matters of sexual conduct. It all began with the Wolfenden Committee, which, in 1957, considered the law in relation to homosexuality and prostitution. The Committee recommended, among other things, that homosexual practices between consenting adults in private should no longer be a criminal offence. (At the time any homosexual practice between males was a criminal offence, but not between females.) The recommendation was not immediately accepted, but some years later the law (in England, and eventually also in Scotland) was changed in the way that the Committee proposed. In justifying this recommendation the Committee said that the function of the criminal law in regard to sexual matters was to preserve public order and decency, to protect citizens from what is offensive or injurious, and to prevent exploitation and corruption, especially of the young. The Committee went on to say, however, that there is 'a realm of private morality and immorality which is . . . not the law's business'. In proposing a relaxation of the law, the Committee restricted itself to *private* behaviour between consenting *adults*, because that does not offend public order and decency nor does it lead to any danger of corrupting the young. The Committee was ready to accept the view that all homosexual behaviour was immoral, or at least to recognize that many people took that view; and similarly it was ready to accept the view that prostitution was immoral. But, it argued, the mere fact that something is immoral is not sufficient reason for making it a criminal offence. *Private* immorality is not the law's business.

The distinction drawn by the Wolfenden Committee has been compared by Professor H. L. A. Hart[6] with Mill's distinction between self-regarding and other-regarding action. Mill says that if a man gets drunk in private, you may disapprove of his conduct but you are not entitled to prohibit it by law if it does not harm other people.

The view of the Wolfenden Committee has been challenged, notably by Lord Devlin,[7] who has argued that 'the suppression of vice' *is* the

[6] H. L. A. Hart, *Law, Liberty, and Morality* (Oxford University Press 1963), 4, 14–15.

[7] Patrick Devlin, *The Enforcement of Morals* (Oxford University Press 1965), especially Ch. 1, originally published as a separate lecture in 1959. For the quotation, see p. 13.

law's business. Professor Hart,[8] who sympathizes with Mill and the Wolfenden Committee, has compared the position of Lord Devlin with that of Sir James Fitzjames Stephen, a notable contemporary critic of Mill. Stephen said that it was the business of the criminal law to be 'a persecution of the grosser forms of vice', and in the context of Professor Hart's discussion we are given the impression that Stephen, like Lord Devlin, was thinking of sexual immorality and believed that it should be subject to the criminal law quite apart from social effects.

In this modern discussion there has been some misunderstanding. In the first place, the position of the Wolfenden Committee is certainly not that of Mill. Mill would never talk of 'private morality and immorality'. In Mill's view conduct comes within the sphere of morality only if it helps or harms other people. Mill thought there was no such thing as a duty to oneself. A man might do himself harm, but that did not make his conduct immoral.

Secondly, the difference between the theoretical position of the Wolfenden Committee and that of Lord Devlin is not as great as appears at first sight. For Lord Devlin argues that the law must protect morality because morality is essential for the preservation of society. That is to say, he takes a utilitarian view of the value of morality and of the purpose of the criminal law. In other words, he thinks that all morality is 'public' morality because its *raison d'être* is the maintenance of society. This being so, when Lord Devlin disagrees with the Wolfenden dictum that there is a realm of private morality which is not the law's business, his disagreement is not over the question whether private morality should be left alone by the law, but over the question whether there is any such thing as private morality as distinguished from public.

Thirdly, when Sir James Fitzjames Stephen wrote that 'criminal law is in the nature of a persecution of the grosser forms of vice', he was not referring to sexual immorality. The quotation comes from a paragraph in which he discussed 'the punishment of common crimes, the gross forms of force and fraud'.[9] Stephen did think, in opposition to Mill, that it is proper to restrain sexual (and other) immorality by the pressure of public opinion, but he considered that the criminal law is usually not a suitable method for dealing with 'vice in general', because the criminal law is a 'rough engine'.[10] Furthermore, in the paragraph where Stephen described the criminal law as a persecution of gross vice, he drew a distinction between *justifying* punishment—on Mill's principles—and recognizing the *fact* that criminal acts are forbidden and punished not only to protect society but also to gratify natural feelings of detestation. The flamboyant

[8] *Law, Liberty, and Morality*, 16.

[9] James Fitzjames Stephen, *Liberty, Equality, Fraternity* (1873), Ch. 4; R. J. White (Cambridge University Press 1967), 152.

[10] Ibid., 140–141, 151.

phrase about persecution refers to the alleged fact, not to the justification. That is to say, Stephen used the phrase to indicate that the criminal law *in practice* follows a retributive and not just a utilitarian outlook.

It seems to me that if we want to relate Mill's principle to the use of the criminal law regarding sexual behaviour, we should look again at his distinction between definite harm (especially to specific individuals) on the one hand and the more vague possibility of general social harm on the other. People who approve of the relaxation in the law about homosexual behaviour are nearly all people who think there is nothing wrong with such behaviour; they are not people who think it is immoral but a 'private' form of immorality. People who are against such relaxation are often (I do not say always) people who are afraid that the permitting of this form of homosexual behaviour will still tend to have an influence on minors and on the possible corruption of minors, which everyone agrees is a bad thing. In other words, the difference of opinion is mainly about matters of fact, whether or not the toleration of one practice will lead to an increase of another practice, the second one being admittedly harmful. The dispute is about utility and disutility. The soft-liners will say, as Mill might well have said, that the dangers of example are so slight and indirect that they are outweighed by the importance of giving some measure of freedom to a formerly persecuted minority group. The hard-liners will say that there is a *definite* risk of social harm, and harm to young people, for whom society should have a special concern.

A more apt analogy to Mill's example of the man who gets drunk in private would be a person who reads pornography in private. Some people will deplore that activity, others will say there is nothing wrong with it. But nobody would want to make it a criminal offence. The Williams Committee on Obscenity has recommended that pornographic material be prohibited if its production has involved the exploitation of the young or actual physical harm to any person. The concern here is of course to prevent such exploitation or harm. Otherwise the Committee has confined its recommendations to restricting the sale or display of the relatively nasty kind of stuff. People like Lord Longford and Mrs Mary Whitehouse want the restrictions to apply to a wider range of pornographic material, but they too are worried about public availability and not about private consumption. They want to drive pornography off the public places, shop windows, the theatre, the cinema, just as the Wolfenden Committee wanted to drive prostitution off the streets. In particular they do not want it thrust before the eyes of the young. They do not for a moment suggest that an adult who chooses to buy a pornographic book should be prevented by law from doing so.

The sexual behaviour that people worry about does not concern isolated individuals. Society has to think very carefully about the regulation of sexual behaviour because it can produce babies, because it can lead to pregnant girls being left in the lurch, because it can lead youngsters of either sex into psychological fixes or venereal disease. Proposals to amend the law, whether about homosexual behaviour or about abortion, have to be backed by argument to show that the changes will benefit individuals and will not harm society. This is all quite different from Mill's argument about conduct that concerns oneself alone.

There are other kinds of conduct that are more relevant to this aspect of Mill's principle. Mill is urging that the law should not be paternalistic. People should be allowed to choose for themselves, and if they choose foolishly they must still be allowed to do so. He took the example of drink. What about the example of drugs? Similar in a way, but more serious because it is so much easier to become hooked on drugs than to become an alcoholic. Are we ready to say that the dangers of drug addiction are outweighed by the value of freedom, of allowing people to choose for themselves? Would you be prepared to see LSD and heroin as easily available as cigarettes and whisky, knowing that this is bound to mean the destruction of many young lives? For that matter, suppose tobacco had just been discovered, and suppose we knew both that it is addictive and that it can cause lung cancer; would you think it right to allow it to be placed freely on the market without any legal restrictions? I would not, and I would certainly not want to see any relaxation of the law on drugs. This much paternalism I gladly hand over to the criminal law.

Let us remember too that there are other ways in which the law is paternalistic. The law requires that all children be sent to school. Well, it may be said, they are *children* and need a paternalistic attitude. Mill himself says that his proposals are for adults, not children. But the law requires *parents* to send their children to school. If you just left it to the initiative of parents, many children would not be educated. In this instance, the restriction on freedom can be justified in the name of freedom itself. Education is a liberator. It develops our potentialities and extends our power of choice and our range of enjoyment. Many of us would not get this if the law did not take a paternalistic attitude to us and to our parents.

Although I have criticized Mill's principle for determining the boundary between liberty and authority, I also want to commend it. As we have seen, Mill's principle does not provide a universal criterion for judging the proper limits of liberty. No single principle can do that. The issues of social life are too complex to allow all conflicts of a particular type to be settled by a single neat principle. Nevertheless it should be recognized, first, that no one has done better than Mill in putting forward a suggested criterion for the limits of liberty and authority, and secondly, that Mill's principle, despite its failings, is still a useful one. If you say that no principle applies, that every case must be decided intuitively on its merits, you have no ground at all on which to argue with those whose intuitions differ from yours. Mill's principle can apply to the great majority of instances, and it is undoubtedly helpful to use it as an initial challenge to any proposed restriction of liberty. Can the proposed restriction pass Mill's test? If not, then it must make out a special case for itself. That is much less of a safeguard than Mill hoped to provide, but it is not negligible.

I have said nothing about Mill's case for freedom of expression, which he evidently thought should be entirely unlimited. His argument on this topic seems to me to be far more dubious. He concentrates on questions of truth and falsity, when censorship has usually been concerned rather with questions of harm. The Williams Committee, in dealing with one of the most obvious candidates for potential censorship, rightly dismisses Mill's arguments in Chapter II of the essay *On Liberty* and utilizes instead his general criterion for limits on freedom of action. That criterion, the prevention of harm to other people, despite its weaknesses as a universal principle, maintains its position as the strongest bastion of liberty that any thinker has given us.

Individual Liberty

J. P. DAY

The philosophical problems of liberty may be classified as those of definition, of justification and of distribution. They are so complex that there is a danger of being unable to see the wood for the trees. It may be helpful, therefore, to provide an aerial photograph of a large part of the wood, namely, the liberty of *individual persons*. But it is, of course, a photograph taken from an individual point of view, as Leibniz would have put it.

1. The Problem of Definition

The chief questions here are those of *the subjects* of liberty and of *the truth-conditions* of liberty.

The subjects of the predicate 'free' are *events* involving *things*, *actions* of persons, and *persons*. Thus, we speak of the degrees of freedom of movement of bodies, of free contracts, of free men, and of free churches. The last two illustrate the distinction between *individual liberty* and *collective liberty*. In this lecture I shall discuss only the former. The significance of attributing freedom to events involving things will appear shortly. But the important subjects of liberty are individual persons and classes of persons.

Different answers are given to the question, When is an individual person, A, truly said to be unfree to do X? According to *the positive or intrapersonal concept of liberty*, A is unfree to do X if A is 'a slave to his passions', i.e. is prevented from doing X by some emotion or desire; e.g. A is unfree to work effectively because A is made unable to do so by his addiction to alcohol.

The creator of the positive concept of individual liberty was Plato, who modelled it on his positive concept of collective liberty. That is, he maintained that the good or free person is isomorphic with the good or free state, in that in both the best part keeps the worst part in subjection. It is, therefore, an essentially political concept. Other protagonists of positive liberty are Spinoza, Rousseau, Kant and Hegel.[1] Of these Spinoza is

[1] See Plato, *Republic* (c. 360 BC); B. de Spinoza, *Ethics* and *Political Treatise* (1677); J. J. Rousseau, *Social Contract* (1762); I. Kant, *Foundations of the Metaphysics of Morals* (1785); G. W. F. Hegel, *Philosophy of Right* (1821) and *Lectures on Philosophy of History* (2nd edn, 1840); I. Berlin, 'Two Concepts of Liberty', in *Four Essays on Liberty* (London: Oxford University Press 1969). Kant uses the expression 'a positive concept of freedom'.

especially interesting since he offers a programme of emancipation from slavery to the passions, which he calls 'human bondage', that anticipates interestingly modern psycho-therapeutic techniques.[2] Some contemporary philosophers also favour this concept of liberty.[3]

Nevertheless, this answer to the question of the truth-conditions of liberty is false. For liberty is *a moral right*, and A can possess a right only against some other person, B, and not against A or part of A. (See section 2.) Liberty is therefore an interpersonal concept and not an intrapersonal one.

According to *the negative or interpersonal concept of liberty*, A is unfree to do X if A is restrained from doing X by B. The name 'negative liberty' was coined by Bentham to indicate that liberty means *the absence of coercion*.[4] B coerces A if B *restrains* A from doing X or if B *compels* A not to do X. (Since these are equivalent, we do not need both 'restrains' and 'compels'.)

B restrains A from doing X if and only if B *makes A unable* to do X. There is a difficulty here, since persons differ in their abilities. It is met by employing the concept of *objective (intersubjective) human possibility* rather than that of subjective human possibility. For example, B is deemed to make A unfree to move if B binds A in a way that would make *the average man* unable to move.

B makes A unfree to do X if and only if B makes A unable to do X with *the intention* of making A unable to do X. For example, if B locks A in a room unintentionally, B makes A unable to leave the room, but not unfree to do so. The reasons for this are that all coercive acts are violations of the moral right to liberty; that all violations of a moral right are morally right or wrong acts; and that all morally right or wrong acts are intentional acts. A violation of a moral right is morally right if and only if the moral obligation to respect the right is overborne by some stronger moral obligation.

Some think that 'free' is *univocal*, so that in the above positive and negative accounts of the truth-conditions of unfreedom 'if' should be replaced by 'if and only if'. But others think that 'free' is *equivocal*, so that the above accounts can stand. Among these are those who think that there are more than two concepts of liberty. Oppenheim has recently distinguished five.[5] But one main thesis of this lecture is that 'free' is univocal and that the negative concept is the only concept of liberty.

[2] See S. Hampshire, *Spinoza* (Harmondsworth: Penguin Books 1951), esp. Ch. 4.

[3] See, e.g., L. H. Crocker, *Positive Liberty* (The Hague: Nighoff 1980); C. Taylor, 'What's Wrong with Negative Liberty', in *The Idea of Freedom*, A. Ryan (ed.) (Oxford: University Press 1979).

[4] See D. G. Long, *Bentham on Liberty* (Toronto: University Press 1977), 54.

[5] F. E. Oppenheim, 'Five Concepts of Liberty', prepared for the European Consortium for Political Research Workshop on Liberty (London: Wiley, 1980).

The creator of the negative concept of individual liberty was Hobbes, who formed it by analogy with the concept of freely moving bodies. It is an essentially physical concept, and its introduction was causally connected with the then rapidly rising science of dynamics. Hobbes' other great achievement in this field was to dissolve *the* (so-called) *problem of free will* by showing that an action can be both negatively free and also determined by law: that negatively free human actions can be explained and predicted by the laws of the social sciences in substantially the same way as the falls of the stones which Galileo dropped can be explained and predicted by his law of falling bodies. With some qualifications, Locke, Hume, Bentham and Mill accept both Hobbes' concept of liberty and his view of the free will question. Respecting the latter, they share Hume's opinion that 'the whole controversy has . . . turned merely upon words'.[6]

Consider now the values that can be taken by the variables A and B in the above negative account of the truth-conditions of unfreedom. The most important value of B is a sovereign, *Rex* (R), a political authority; when the corresponding value of A is a citizen (C). The species of liberty involved here is *political liberty*. There is also non-political liberty, because coercion is also exercised by, e.g., parents and teachers on children. Again, C_1 may make C_2 unfree by kidnapping him, and it is one of R's duties to deter or prevent such violations of liberty by his subjects. Mill considered 'the coercion of public opinion', i.e. *social liberty*, to be as serious a matter as political coercion; but he lacked our sad experience of how coercive governments can be.[7] If the state should wither away, political liberty would cease to be the most important species of liberty. At present, however, it is so; just as political justice is the most important sort of justice, and political punishment is the most important sort of punishment.[8]

R coerces any C in three main ways. First, by *simple coercion*, e.g. incarceration. Here, R restrains some C from doing *a simple action*, namely, moving out of prison.

Secondly, by *legislation*, above all by *criminal law*. For example, R addresses to all C a command not to kill any fellow-C, and backs his

[6] See T. Hobbes, *Leviathan* (1651); J. Locke, *Second Treatise of Civil Government* (1690) and *A Letter concerning Toleration* (1689); D. Hume, *An Enquiry concerning the Principles of Morals* (1777); J. Bentham, *An Introduction to the Principles of Morals and Legislation* (2nd edn, 1823) and *Of Laws in General* (1782); J. S. Mill, *On Liberty* (1859) and *A System of Logic* (8th edn, 1872); D. J. O'Connor, *Free Will* (London: Macmillan 1972), esp. Ch. 9. It is a curious paradox that the concept of liberty which is indispensable for political thought is not the political one, positive liberty, but the physical one, negative liberty.

[7] *On Liberty*, Ch. 1.

[8] Bentham uses the expressions 'political liberty' and 'political punishment', and Godwin uses the expression 'political justice'; see note 29.

command with *a threat* that he will *punish* any C who disobeys it by killing him. It is the effective threat and not the command which coerces all C, and it does this by restraining any C from doing *a complex (conjunctive) action*, namely, both taking a fellow-C's life and also keeping his own life. The effect of this restraint is *to deter* any C from doing the simple action, killing a fellow-C.[9] Coercion by legislation is therefore *complex coercion*.

Thirdly, by *manipulation*. Here, R proceeds typically as follows. He covertly compels all C to hear the proposition, P, that any C who kills a fellow-C will die immediately. He also covertly prevents all C from hearing not-P. Consequently, all C believe P, and so desire not to kill any fellow-C, and so refrain from doing so. Note that P is *a prediction* and not a threat. Moreover, since R is engaged in political propaganda, it is a prediction which he knows to be probably false. If R were to compel all C to hear the proposition, Q, that any C who kills a fellow-C will die immediately *by R's hand*, that would be in effect coercion by legislation, not coercion by manipulation, and identical with the example of it given above. Like incarceration, eviction, etc., coercion by manipulation is simple coercion.

The differences between coercion by legislation and coercion by manipulation are therefore as follows. First, in coercion by legislation, R prevents all C from doing a complex action, whereas in coercion by manipulation R restrains all C from doing a simple action; for example, hearing not-P. Secondly, in coercion by legislation, any C who wants to kill a fellow-C is made *to feel unfree* by R's threat of punishment, because he is restrained from doing what he wants to do, namely, both take a fellow-C's life and also keep his own life. But in coercion by manipulation, no C is made to feel unfree, because all C do what they want to do, namely, refrain from killing any fellow-C. Thirdly, coercion by legislation must be overt, since R's threat will not deter unless it is published to all C. But coercion by manipulation must be covert, since R's propaganda will not work if all C realize that they are being manipulated by him.

Which of the three modes of political coercion now curtails liberty most? Not simple coercion, such as incarceration, since the proportion of all C whose liberty is curtailed in this way is relatively small even in extreme tyrannies. Coercion by manipulation is superior to the other two modes. For whereas incarceration and legislation normally make some C feel unfree to do X and so disposed *to resist* R, manipulation makes no C feel unfree to do X and so disposed to resist R. It is not surprising, therefore,

---

[9] This account of a penal statute is due to Bentham, who created *the imperative theory of law*. See Bentham, op. cit.; H. L. A. Hart, 'Bentham's *Of Laws in General*', *Rechtstheorie* **2** (1971). On how threats coerce, see J. P. Day, 'Threats, Offers, Law, Opinion and Liberty', *American Philosophical Quarterly* **14** (1977). Although criminal law is the chief instrument of political coercion, it must be remembered that *civil law* is also coercive, since the orders of civil courts are backed by a threat of punishment for contempt in the event of recalcitrance.

that it is coercion by manipulation which has fired the public imagination.[10] But, while the present power of propaganda, brainwashing, etc., should not be underestimated, the full exploitation of these techniques still lies in the future. Today, coercion by legislation is still the main cause of unfreedom. Indeed, the situation in this respect has long been deteriorating. The monstrous multiplication of possible offences in this and other countries in modern times is due chiefly to R's obsessions with internal and external security (the public safety) and with collectivism. These obsessions in turn have been created mainly by the two world wars. This, therefore, is the problem which I address in the present lecture.

2. The Problem of Justification

It is necessary to distinguish, first, arguments for *liberty* (singular) from arguments for *liberties* (plural); and secondly, arguments for liberty as *a moral right* from arguments for liberty from *consequences*. It will be convenient to discuss the second distinction first.

Political liberty is *a negative, general, individual, moral right*. It is individual, because it is held by individual persons.[11] Since political liberty is the subject under discussion, the right is held by an individual in his role as a C, and is held by him against R. The right is general, because it is held by any C in his role as a citizen, and not because of some special relationship between him and R. Such a special relationship would exist if, for example, R had promised all C that he would assure their political liberty.[12] General rights are therefore also called 'human rights', 'natural rights' or 'the rights of man and of the citizen'. Finally, it is negative, because it is *a right not to be injured. A positive right* is *an (alleged) right to be benefited*. I shall touch on the subject of positive rights later. (See section 3.)

Arguments for liberty as a moral right preceded arguments for it from consequences. The notion that political liberty is a negative, general,

[10] See, e.g., A. Huxley, *Brave New World* (London: Chatto & Windus 1932) and *Brave New World Revisited* (London: 1959); G. Orwell, *Nineteen Eighty-four* (London: Secker & Warburg 1949); V. Packard, *The Hidden Persuaders* (London: Longman 1957). Rousseau was the first to grasp the concept of political coercion by manipulation; see his *Discourse on Political Economy* (1758). Bentham call it 'indirect legislation'; see Long, op. cit., Ch. 8. B. F. Skinner's reflections on social control provide the most thorough contemporary treatment of the topic; see his *Beyond Freedom and Dignity* (London: Cape, 1971).

[11] There are also *collective rights* held by groups, e.g. women and Negroes. See N. Glazer, 'Individual Rights Against Group Rights' in *Human Rights*, E. Kamenka and A. E. Tay (eds) (London: Arnold 1978).

[12] See Hart, 'Are There Any Natural Rights?', *Philosophical Review* **64** (1955). One consequence of the theory of *a contract of government* is that it transforms liberty and other natural rights from general political rights into special political rights.

individual, moral right is causally linked with the connected phenomena of Protestantism and capitalism.[13] Locke, who first claimed political liberty as a natural right, was sympathetic to both these movements. From him, the idea passed into the English, American, French and other classic declarations of the rights of man and of the citizen.[14]

Consequential arguments for liberty were introduced by Bentham and Mill.[15] They are intended to show that negative individual political liberty benefits all C (is in the public interest, that is, promotes the general happiness or common good). So the essential difference between arguments for such liberty as a right and arguments for it from consequences is as follows. The former are designed to show that such liberty *averts injury from each C individually*, whereas the latter are designed to show that it *confers benefit on all C collectively*.

Let us consider first an argument for liberty in general (singular) which is an argument for it as a moral right. When R coerces all C by legislation, they often feel unfree. But the feeling of unfreedom, or frustration, is painful and injurious.[16] This argument is sound, but subject to the important qualification that a C does not always feel unfree when R makes him unfree. First, a C does not feel unfree to do X when R restrains him from doing X if that C believes falsely that he is free to do X. Secondly, a C does not feel unfree to do X when R restrains him from doing X if that C does not desire to do X.

Confusion between feeling unfree and being unfree vitiates the Stoic theory of individual liberty. The slave Epictetus taught that the remedy for a slave is to suppress his desire to be free.[17] But although a slave who did that would cease to feel unfree, he would not cease to be unfree.

The facts that coercion tends to make coercees feel frustrated and that liberty is a moral right justify Mill's judgment that 'all restraint, *qua* restraint, is an evil'. They also justify *the presumption* in favour of liberty which imposes *the burden of justification* on the coercer.[18]

[13] See M. Weber, *The Protestant Ethic and the Spirit of Capitalism*, trans. T. Parsons (London: Unwin 1930); R. H. Tawney, *Religion and the Rise of Capitalism* (London: Murray 1926).

[14] See Locke, op. cit.; E. Kamenka, 'The Anatomy of an Idea', in Kamenka and Tay, op. cit.

[15] But there is a strong utilitarian (consequential) strand in Locke's political thought too, e.g. 'The public good is the rule and measure of all law-making' (*A Letter concerning Toleration*).

[16] See J. P. Plamenatz, *Consent, Freedom and Political Obligation* (Oxford: University Press 1938), Ch. 6.

[17] *Discourses* (c. 100).

[18] *On Liberty*, Ch. 5. See also S. I. Benn and R. S. Peters, *Social Principles and the Democratic State* (London: Allen and Unwin 1959), Ch. 10; Day, 'Presumptions', *Proceedings of the Fourteenth International Conference of Philosophy*, Vol. 5 (Vienna: Herder 1968).

I turn now to arguments for liberties (plural). Liberties are differentiated as liberties *to do X, to do Y, to do Z,* etc.; where doing X, doing Y doing Z . . . etc., are *sorts of actions*, not *particular actions*. We shall need to consider the liberty of expression, 'the liberty of tastes and pursuits'[19] the liberty of association, religious liberty and economic liberty.

The expression *religious liberty* is ambiguous. Usually it means *ecclesiastical liberty*, which is the liberty of a Church *vis-à-vis* R.[20] This is a collective liberty, consideration of which lies outside the scope of this lecture. Sometimes, however, 'religious liberty' means the liberty of an individual to join any Church or none, or to leave any Church. This falls under the liberty of association, which I shall discuss shortly.

Economic liberty, too, is a collective liberty, since economic operations are carried on mostly by groups, such as family businesses, partnerships and joint-stock companies, rather than by individuals. Discussion of this liberty therefore also falls outside the scope of this essay.

The argument for *the liberty of expression* as a right consists in pointing out that not only the professional author (*the individual producer*) but also the common speaker need to express their thoughts. If R deters or restrains them from doing so, he injures them by denying their need and by frustrating their potentiality for self-development. But Mill, in his classic defence of this liberty, uses consequential arguments which point out the benefit of this liberty to all readers (*the consumers collectively*). If R deters or prevents geneticists from publishing their results, the progress of the science of genetics towards *truth* will be slowed or arrested. If he disallows criticism of religious doctrines, they will lose their *meaning* and become 'dead dogmas'.[21]

Similarly, the argument for *the liberty of tastes and pursuits* as a right consists in pointing out that R injures each individual C if R deters or prevents him from his *pursuit of happiness*. But Mill emphasizes the public benefit of R's respecting this right, since the happy few who realize their potentialities will set the rest 'the example of more enlightened conduct, and better taste and sense in human life'.[22]

The liberty of association (singular) is the *individual* liberty of each C to associate or not to associate with, or to dissociate from some other C. It must be distinguished from *the collective liberty of associations* (plural) to do X, to do Y, to do Z . . . etc., e.g. the liberty of Churches to profess their faiths and to practise their rites, and the liberty of joint-stock companies to engage in free enterprise and free trade. The argument for the

[19] Mill, *On Liberty*, Ch. 1.

[20] Locke uses the expression 'ecclesiastical liberty' in his *Letter concerning Toleration*.

[21] *On Liberty*, Ch. 2; see also T. Scanlon, 'A Theory of Freedom of Expression', *Philosophy and Public Affairs* **1** (1972).

[22] *On Liberty*, Ch. 3.

liberty of association as a right consists in pointing out that each C is a social animal who needs the company of his fellows in clubs, etc. More importantly, that each C can only achieve many of his main goals in co-operation with others. He cannot play cricket without being a member of a team, and he cannot engage in economic operations on any scale without joining a partnership or a joint-stock company. Hence, R will injure each C gravely if he does not respect this right. Consequential arguments for this liberty point out the benefit to all C of free associations, such as joint-stock companies and trade unions. Showing that joint-stock companies and trade unions benefit the public is a matter of justifying collective economic liberty. Here, the point is simply that, without the individual liberty of association, such organizations could not exist.[23]

3. The Problem of Distribution

This problem is that of deciding what *kinds* and what *amount* of each kind of liberty are normally justified. Important principles have been proposed to answer it.

The most famous of these is Mill's 'principle of individual liberty', which he applied to social liberty as well as to political liberty.[24] (See section 1.) Being interested only in political liberty, I shall consider (1) *the* (corresponding) *principle of negative individual political liberty*. This states that, if any C does not injure some other C by doing X, then R is not morally justified in legislating against any C doing X.

The following remarks will clarify the meaning of principle (1). First, 'some other C' means not only some other individual C, but also alternatively some proper subset of the set of all C, or the set all C. Secondly, 'some other C' excludes any C himself. So, since the principle says nothing about cases where some C does not injure himself or others, or about cases where some C does injure himself but not others, it is against legal paternalism. (See principle (4), below.) Thirdly, the principle states that harm to another is a necessary condition, not a sufficient condition of morally justified political coercion. The following examples illustrate this point. (i) A penal law against homosexual conduct between consenting adults. Since such conduct harms no other, the principle applies and condemns such a law as morally unjustified.[45] (ii) A penal law against murder. Since murder harms another, the principle does not apply. (But the law is

---

[23] On the liberties of association and of associations, see A. V. Dicey, *Law and Opinion in England* (London: Macmillan 1905), lectures 5, 6, 8, appendix, note 1; Benn and Peters, op. cit., Ch. 13; *Nomos XI: Voluntary Associations,* J. R. Pennock and J. W. Chapman (eds) (New York: Atherton Press 1969).

[24] *On Liberty,* Ch. 1.

[25] See Hart, *Law, Liberty and Morality* (London: Oxford University Press 1963).

morally justified because it is R's duty to maintain the right to life of all C.) (iii) A penal law against economic competition. Since such competition harms others, namely, the losers, the principle does not apply. (But Mill, as a classical economist, maintains that this law is not morally justified because free competition is in the general interest.[26])

The truth of principle (1) is contested. I shall consider the commonest objection to it with a view both to defending it and to bringing out an important point which tends to be overlooked in these debates.

Consider a penal law which requires motor-cyclists to wear protective helmets. Some say that this law is not morally justified because a motor-cyclist who has no dependants and who does not comply with it is likely to harm himself but not others. The commonest objection to this claim is that, on the contrary, his conduct is likely to harm others. For if he is injured as a result of not wearing a helmet, other C will have to pay for his medicare in taxation; which involves violating their property-right and their liberty to dispose of their property as they wish. But the reply to this objection is that it is true only in a collectivist state with socialized medicine. It is true because it is made to be true by political coercion. The important general point is that principle (1) applies only to states which are free, in the sense that all C already have a large amount of negative individual political liberty.

I turn now to (2) *the principle of Good Samaritan legislation*. This states that R is morally justified in legislating so as to benefit some proper subset of the set all C at the expense of the complementary set of that subset: for example, in providing education for the children of those C who cannot afford to pay for it by taxing the other C.

Like principle (1), principle (2) is highly controversial. It is implicit in the laws of some collectivist states, such as the people's democracies of Eastern Europe, but not in those of mainly non-collectivist states such as Great Britain and the USA.[27]

A common defence of it is the contention that there is a positive right to be benefited. (On the difference between positive and negative rights see section 2.) A typical negative right is the right to life, and a typical alleged positive right is the right to the means of livelihood. There are two essential differences between them. First, in the case of the right to life, there is a perfect reciprocity between right-bearers and right-respecters. Every C can and ought to respect every other C's right to life. Similarly with liberty and other negative rights. But in the case of the right to the means of livelihood, there is no such reciprocity. Some C cannot, and so

[26] *On Liberty*, Ch. 5.
[27] See S. I. Benn, 'Human Rights—for Whom and for What?', in Kamenka and Tay, op. cit.; E. Mack, 'Bad Samaritanism and the Causation of Harm', *Philosophy and Public Affairs* **9** (1980).

have no obligation to, contribute to the means of livelihood of other C.[28] Similarly with the right to holidays with pay and other alleged positive rights. Secondly, if R coerces C_1 in order to deter C_1 from violating C_2's right to life, R violates no right of C_1, since C_1 has no right to violate C_2's right to life. Similarly with liberty and other negative rights. But if R coerces C_1 in order to deter C_1 from not contributing to C_2's means of livelihood, R does violate some right of C_1, namely, his property-right. Similarly with the right to holidays with pay and other alleged positive rights.[29]

Principle (2) must therefore be justified, if at all, by consequential argument and not by argument from rights. I submit that the true principle is *the principle of the coincidence of particular and general interests*. This states that principle (2) is true only if such legislation also benefits the set all C.[30] This principle of coincidence is satisfied in the education example (above), since it is to the interest of all C that all C should be educated. But this principle is not satisfied if R imposes a protective tariff on footwear of foreign manufacture. The essential difference between the two cases is as follows. In the education case, the complementary set are not injured, since it is to the interest of all C that all C should be educated, and they are a proper subset of the set all C. But in the tariff case, the complementary set are injured, since they have to pay more for their footwear than they need to do, and receive no benefit in return for this injury. A subsidy to General Motors by the US government would be

---

[28] See Antony Flew, 'What is a Right?', the *Georgia Law Review* **13** (1979).

[29] The spread of the belief in positive rights is obviously connected with the growth of the welfare movement; see Benn, op. cit. (note 27, above). But, in England, the belief is already to be found in the writings of, e.g., Paine and Godwin, and in legislation of the sixteenth century. See Thomas Paine, *The Rights of Man* (1792), Pt 2, Ch. 5; William Godwin, *Enquiry concerning Political Justice* (3rd edn, 1798), Bk 2, Ch. 5 and Bk. 8; Elie Halévy, *The Growth of Philosophic Radicalism*, trans. M. Morris (London: Faber and Faber 1928), Pt 2, Ch. 2, sec. 1.

[30] This principle should not be confused with *the principle of the natural identity of particular and general interests*. This states that individuals and groups promote the general interest by pursuing their particular interests. Its most famous formulation is A. Smith's doctrine of 'an invisible hand' in his *Wealth of Nations* (1776). An essential difference between the two principles is that Smith's is descriptive whereas mine is normative. Different again is *the principle of the artificial identification of particular and general interests*. This states that the legislator ought to enact penal laws which will make it to the interest of individuals and groups to promote the general interest; and that the instructor ought to inculcate in his pupils beliefs which will make them desire to promote the general interest, and consequently do so. Plainly, this Benthamite view of *education*, which derives from C. A. Helvétius, represents it as propaganda, i.e. as a sort of coercion by manipulation. (See section 1.) This principle too is normative and not descriptive. See Halévy, op. cit., Pt. 1, Ch. 1.

justified only if what is good for General Motors in this respect is indeed good for the USA. Bentham called particular interests which do not coincide with the public interest 'sinister interests'. The purpose of most lobbies and pressure groups is to promote sinister interests.

According to (3) *the principle of utilitarian legislation*, R is morally justified in legislating so as to benefit all C at the expense of some proper subset of the set all C, e.g. in conscripting young C for the defence of the realm, or in taxing C who are not poor in order to provide and maintain roads. As these examples suggest, this principle applies particularly to the provision of goods and services which benefit all C collectively.

We have just seen that principle (3) is justified by the fact that the proper subset are not injured precisely because, being a proper subset of the set all C, they too receive benefit in return for their injury. We have also just seen principle (3) justifies a qualified version of principle (2) by the mediation of the principle of the coincidence of particular and public interests.

The difficulty with it lies in achieving an equitable trade-off between the public interest and individual rights, e.g. *how far* may R justifiably violate the property-rights of some proper subset of all C by taxation in order to provide and maintain roads? It is not possible to answer such a question by appeal to any one principle. One has to appeal to a number of fairly obvious considerations, such as that the level of taxation imposed by R on some proper subset of all C for all goods and services which benefit all C collectively must not be so high as to deter that subset from producing the wealth out of which the taxes must be paid.

I pass now to (4) *the principle of paternalistic legislation*. This states that, if any C injures himself by doing X, then R is morally justified in legislating against any C doing X. Thus R would be morally justified in legislating against C taking heroin. This principle seeks to mandate *prudence*. The commonest liberal objection to it is based on *the principle of rational self-interest*. This asserts that A is the best judge of A's interests; so that R does not know what is good for any C better than he himself does. But the reply to this objection is that, as a matter of fact, the gentleman at Westminster does know best.

I have three observations to offer on this dispute. First, the principle of rational self-interest is often rendered 'A knows best what A wants'. But 'A wants X' means either 'A desires X' or 'It is in A's interest that A should have X'. It is approximately true that A knows best what A desires, so that the principle may look obvious. However, the principle is in fact about A's interests and not his desires. And it is questionable whether it is approximately true that A knows best what A's interests are. Secondly, Mill uses this principle to justify economic liberty or *laisser faire*. He therefore means by it that A is the best judge of A's *economic interests*. This may be true, and yet it may be false that A is the best judge of A's non-economic interests. On the other hand, thirdly, there is no reason to believe that R, the political authority, possesses *as such* expert knowledge of, e.g., the educational needs of any child of any C. If he has it, it is because he has consulted an expert on this subject. But any C can do this himself, and satisfy his children's needs accordingly. Such a system is superior in point of cost, flexibility and preservation of liberty to one in which R monopolizes the supply of education.[31]

In any case, there is a deeper objection to legal paternalism which bypasses this controversy. Even if R were to know what is good for any C better than he himself does, it would not follow that R ought to legislate against actions whereby any C injures himself. For it is assumed that all C are adults; and if adults are treated as children, children they will remain. It is an essential part of growing-up and of education that A should learn from his own mistakes. Indeed, he is unlikely to learn in any other way. For, although A can learn from A's mistakes, he is unlikely to learn from B's mistakes.[32]

The last principle of distribution for consideration is (5) *the principle of moralistic legislation.* According to it, if any C acts immorally in doing X, then R is morally justified in legislating against any C doing X. As principle (4) seeks to mandate prudence, so principle (5) seeks to mandate *morality*.[33] Moreover, these two principles are compatible. The puritans who foisted prohibition on the USA seem to have been at least as much interested in saving their fellow-Cs' souls as their bodies.

Like principles (2), (3) and (4), principle (5) is exposed to the objection that it curtails liberty. But there are two further strong objections to it. First, it is impracticable. Certainly, some immoral acts, such as murder, can be and are also treated as crimes. But it is equally certain that other immoral acts cannot be so treated. Ingratitude is a black vice; but the notion that acts of ingratitude could be treated as legal offences is too obviously absurd to require discussion.[34] Secondly, principle (5), which is intended to strengthen morality, actually weakens it. For suppose it were practicable to mandate gratitude: for R to threaten C_1 with punishment

---

[31] See Mill, *Principles of Political Economy* (7th edn, 1871), Bk 5, Ch. 11; Dicey, op. cit., lecture 6; Day, 'On Liberty and the Real Will', *Philosophy* **45** (1970).

[32] I an grateful to Professor E. Mack for pointing out to me this deeper objection to legal paternalism. See also J. Feinberg, *Social Philosophy* (Englewood Cliffs: Prentice Hall 1973), Ch. 3.

[33] See J. F. Stephen, *Liberty, Equality, Fraternity* (2nd edn, London: Smith, Elder 1874); P. Devlin, *The Enforcement of Morals*; Hart, *Law Liberty and Morality*; Feinberg, op. cit.

[34] In fact, that is. In fiction, things are different—'Among the Lilliputians ingratitude was a capital offence' (A. D. M. Walker, 'Gratefulness and Gratitude', *Aristotelian Society Proceedings* **80** (1980).

if C_1 fails to return good to C_2 in return for the good which C_2 gave to C_1. Then C_1's returning good to C_2 would be less meritorious than it would be if there were no such penal law; since at least part of C_1's motive would be a desire to avoid punishment as opposed to a desire to discharge a moral obligation to C_2. A similar objection applies to principle (4). Moderation in drinking, as in other things, is commendable; but it is less commendable when the motive for practising it is, at least in part, a desire to escape punishment.

Although legal moralism is usually discussed with reference to criminal law, it is important to note that civil law too mandates morality. Consider the moral obligation to fidelity. Suppose C_1 knows that, if C_1 breaks his contract with C_2, then C_2 can sue C_1 for damages; and that, if C_1 fails to pay the damages which R awards to C_2, then R will punish C_1 for contempt. Clearly, C_1 has a strong motive for honouring his contract with C_2. (See note 9.)

In conclusion, I shall touch on a principle of individual liberty which is not a principle of distribution but a principle of historical interpretation. Mill believed in a 'general tendency ... towards a better and happier state'.[35] Now, as he understood 'happiness', more happiness involves more negative individual liberty as a necessary condition thereof. Many other liberals of Mill's time accepted this *negative individual liberal interpretation of history* and conception of *progress*. We have noticed, however, that in fact the general tendency has long been towards more political coercion. (See section 1, end.) Yet Mill's belief was natural, since his life coincided with a period of individualism. Only after his death was this succeeded by a period of collectivism which has endured until very recently.[36] For there is now mounting evidence that men, disillusioned by the failure of more than a century of collectivism to yield its promised benefits, wish to revert to a freer political order. Yet the obstacle in the way of doing so should not be underrated. For, 'as our history only too clearly shows, it is comparatively easy to make criminal law and exceedingly difficult to unmake it'.[37]

[35] *A System of Logic*, Bk 6, Ch. 10.
[36] See Dicey, op. cit.
[37] Hart, *Law, Liberty and Morality*, Preface. I am grateful to Professors A. G. N. Flew, H. L. A. Hart and J. O. Urmson for their comments on an earlier version of this lecture.

The Social Liberty Game[1]

MARTIN HOLLIS

It might surprise someone, who knew only *On Liberty*, to hear J. S. Mill called the father of British socialism. That would sound a careless bid for a respectable pedigree, on a par with hailing King Canute as father of the British seaside holiday. Mill is passionate there about making the individual a protected species, not to be interfered with even for his own good, unless to prevent harm to others. He is so passionate that government seems at times to have no other task than to protect. *The Principles of Political Economy*, on the other hand, displays clear, if intermittent, socialist leanings. There too 'there is a circle round every individual human being, which no government . . . ought to be permitted to overstep' (*PPE* V.xi.2, p. 306).[2] But, subject to this constraint, government is urged to do all the utilitarian good it can and some nasty worries for democratic socialists surface instructively. They centre on the social aspects of individuality and give rise to problems in what my title calls the Social Liberty Game. British socialism, with its Lib-Lab origins and tolerant respect for individual liberty, embodies a tension between the rights of each and the good of all, which makes the *Principles* a living part of its intellectual history.

The tension is present in *On Liberty* too and it may be as well to start with a word about the relation of the two books. It is not as if the utilitarian concerns of the *Principles* were simply pushed aside in the later work. The 'very simple principle' of *On Liberty* is not a definition of the proper ends of government. It does not try to confine government to protecting. The wording is 'that the sole end for which mankind are warranted individually or collectively in interfering with the liberty of action of any of their number is self-protection', which leaves government a free hand wherever individual liberty is not infringed. Otherwise *On Liberty* would be in a hopeless muddle, when it comes, for instance, to education. Perhaps it could be argued that to educate is to protect but it would be a tortuous argument and I see no need to saddle Mill with it. A utilitarian case for an

[1] I am warmly grateful to Professor A. Phillips Griffiths for his helpful criticisms of an earlier draft. The present version, especially in its later parts, owes him much.
[2] For ease of reference I shall be citing the 1871 edition, page numbers being taken from the Penguin text of Books IV and V, edited by D. M. Winch (Harmondsworth: Penguin Books, 1970).

educated people, coupled with a proof that it respects or enhances the liberty of individuals, has more to commend it.

The core of *On Liberty* is, I take it, less liberty than individuality. Mill is not concerned to help each of us make a mess of his own life in his own way. He does not forbid it but he offers no encouragement and, indeed, proposes much to prevent or pre-empt us. The essay tills the soil in which individuality can flourish. That metaphor is deliberate. Individuality is the prize of a person who functions not like a machine but like a tree, Mill says, and who is a moral being concerned as a matter of course for others.[3] It is the precious and precarious attribute of human beings in the maturity of their faculties. It flourishes only if government cultivates the soil and tends the maturing plants. So, although 'liberty consists in doing what one desires' (*On Liberty*, Chapter V), that is no invitation to license. Mature persons will not make an orgy of it, since their desires will be schooled (any more than a devout person will abuse the instruction *fac quid vis*). I do not at all deny that there is a tension between individual and social in *On Liberty*, which stirring words about individuality leave unresolved. It is the same tension which the *Principles* grapples with.

Both books, then, bid government further the real interests of individuals. Both require a robust notion of individuals and their interests. This is less plain in the *Principles*, where Mill usually speaks of 'individuals' in the idiom of *laissez faire* political economy or what would now be called rational-man models; and I take *On Liberty* to advance his reflections on this score. But the *Principles* has much to say about the economic, social and political framework best suited to individual liberty and here *On Liberty* is naughtily silent. However, that is enough of a post-mortem before we have even eaten the meal and I turn now to 'the circle round every individual human being' in the *Principles* and the utilitarian duties of government in guarding it.

To introduce the tension, here are two lapidary statements made while discussing the proper scope of government. One is the maxim offered at *PPE* V.xi.7 (p. 314) to round off a series of reasons to restrict government intervention in the business of a community:

> *Laissez faire*, in short, should be the general practice: every departure from it, unless required by some great good, is a certain evil.

The other, from section 15 of the same chapter (p. 344) reads:

> It may be said generally that anything, which it is desirable should be done for the general interests of mankind or of future generations or for the present interests of those members of the community who require external aid but which is not of a nature to remunerate individuals or

[3] Cf. *Utilitarianism*, Ch. 3, where the complete individual is described as 'a being who *of course* pays regard to others'.

associations for undertaking it, is itself a suitable thing to be under-taken by government.

In between there is a trumpeting of 'the great principle of political economy that individuals are the best judges of their own interest' (*PPE* V.xi.12, p. 331, and kindred versions in several other places). It is bound up with 'the practical maxim, that the business of society can best be performed by private and voluntary agency' (*PPE* V.xi.16, p. 345, and elsewhere). Crucially, however, there is also a string of exceptions to the principle or the maxim (and we shall ask which), bidding fair to subvert both alto-gether.

I shall next trace Mill's passage along this tightrope in readiness for the finer points of the Social Liberty Game.

Book V of the *Principles* opens by distinguishing the functions of government into the necessary and the optional. But 'optional', it soon emerges, means only that there is room for rational debate about how desirable they are. It is not as if a function is necessary, only if involved in protecting the circle round each individual. For 'it is not admissible that the protection of persons and that of property are the sole purposes of government. The ends of government are as comprehensive as those of the social union. They consist of all the good, and all the immunity from evil, which the existence of government can be made either directly or indirectly to bestow' (*PPE* V.ii.2, p. 156). Government has broad utili-tarian duties; but there is a key difference between authority and influence. When intervening with authority, government controls the free agency of individuals by commands and penalties. When merely using influence, it is content to provide information, advice and facilities for those willing to use them. The latter role gives large scope—national banks, schools, hospitals, church establishments, post offices, for example—but, Mill assumes, poses no threat to liberty, so long as no attempt is made to suppress private provision. (A century later even the mildest social demo-crat might wish to doubt that assumption but I put the thought aside.) The hard questions, in his view, are set by the use of authority to inter-vene, whether people want it or not.

Mill is not directly concerned with people's wants, however, but with their interests. One source of conflict between utility and liberty is thus swiftly removed. Just because an intervention is unpopular, it is not thereby an intrusion on liberty. Here Mill's paternalist side is showing but there is no doubt that he means 'interests' and not merely 'wants' (witness also *On Liberty*). So far the utilitarian is faring better than the libertarian. But the 'great principle of political economy' redresses the balance by recognizing the individual as, on the whole, the best judge of his own interests—the word used is not 'wants'—and sovereign when only his own interests are at stake. The broad idea is to harmonize utility and liberty by making *laissez faire* the general practice, since that puts the best judges of our interests in the driving seat and so maximizes general utility too.

But the great principle has 'large and conspicuous exceptions', as Chapter xi of Book V makes crushingly plain. Mill lists seven, all worth discussing but turning crucially on the fourth. Since it is the fourth which prompts my title, I shall concentrate on that. Briefly, however, let us note the other six for purposes of context and of reference later.

Firstly (*PPE*, V.xi.9), people are not the best judges of their own interest, unless they are mature and sane adults. Lunatics, idiots and infants are a proper concern of the state, which can, for instance, control the hours and conditions of child labour. So too are 'those unfortunate slaves and victims of the most brutal part of mankind, the lower animals' (p. 323). Women, however, Mill stubbornly refuses to lump with children and idiots, in accordance with his scandalous view of them as fully fledged individuals.

The second exception (V.xi.10) is 'when an individual attempts to decide irrevocably now what will be best for his interest at some future and distant time' (p. 325). The law should look askance at such engagements, either refusing to sanction them or at least insisting on an escape route for later 'on a sufficient case being made out'. Marriage is an example.

The third (V.xi.11) occurs where individuals have delegated their agency to others, as with joint stock associations, whose directors and managers do not have quite the stockholders' direct concern with the stockholders' interests. Government can intervene on behalf of persons who have delegated control of their own interests.

Fifthly (V.xi.13), persons acting in the interests of others are a proper target of government. Philanthropic institutions, for instance, do not always act in an impersonal way with an eye to the general good and it is for government to guide their activity. But private bodies nevertheless do some things better and charity needs a mixed economy, for example, with government deciding the rules and scale of subsistence for poor relief, while leaving it to private bodies to identify the deserving and undeserving poor. Similarly colonial development is best handled as a mixed enterprise.

Sixthly (V.xi.14), acts, which individuals judge correctly to be in their interest, may have consequences extending indefinitely beyond them. Society as a whole has a stake in whatever affects the nation at large or posterity. The colonies are again cited but the point is still relevant. North Sea oil shows it well. Multinationals are no doubt excellent judges of their own interest, without its being obvious that what is good for the moguls is thereby good for mankind.

The seventh exception (V.xi.15) extends the sixth to areas where 'important public services are to be performed, while yet there is no individual especially interested in performing them' (p. 342). Mill mentions voyages of exploration, lighthouses, harbour buoys and the creation of professorships. The modern eye here discerns a familiar issue in the theory of public choice, of how rational men are to provide themselves with public goods.

The reader is struck by the unsystematic character of this list of exceptions. The general rule which they breach is that 'most persons take a juster and more intelligent view of their own interest, and of the means of promoting it, than can either be prescribed to them by a general enactment of the legislature, or pointed out in the particular case by a public functionary' (V.xi.9, p. 322). Breaches occur whenever the actions of individuals, whether competent or incompetent as judges of self-interest, fail to produce the general interest. Since the list has neither system nor closure, it threatens to reduce the great principles and maxims of political economy to jelly. Indeed, as Mill observes presently, 'In the particular circumstances of a given age and nation, there is scarcely anything really important to the general interest, which it may not be desirable, or even necessary, that the government should take upon itself, not because private individuals cannot effectively perform it, but because they will not' (V.xi.16, p. 345). So broad a licence to intervene is a surprise, until we realise that Mill has hit upon the central paradox of the modern Theory of Rational Choice and, I think, failed to spot how devastating it is. At any rate the paradox is there and has never been better stated than in the fourth exception, which I now introduce.

This exception (V.xi.12) is for matters where the force of law is needed, not to overrule the judgment of individuals but to give effect to it. Mill discusses it apropos of wage levels and of colonization. Suppose that a general reduction in daily hours of work from ten to nine would benefit all workers, in that they would still receive the same pay despite the reduced hours. Suppose also that it would come about, if all refused to work the tenth hour. None the less it will not happen. For, while some work for ten hours, anyone who refuses will be either fired or forced to accept less pay. So no small group has any interest in trying to pioneer the change. Could all the workers collectively not agree among themselves to work for only nine hours? They could; but that too would not give them success. The immediate interest of each would lie in violating the scheme and 'the more numerous those were who adhered to the rule, the more would individuals gain by departing from it'. For, while only a few work the tenth hour, they can count on being paid extra for it, thus gaining all the benefits of others' restraint and extra pay besides. Admittedly that might be a satisfactory outcome, if it were stable, since all would be better off and some very much better off. But it would not be stable, because more and more will be tempted by the tenth hour, until the benefit is eaten away and the previous situation restored. Hence the only solution which advances the interests of all is to make the agreement to work the shorter day enforceable. It needs the force of law.

Mill's reasoning can be crisply rendered in the argot of games theory. To start with let each worker have an independent choice between ten hours and nine and let each order the possible outcomes from his own point of view thus:

	Self	*Others*
1st	10	9
2nd	9	9
3rd	10	10
4th	9	10

The ordering reflects the point that all do better if all choose 9 than if all choose 10. But it also lets us deduce that each will rationally choose 10. Each can reason that, if others choose 9, he does better from 10 than from 9; and that, if others choose 10, he still does better from 10 than from 9; and hence he does better from 10 *whatever others choose*. Nor does it matter how many others choose 9. For, although the benefit from the 10th hour varies, it remains an improvement on the reward for 9. While few work 10, each of them gains from being the odd man in; while many do, each would lose by being the odd man out. Equally no one has an interest in trying to set an example by working the shorter hours.

That a gentlemen's agreement will not suffice can be shown formally by ranking the merits of keeping and of breaking it from the standpoint of each worker:

	Self	*Others*
1st	Break	Keep
2nd	Keep	Keep
3rd	Break	Break
4th	Keep	Break

By parity of reasoning 'Break' drives out 'Keep', until the Keepers vanish entirely and *all* are worse off than needs be. This frustrating line of thought echoes Hobbes' grounds for saying that 'covenants without the sword are but vain breath' and continues to vex social democrats wanting a voluntary incomes policy. Mill spots its bearing but fails to see that he has a tiger by the tail. There are, I think, at least two reasons why he underrates it.

In the first place he is not quite clear what principle or maxim is at stake. I have mentioned both 'the great principle of political economy that individuals are the best judges of their own interest' and 'the practical maxim that the business of society can best be performed by private and voluntary agency'. The text of the *Principles* reads easily, if principle and maxim simply complement each other. The judgment by each of his own interest would sum painlessly to the best performing of the business of society. But the fourth exception puts a stop to such optimism. *Laissez faire* cannot be the rule on grounds of both liberty and utility, when it leaves *all* worse off than *all* need be. Wage levels and the colonies show how there can be an all-round advance on the results of rational free choice. The same may be said of public goods, like lighthouses, under the seventh exception, where there is a benefit to all which soundly judged individual interest will not provide.

Mill hopes to re-align utility with liberty by an enforced contract, which each man judges to be in his interest, provided that others abide by it too. The contract, however, is not just a new way of furthering present interests, since it affects future options and, more generally, raises questions of individual autonomy. So we must know the exact warrant for the fourth exception. Is the fact that enforcement raises everyone's utility necessary or sufficient for each man rationally to assent? If it were sufficient, utility would be trumps and Mill would find himself forcing people to be free—the spectre of Rousseau which he recoils from in *On Liberty*. If it were merely necessary, what more would be needed for a warrant? The liberal answer seems to be Consent. But that is threatened by the second exception, whereby government is to *prevent* an individual deciding 'irrevocably now what will be best for his interest at some future and distant time'. Thus, with the principle and the maxim in tension, benevolent government cannot be treated as a useful *deus ex machina* and we are owed more of a theodicy of government intervention.

The second reason why Mill underrates the exception, I submit, is that he is not yet working with the kind of 'individuals' which *On Liberty* commends. In the *Principles*, as noted, he usually assumes the rational, self-interested maximizing bargain-hunter now standard for analytical economics and the theory of games. 'Self-interested' means neither 'selfish' nor 'short-sighted' but does require that each actor maximize the (overall and duly discounted) benefit to himself. Hence it cannot be obvious—even if it were in the end true—that what is best for each is best for all. The fourth exception threatens to prove out of hand that *laissez faire* is not the best general rule for self-interested maximizers. This may be plainer, if we turn to Mill's other example of the fourth exception, colonization. Each immigrant to a new colony, he observes, will tend to grab whatever land he can as early as possible and to set about working it with his family. As a result there is no pool of labour to help on older farms and to build roads, canals and the rest of a public infra-structure. Yet all would gain, if new immigrants worked for hire for a period and so, when their turn came to be owners, could then find workers for hire. But 'it can never be in the interest of an individual to exercise this forbearance, unless he can be assured that others will do so too . . . It is the interest of each to do what is good for all, but only if others will do likewise' (V.xi.12, p. 332). Assurance, I suggest next, is not enough.

It is better for each that all forbear than that none do. But it is better still for each that others forbear while he does not. Similarly it is better for each new immigrant, if all must work for hire than if none do; but it would be better still, if the rule came into effect a few years after his arrival. For familiar Prisoner's Dilemma reasons therefore it is not in the interest of each to do what is better for all, including him. The *logic* of this brand of individualism requires everyone to cut off his nose to spite his face. It can be held at bay only by removing the troublesome top option by passing and enforcing laws. Yet those laws are not (usually) in the interests of all affected. The state of a colony, for instance, affects old immigrants, new immigrants, future immigrants and possible immigrants (to say nothing of native inhabitants and their descendants). Once the colony is under way, these groups have differing interests and no Pareto-improvement, in the sense of a change which leaves some better and none worse off, need be possible. Especially when future immigrants are to be considered, government will have to intervene more highhandedly than Mill notices, no doubt appealing to the sixth exception (for acts which have consequences extending indefinitely beyond them). The same point arises for the more recent case of productivity bargaining in industry, where an arrangement, which suits the present workforce nicely thank you, may help to sabotage the future of school leavers.

Government thus has to legislate on a large scale to prevent rational bargain-hunters maximizing the drawbacks of *laissez faire*. This plays havoc with the main line of Mill's argument, as he all but grants in the final paragraph of V.xi.12, ending with the comment, 'Penal laws exist at all chiefly for this reason—because even an unanimous opinion that a certain line of conduct is for the general interest, does not always make it people's individual interest to adhere to that line conduct' (p. 332). There is, in short, no guarantee whatever that *laissez faire* ensures that rational free choice by each will maximize the utilitarian good of all, each or even any individual. Provisionally, then, utility is at odds with liberty and, it seems so far, should be preferred.

'Provisionally' needs underlining. It remains possible that we are trying to play the Social Liberty Game with the wrong counters. The individuals described in the 'Individuality' chapter of *On Liberty* are not the rational economic men of the *Principles*. So it may be that *laissez faire* can be the general rule for fully fledged individuals who are concerned for others as a matter of course. But, before turning to that thought, I want to take up the point about rules, options and interests. Interests are partly a function of rules and partly not. New colonists, for instance, have an interest in grabbing land, when not penalized, and an interest in a forbearance scheme, if enforced by law. So, when rules change, interests can change. On the other hand each colonist has an interest in his own prosperity which is constant. So rules can be assessed for how well they give effect to constant interests. Hereby hangs an awkward tale for individualists.

There is some distinction between immediate and more general interests without doubt. For example, new parents acquire an interest in the provision of playgrounds, as distinct from whatever general interest they may continue to have in a balanced provision of public services. But it is not plain that even general interests are independent of rules. Schematically, if we call the existing rules R_1 and the rules after some proposed change in them R_1', we can see that people's interests under R_1 may differ from those under R_1'. Then it is natural to ask which set of rules serves their wider interests better. The enquiry makes ready sense, if there is some larger frame of rules R_2, within which to compare R_1 with R_1'. For example R_1 might encourage people to have more children and R_1' discourage it, with R_2 being the norms of a tribal society to judge the merits of procreation against. But then R_2 can be challenged in turn and compared with R_2'. There is the start of a regress, which individualism must presently block by maintaining that for some set of rules R_n, there is no wider set $R_{(n+1)}$ within which R_n can be compared with R_n'. In plainer English, the interests of individuals must be identifiable independently of all rules so that any social system can be assessed by how well it serves those final interests. What sort of interests are these?

Various individualistic answers have been offered, divisible on to the substantive and the formal. By 'substantive' I refer to accounts which postulate specific motives in human nature, as, for example, Hobbes does. By 'formal' I refer to those which specify only a shape or direction, for example by ascribing to all a human interest in having one's desires satisfied, without saying what they are. The more mathematical versions of utility theory are an example. Mills' own answer is, I take it, substantive. But he differs from Hobbes in instructive ways which bring him near to Rousseau and cast doubt on all individualist views of the relation of rules to interests.

The *Principles* takes a different line from *On Liberty*. The proposition that individuals are (on the whole) the best judges of their own interests expresses, as noted, the standard assumption about rational egoists, who maximize a utility function subject to constraints. For this kind of individual, attitudes to rules and even to other people are instrumental. Each homunculus has private, separate interests which are better or worse served by various rules. Social relations with other people are, in theory at least, contractual and need the cement of mutual self-interest. *On Liberty*, on the other hand, is written to foster engaged, interdependent, morally concerned individuals. The difference is not, in fact, as abrupt as that makes it sound, since a homunculus need not be brutally selfish and moral concern underlies the *Principles* too. But there is still a shift of approach, which is worth exploring.

The shift is less from individuals as egoists to individuals as utilitarians than from the Social Liberty Game as instrumental to the Social Liberty Game as expressive. To show it, let us return to the matter of hours of work. Mill sees clearly that the reason why individuals cannot arrive at shorter hours all round is not that each takes too narrow or selfish a view of his self-interest. Nor is it because there is a limited fund of wages, so that no efforts could raise total pay—Mill's opinion about that changed but, in any case, is not relevant here. The reason is that each and all are trapped in a Prisoner's Dilemma. The solution is for government to do what each would rationally will it to do, once convinced that he cannot hope for a law which constrains others without constraining him. This solution is incoherent, however, as becomes plain when the wider Social Liberty Game is reviewed.

The game described in the *Principles* is not, on reflection, among pre-social individuals but among workers and employers, with legislators involved too. Government has a duty to intervene when it can advance the interests of *all* players. Now it could be held (as Marx perhaps did) that employers also had an interest in shorter hours and better pay for workers, owing to a link between underconsumption and falling profits. (If it is asked why, in that case, employers resisted attempts to raise wages, one reply could be that they too were caught in a Prisoner's Dilemma, with each rationally forced to resist what it would all pay to concede.) Mill does not maintain this, however, and I take it that we are to regard the workers' gain as the employers' loss. So, with *laissez faire* as the general rule, government should not intervene, at least not in the name of the seven exceptions.

For *laissez faire* to be the general rule, there needs to be an ultimate harmony of interests, at least in a properly organized society. But it is, I think, beyond the apparatus of the *Principles* to prove one. Like Rousseau, Mill takes men as they are and laws as they might be; unlike Rousseau, he ascribes to men a pre-social interest in personal prosperity, which makes their social activity instrumental. This stops him giving government a general brief to raise total or average utility, since it prevents any blanket use of law to transfer utility among individuals or groups. Instead he is confined to the milder test of good law, that it raise the utility of some without reducing that of others, while preserving the circle round each individual. This is so weak that, for a society with conflicting interests, government seems likely to have very little to do. For, with power unevenly distributed, the have-nots can advance only at the expense of the haves, who will usually therefore be left worse off, even if total utility rises. But Mill's baseline is not, presumably, the actual state of an existing society. It is, rather, the distribution of utilities which would occur in the absence of law among persons who are competent judges of their own interests. The role of government is then determined by asking what produces the greatest advance beyond the baseline, without infringing liberty. Since all gain (or some do, without anyone losing), each could be deemed to have willed the resulting intervention.

There are, no doubt, objections to the very notion of a determinate baseline in the absence of law. But that is beyond my scope here and I propose to grant the baseline. Let us focus on the idea of justifying government as an improvement on it. Suppose there are two ways of improving, one doing better for employers and the other for workers. By the test in the last paragraph, government is warranted in imposing either and, in doing so, can be deemed to have the consent of all. But that is absurd, while the less favoured persons can point to another scheme, which meets the test and gives them much more. Even if there is just one scheme which makes a greater advance on the baseline than all others, there will still be persons who would have done better under another. Where, then, is the needed harmony of interests?

A familiar move here is to make the distribution anonymous or as if by lot. If the best scheme is also the one which rational persons would agree to before knowing who in particular would get what out of it, perhaps government is warranted in improving it. That too, however, opens longer avenues than I can explore now. Instead let us try a line which would link the *Principles* to *On Liberty* by locking individual interests together in an earlier and deeper way. Not seeing how to show a harmony of interests among the pre-social individuals of the *Principles*, I suggest substituting the kind of individuals who inhabit the free society of *On Liberty*. Perhaps they can be deemed rationally to consent to government which makes the largest advance on the baseline?

'The only liberty which merits the name is that of pursuing our own good in our own way' (*On Liberty*, Introduction). The first person-plural hints at interdependence as well as asserting independence. Equally the utility in Mill's utilitarianism is that of a human flourishing, a welfare calculated but not captured in measures of market consumption. From this standpoint 'the great principle of political economy' governs a different notion of 'interests' to that of the *Principles*. Rational Economic Man is no longer the best judge of his interests but a mature individual is. The contrast is, I granted earlier, not wholly sharp and the *Principles* is not thoroughly mechanical about market gain as the basic human interest. But, in so far as interests are given humane treatment there, a tension is left unresolved. *On Liberty* resolves it squarely in favour of humanity, with pure marketeers tolerated only because we are entitled to indulge our own ignorance of our interests, short of harming the interests of others. Even so, however, each individual still has a stake in his own happiness. Each presumably still distinguishes a larger total utility in which he has a smaller share from a smaller total from which he gets more. If the free society of rational individuals in *On Liberty* breeds utilitarians, it needs proving.

Well, it looks as if the fourth exception, which justified government in rescuing bargain hunters from the Prisoner's Dilemma, should at least be less pervasive. Previously each worker most preferred that he worked ten hours, while others worked nine; and each colonist most preferred that the new land-owning system not operate until he was ready to benefit. These fatal top preferences arose because interdependencies were solely instruments of personal gain. The mature individuals of *On Liberty*, however, can see positive, expressive virtue in interdependence. Each will positively prefer an arrangement, where he helps all, to one where he alone profits. So cases of the fourth exception become rarer, with the labour market and the colonies in particular now working as the Assurance Game, which Mill too casually claimed them to be among Rational Econmic Men. Here government is no longer intervening from on high. It is merely stopping market egoists from acting as bad apples in the barrel. It now prevents the ill effects of imperfect compliance with the principle or maxim properly understood, where before it had to impose a solution on people who all complied perfectly with what they understood wrongly. In practice, no doubt, there will still be bad apples and intervention may be needed almost as often as before. But at least the need is now transitional and will much diminish, when truly enlightened self-interest comes to prevail.

It looks, then, as if liberty and utility can be reconciled by interlocking the true interests of human beings before they ever reach the market. If each would be truly served by a situation where it was not in his interest to work ten hours, while others worked nine, then government is enforcing liberty as well as greater utility. But this is not enough to make the truly rational individual into a compleat utilitarian. We have been supposing that the Social Liberty Game, as instanced by the nine-hours-or-ten question, is at least an Assurance Game, whose proper outcome is nine hours for all. But that, on reflection, need not be so. Mill himself allows that ten hours for some and nine for others might be a good outcome, were it stable. Indeed, any outcome which improves life for some, without worsening it for others, is an advance on the proper outcome of an Assurance Game. (The citizens of *On Liberty* are, I presume, untroubled by envy.) In other words, where total utility can be raised by uneven distribution but without loss to anyone, utilitarianism approves. This point crops up often, notably for instance with promise-keeping and truth-telling, wherever a few lies or broken promises can raise the total good. In so far as utility demands such outcomes from the game of life, universal prohibitions will not be for the best.[4]

---

[4] The practical importance of the matter is roundly shown by Fred Hirsch's discussion of 'Positional Goods' in *Social Limits to Growth* (London: Routledge & Kegan Paul, 1977).

While *laissez faire* remains the general rule, the next move is presumably through incentives. It has to be worthwhile for a few to work for ten hours and for most to work nine. There are various schemes for taxes, allowances and prices which might produce the uneven marginal improvements which Utilitarianism seeks. It is too late in this essay to try to pronounce definitively. But the odds are against Mill's finding a *laissez faire* scheme which maximizes utility, thanks to the sheer variety of his seven exceptions. He has given government too many legitimating grounds on which to try to maximize utility by intervention. He has no total faith in market mechanisms alone, will not settle for what they yield and has listed warrants for intervening which go far beyond mere tinkering. When *On Liberty* is added in, the market freedom of individual economic actors becomes the moral freedom of individual citizens. The 'business of society' is by now to maximize the good of all and that sounds to me uncommonly like Rousseau's General Will.

I started by asking how the author of *On Liberty* can be hailed as the father of British socialism. The initial answer lies in the *Principles*, in part for its awareness that there are economic preconditions for pursuing our own good in our own way and in part for the coach and four it drives through its own great principle of political economy. This may seem an odd comment on a work which starts by remarking that 'the efficiency of industry may be expected to be great in proportion as the fruits of industry are insured to the person exercising it' (I.viii.6) and, in general, seems to regard production as governed by iron laws of egoistic human nature. But Mill himself notes that 'history bears witness to the success with which human beings may be trained to feel the public interest as their own' (II.iii.1) and hints that the iron laws may not be timeless. Even if state socialism is a chimerical notion, syndicalism might be workable. Putting this open-mindedness together with the concern for the general good which inspires the seven exceptions, I think that the *Principles* flirts with a mild socialism but offers no promise of marriage. In *On Liberty*, however, the major obstacle is removed. It ceases to be true that men are by nature at all the self-interested economic homunculi of the laws of political economy. All depends on whether social life turns men into machines made after a model or provides the soil in which they can develop like trees. The talk there of culture and horticulture is utopian, no doubt, but the *Principles* stills offers a shrewd corrective. Meanwhile it is *On Liberty* which contains Mill's mature view of individual human nature and thus, in final irony, the book which remains the gospel of liberal passion is the more socialist of the pair.

The Social Liberty Game for Mill, however, is played by individuals for individuals. Its outcome must enhance individuality, not subvert it. So the tension between liberty and utility remains to worry social democrats and democratic socialists. The 'business of society' may demand stage management of the economy but 'liberty' still lets the citizen spit in the eye of management when individuality is threatened. Utility must still respect the circle round each individual. The Game is as tricky as ever. Since Mill's day the seven exceptions have become almost the rule. (1st) The state is now the accepted guardian of those who are not best judges of their own interest, like children and the mentally handicapped. (2nd) It will often terminate contracts, like marriage, however thoroughly the parties freely bound themselves originally. (3rd) It casts an interfering eye on all sorts of delegated agencies. (4th) Not even the born-again market Conservative supposes that the market by itself will give effect to all the sound judgments of individuals; *laissez faire* is no longer the general rule of industry, still less of the public sector, which employs over half the work force. (5th) The welfare organs of government now dispense the lion's share of philanthropy. (6th) The interlocked character of economic life gives all major decisions consequences extending indefinitely beyond them. (7th) The state has become the unquestioned provider of endless public goods. Is the circle still intact?

The question is hard for Mill's social-minded successors because of their semi-social view of human beings. On the one hand individual interests are not prior to all rules and a liberal theory of social justice is, they believe, stuck for want of an intelligible baseline. On the other hand rules can be judged as a vehicle of expression for human nature and it is wrong, they hold, to brandish a bright red flag in the name of thorough social engineering. They hover between a liberal reading of Rousseau and a socialist reading of Mill. Individuality has social and economic pre-conditions but individual persons are still the inviolable units of social policy. A person's relations with others are neither merely instrumental nor wholly definitive of his being. This is the muddy pitch where the Social Liberty Game is to be played. The central puzzle of the game is when government shall intervene to change the outcome, which existing preferences of the players would produce. Its solution is not finally in Mill but I do not myself find it anywhere else and Mill remains a provoking source of all that makes it difficult.

'Freedom is Slavery': a Slogan for Our New Philosopher Kings

ANTONY FLEW

> But if you want to be free, you've got to be a prisoner. It's the condition of freedom—true freedom.
>
> 'True freedom!' Anthony repeated in the parody of a clerical voice. 'I always love that kind of argument. The contrary of a thing isn't the contrary; oh, dear me, no! It's the thing itself, but as it *truly* is. Ask any die-hard what conservatism is; he'll tell you it's *true* socialism. And the brewer's trade papers; they're full of articles about the beauty of true temperance. Ordinary temperance is just gross refusal to drink; but true temperance, *true* temperance is something much more refined. True temperance is a bottle of claret with each meal and three double whiskies after dinner . . .
>
> 'What's in a name?' Anthony went on. 'The answer is, practically everything, if the name's a good one. Freedom's a marvellous name. That's why you're so anxious to make use of it. You think that, if you call imprisonment true freedom, people will be attracted to the prison. And the worst of it is you're quite right.'
>
> Aldous Huxley, *Chrome Yellow*

I

I thank Professor C. L. Stevenson for drawing this percipient passage to the attention of philosophers of my generation. I now demonstrate the sincerity of that appreciation by refreshing their memories; as well perhaps as by displaying it for the first time to one or two juniors who may have read neither the novels of Aldous Huxley nor *Ethics and Language*. The phenomenon of persuasive definition thus luminously delineated is, of course, still very much alive and well. So the present series of lectures needs to include at least one review of the work of someone persuasively redefining 'freedom' or 'liberty' as perfect obedience to those likeminded with themselves. To liberate, an exultant Marcuse used to tell the student mobs, is to emancipate from 'repressive tolerance'; in *1984* under Ingsoc (English Socialism) the telescreens will surely blare out the slogan, 'Freedom is Slavery'; while already, with shameless persistence, what an old song used to call 'Lenin's lads' characterize the collective absolutism of the right left people as rule in accordance with the principles of democratic centralism.[1]

The book upon which I propose to work is *Freedom and Liberation* by Benjamin Gibbs. It is, the Preface says, 'the substance of lectures given at Sussex University in 1973 and 1974' (p. 8). It was first published in 1976 by the Sussex University Press as the second member of a series edited by Professor Roy Edgley under the general title 'Philosophy Now'. But it is now handled by the Harvester Press of Brighton. (The more it changes, perhaps, the more it is the same thing?)

In view of this ambience it is perhaps surprising that the intellectual debts of the kind of authoritarianism advocated by Gibbs are far more to Plato than to Lenin. Certainly many very general expressions of hatred and contempt are directed against capitalists, capitalism, and 'your typical smug pillar of commercial society' (p. 105). Thus, with precious little reason given, Gibbs utters a comprehensive condemnation: 'The profit motive debases methods of production, the nature of what is produced, and the character of the producers' (p. 138). J. S. Mill too falls under a bit of cloud for what he says ('showing his bourgeois streak?') about the irrevocability of contracts 'relating to money' (p. 92). This happens notwithstanding that he had earlier appeared to be among the elect: 'Like most bourgeois intellectuals (including Marx) Mill detested the avaricious society that had made him' (p. 85).

Nevertheless—for all this fury and ferocity against 'senescent capitalism, putrid with greed, luxury and lawlessness' (p. 140)—*Freedom and Liberation* seems to contain only one reference either to socialism or to any of the existing socialist societies. That reference is not wholly happy: 'The Russians produce novels, symphonies and rockets at least as good as ours. The leaders of modern China have controlled the lives and thoughts of their people more than Mill would have conceived possible; yet the social and technological achievements of that same people during the same period have astonished the world' (p. 95). To commend the Soviet regime for inspiring such novels as *Cancer Ward* and *A Day in the Life of Ivan Denisovitch* would be a backhanded and, I should have thought, grating tribute; while the present masters of China might be themselves even more astonished than displeased were they to be presented with a list of spectacular achievements under the notorious Gang of Four.

It is, however, time to make good on the claim that Gibbs is persuasively redefining 'freedom' into something very different, if not exactly opposite.

[1] It is in the present context worth remarking that when Lenin first developed his proposals for a party of a new type he made no bones about their totally undemocratic character. Instead he argued that this defection from the theoretical ideal was practically essential in a period of illegality. See my 'Russell's Judgement on Bolshevism', in G. W. Roberts (ed.) *Bertrand Russell Memorial Volume* (London: Allen and Unwin, 1979).

He himself asserts in his Preface: 'The theory of freedom expounded in this book might be described not entirely inaptly as a form of liberalism' (p. 8). Yet I am at once reminded of Joseph Schumpeter's remark, often quoted by F. A. Hayek, about the socialists who 'as a supreme but unintended compliment . . . have thought it wise to appropriate this label'; and who are too easily allowed to keep it.[2] After explaining that he is himself, since 'the term has been pre-empted by defenders of a shallow and inadequate doctrine', willing to relinquish it, Gibbs concludes his preliminaries: 'It will be sufficiently obvious that this is not a tract *against* freedom' (p. 8, italics original).

Yet as soon as we get into the main text it becomes clear to the critical reader that—apart from two or three pages of inconsistent backsliding, occasioned by recalling belated insights in Plato's *Laws* (pp. 112 and 132ff) —'a tract *against* freedom' is precisely what this is. Such a reader will have formed strong suspicions by, at latest, the time when Gibbs quotes and— with a characteristic explosion against 'heartless *laissez faire* policies'— dismisses Berlin's definition: 'Political liberty . . . is simply the area within which a man can act unobstructed by others' (p. 24, quoted from p. 122 of *Four Essays on Liberty*). By the bottom of this page Gibbs has already begun to assure us that 'complete freedom is more than merely being *made* to do what is good; it consists in recognizing the good and doing it willingly' (italics mine). So that first suspicious disquiet consolidates into certain conviction.

It is now no surprise to find poor Mill again being hauled over the coals, this time for not owning up to having realized that 'freedom in the sense of personal autonomy is a very different thing from being allowed to do what one desires' (p. 93). Nor are we startled by the revelation that 'Moral freedom involves conformance [*sic*], not so much between what one is and what one wants to be, as between what one is and what one *ought* to be' (pp. 105–106, italics original). Finally Gibbs gives an account of a free society which should, surely, win some sort of award for working three uses of

[2] Recently I have myself seen both Jane Fonda and J. K. Galbraith described in the *Los Angeles Times* as liberals. This was in defiance of the fact that Galbraith is a self-confessed socialist, on the record as saying: 'I am not particular about freedom.' Miss Fonda's commitment is so hard and, we might add, so callous that she refused to abandon her stated principle of never criticizing socialist countries even in order to join Joan Baez in protesting the holocaust wrought by Pol Pot and the Khmer Rouge. That Galbraithian nugget was one of several extracted by Sir Keith Joseph from an interview given to *Die Zeit*, and shared by him with readers of the *The Times* of London in letters published on 1 April and 4 May 1977. Asked by his interviewer how he could say such things within sight of the Berlin Wall, Galbraith showed that he at least suffered no hesitations in *The Age of Uncertainty*: 'I think the wall is a good thing; at least it has maintained the peace'.

the word 'make' into its two short sentences: 'A free society is not simply one that *makes* its people do what is right and good. It is a society that *makes* them do what is right and good by *making* them desire to do it understanding that it is right and good' (p. 109, some italics supplied and others removed).

Throughout *Freedom and Liberation* much is also disclosed, both directly and indirectly, about the Guardian élite which is to do all this making—the new philosopher kings who will, if all goes well, create, and impose their own values upon, what Gibbs wants to honour as 'A free society'. Although Gibbs does not actually employ these particular Platonic technicalities, their introduction here is nevertheless appropriate and fair. Certainly, by quoting twice from Marx and making one further wry reference to him, Gibbs does just enough to keep on terms with, if not to be received into, the Radical Philosophy Group.[3] Nevertheless it is everywhere apparent that his own inspiration is primarily Platonic.

However, in order to get themselves upon their thrones, the Gibbs Guardians will have to effect a revolution—and this *is* a little incongruous—a revolution specifically against capitalism; one involving 'fundamental changes in the economic framework'. For, Gibbs goes on, 'The institutions of capitalism do not compose a stable system . . . Calliclean libertinism is adopted as a principle of conduct' (p. 139).

What is to be done? 'Without doubt, this charmless, decaying polity needs some kind of revolution to restore its equilibrium and vigour . . . But where are the engineers of revolution? Every great melioration that takes place in human affairs is initiated by some resolute organization, endowed with political wisdom. A revolutionary movement, if it is to succeed, must be in possession of a clear design for the social order it wishes to establish, and must be able to gain command of the means (including sufficient military power) to enforce execution of that design' (pp. 139–140). As the red dawn draws near, Plato, it appears, is yielding place to Lenin, the golden man to the iron Bolshevik. But then, through another strange turn, it emerges that the true revolutionary party has still to be constituted: 'There are a few enlightened groups and persons of influence, who understand what is involved in a truly liberating reformation of society, and who are endeavouring to bring it about. We can only hope that their numbers increase and that they find ways of uniting. With luck, they might still win the day' (p. 141).

II

1. Now that we have seen what Gibbs really is doing we are ready to

[3] He quotes *Capital* on Mill (p. 85) and *The Eighteenth Brumaire of Louis Buonaparte* on the *lumpenproletariat* (p. 140), while the unquoting reference is to Marx maintaining 'the habits and manners of respectable bourgeois citizens'.

discover how he does it. Our first clue lies in the repudiation of minute philosophy in the opening manifesto from the General Editor, and in his identifying with this repudiation a demand for—if a word of cant may be excused—relevance: 'The books in this series are united by nothing except discontent', with an activity, 'submissively dwindled into a humble academic specialism, on its own understanding isolated from substantive issues in other disciplines, from the practical problems facing society, and from contemporary Continental thought' (p. 6).

The author himself has a little more patience with logical analysis. Perhaps he at least half remembers that Plato wrote not only the *Republic* and the *Laws* but also the *Theaetetus*. Nevertheless Gibbs still wants to mix up questions about meaning with questions of other quite different kinds. He allows that 'Part of the enterprise must consist in reflecting on what may seem rather dull facts about the meaning of words', and that 'An adequate theory of freedom must have some congruity with ordinary linguistic usage ... ' But then he completes that second sentence by insisting: '. . . the problems are to a large extent psychological, moral and political problems' (p. 10).

It is this insistence which leads him to reject Berlin's definition of 'political liberty', offering as his reason what is, among its other faults, and in an understanding which is not cant at all, simply irrelevant. 'Berlin's idea of freedom', he wails, 'could be invoked *as it stands*, without being misrepresented in any way, to justify heartless *laissez faire* policies' (p. 23, italics original).[4] Yet, whatever the truth about this, it remains neither here nor there. Given ingenuity, almost any term could be put to work in the development of a justification of almost anything: the proper question about a suggested descriptive definition is, rather, that of its 'congruity

[4] Another gross fault is that what Gibbs denounces as 'heartless *laissez faire*' is not a free, competitive and pluralist economy. It is what Marx labelled oriental despotism, making desultory and ineffective efforts to squeeze this uncovenanted discovery into his already supposedly complete schema of inexorable historical progress. Thus the Gibbs specification runs: 'If a ruler owns all the land and means of production, he need not burden his people with a multitude of laws and taxes. He need not make explicit demands, because his subjects have no choice but to sell him their labour in order to survive' (p. 24). Had our Radical Philosophers any sincere interest in liberty and liberation as popularly conceived they would surely remark that this is very like the situation under socialism; the difference being that there the despot is not an individual but a collective. Radical Philosophers will not listen to any 'bourgeois liberal' critic. But to Trotsky they might: 'In a country where the sole employer is the State, opposition means death by slow starvation. The old principle, who does not work shall not eat, has been replaced by a new one: who does not obey shall not eat.' This passage, to which I was directed first by F. A. Hayek, comes in *The Revolution Betrayed*, translated by Max Eastman (Garden City, NY: Doubleday, Doran, 1937), 76.

with ordinary linguistic usage'. The reason why Gibbs thinks that his outraged cries are relevant lies in his forever hankering after a peculiar conception of what he proposes to go on calling freedom or liberty; a conception which will enable him to welcome this as always and every-where, in all circumstances and without qualification, good. Indeed at times he appears to want to go even further, maintaining that it must itself embrace all goods of every kind. For his final chapter, 'Liberation and Politics', begins: 'If perfect freedom encompasses the whole spectrum of human goods', which I take him to be suggesting that it does; then, 'a fully fledged political philosophy is needed to give an account of it' (p. 129).

This same ruinous insistence that nothing can truly be liberty, or true liberty, or perfect freedom, unless it is something which Gibbs could hail as, if not the sum of all goods, then at least a good without qualification, occurs not once only, nor yet once and again, but again and again and again. A page or so earlier, for instance, he writes: 'When a person can select any of several apparently flawless apples he *thinks* he has a free choice, but he will not think so if some of the apples are discovered to be rotten . . . Being free to choose between likeable things is of no advantage if, through ignorance or misjudgment, one is led to desire and choose things which are harmful. We want, surely, to be free to choose things that not only seem good but which really are good' (pp. 21–22, italics original).

No doubt this is what, on a great many occasions, we do want to be free to choose. However, before proceeding with the argument, I have by the way to record that I am construing this 'we' as including the vulgar. That would certainly not be correct in some other cases. For example: at the end of a chapter on 'The Direction of Desire' Gibbs speaks with reproachful tolerance of 'depravity among adults whose desires have been irretrievably corrupted, and who would suffer great misery if they were forced to alter their ways . . . Let us follow Mill's principle, permitting them to do as they like so long as they do it in private, and no one else is harmed' (p. 112). There the 'we' presumably has a more exclusive reference to the Guardian elect, who share with Gibbs all the right and good pre-ferences.

It may be interesting further to interject that these, it seems, are: in opera, for *The Marriage of Figaro* over *Madame Butterfly* (pp. 19–20); in pubs, for real ale rather than the 'standardized pressurized, sweet indi-gestible muck that the big national breweries, with an eye to their profit, have conditioned the public to prefer' (p. 89); and, after 'one has been philosophizing all day', for 'taking a cross country run' (p. 130). Tempted though I am both to sound off about the unhappy experience of consumers under socialism and to point out that it is precisely 'with one eye to their profit' that the many firms which have identified the demand are now supplying real Guardian ales, I will instead say only, and more generously, what a great joy it is to these old eyes to see the spirit of the public school house run so vigorously alive among our Sussex revolutionaries.

No doubt—to return to the choosing of apples—we do indeed, on many occasions, all want to choose between alternatives which do not merely seem to be but really are good. Yet this is no reason at all for saying that persons so unfortunate as to have chosen rotten apples, under the mistaken impression that these were all in splendid condition, have not freely and without coercion chosen whatever apples they have in fact chosen. If they think they have not so chosen, then they are in error. We might add too that—in their wingeing and whining refusal to accept responsibility for doing what, however excusably, they most manifestly have done—they display in a trifling matter a mean-souled lack of moral fibre.

Nor is it anywhere to the point to protest: 'Being free to choose between likeable things is no advantage if, through ignorance or misjudgment, one is led to desire and choose things which are harmful'. Whether or not it is an advantage is once again neither here nor there. The question is: not whether it is in such circumstances an advantage to be free to choose; but whether people in those same circumstances do have a free choice. And they do.

This is something of which on other occasions, Gibbs himself is well aware; as indeed, he could scarcely fail to be. At the very beginning of this first chapter, and notwithstanding that he is going a mere dozen pages later to put down Berlin's negative definition of 'political liberty' as describing a 'merely nominal liberty' (p. 24), Gibbs recognizes that he christens 'prescriptive freedom' as something which is presumably not merely nominal: 'the idea of exemption from servitude and being allowed to do as one pleases ... Prescriptive freedom is freedom from rules and rulers ... ' (pp. 12–13). It is this same old original freedom—and again with no suggestion that it is to be sneered at as negative, unreal, or merely nominal—of which Gibbs is speaking when he refers to Luther 'denouncing the German peasants, when they revolted against their princes and sought liberty for themselves' (p. 82). Most remarkably, it is still the same old original, genuine freedom which is under discussion in those curious backslidings in his final chapter.

There—sandwiched between the previously quoted proclamation that 'perfect freedom encompasses the whole spectrum of human goods' (p. 129) and the concluding call for the Guardian élite to gather its forces ('including sufficient military power') in order to overthrow by revolutionary violence 'senescent capitalism, putrid with greed, luxury and lawlessness' (p. 140)—we can find an incongruous admission: 'The liberal political tradition is right to insist that human welfare requires a fair degree of liberty, understood simply as being allowed to do as one pleases, for good or ill ... ' (p. 134). Earlier, at pp. 109–110, he makes an even more remarkable admission: 'There may never have existed a society which granted its members more liberty than we citizens of England enjoy'.

Yet none of this liberal backsliding is permitted to detract from his bold convictions: that a truly free society is 'one that makes its people do what is right and good'; while also 'making them *desire* to do it *understanding* that it is right and good' (p. 109, italics original). Nor does it insinuate into his mind the slightest doubt whether his fellow revolutionaries will in practice allow it to be 'patent sophistry to argue that, in a juster, freer society than the one we know, the traditional liberties might be abolished completely' (p. 136). This patent sophism, after all, has been and is both presented and accepted by every Jacobin from Robespierre and Saint-Just, through Lenin and Trotsky, right up to Castro and Ho Chi Minh.

His brief encounter with 'insubstantial and sterile . . . liberal ideology' (p. 128) thus fails to produce any salutary effects upon Gibbs. The main reason for this failure lies in that prime, besetting confusion: between, on the one hand, questions of what liberty and freedom are; and, on the other hand, questions whether some particular exercise or kind of exercise of either is or was or will be—in the phrase made famous by *1066 and All That*—'a good thing'. He asserts, it seems without a qualm: 'Liberty is simply the area within which individual conduct *should* be free from legal and bureaucratic coercion' (pp. 136–137, italics mine). About this, as Berlin notes, Bentham said what should be, but obviously will not be, 'the last word: "Is not liberty to do evil, liberty? If not, what is it? Do we not say that it is necessary to take liberty from idiots and bad men because they abuse it?"' (p. 148).

2. A second source of trouble is not the same as but related to that examined in the previous section. Gibbs, though not so impatient of philosophical underlabouring as his General Editor, is still in much too much of a hurry to get on to what he proudly proclaims to be 'the theory of freedom expounded in this book' (p. 6). In that, though not in its modest bulk, *Freedom and Liberation* is reminiscent of *A Theory of Justice*. For John Rawls expresses his happiness 'to leave questions of meaning and definition aside and to get on with the task of developing a substantive theory of justice' (p. 579). In both cases this impatience makes it easier to present what is at least in part an essay in persuasive redefinition as something other than it is.[5]

Thus Gibbs begins: 'All men yearn to be free . . . Yet there is no general

[5] See Wallace Matson, 'What Rawls Calls Justice', *The Occasional Review* No. 8/9 (Autumn 1978) (San Diego: World Research, 1978); and perhaps compare Chapter III of my *The Politics of Procrustes* (London: Temple Smith, 1981).

agreement about what, in its essence, freedom is' (p. 9). Although the next four chapters are going to deal with the Freedom of the Will, all the examples provided here are of political liberty. Without for one moment attempting to sort out what actually is being said in any of these various particular cases, Gibbs goes on at once in very general terms to outline his first answer: 'Certainly it is possible to be confused or mistaken, and to deceive people, about what being free or being set free consists in. But ... "freedom" means different things in different contexts ... because it has a number of meanings which, though distinct, are ... related to each other in specifiable ways ... there is no single correct concept of freedom ... ' (p. 9).

I speak of 'very general terms' and of 'his first answer' advisedly. For neither now nor later is any set of distinctions between related senses applied to these initial examples. What is, however, much more serious is that, in the very same paragraph in which we have just now been told that 'there is no single correct concept of freedom'—that very same paragraph in which we are also about to be warned that 'We are prone to misconceive and misrepresent this perplexingly polymorphous notion, to abstract from it something ... which we take to be the real essence of freedom'—we are then told that, in the event, 'What is brought into being may be a negation of true freedom' (p. 10). Whatever can this 'negation of true freedom' be if it is not the negation of that allegedly non-subsistent 'single concept of freedom'?

So long as it is to be interpreted as rebuking the kind of exercise in persuasive redefinition which is supposed to justify the revolutionary destruction of a system guaranteeing liberties perhaps more numerous than any other people have ever enjoyed, then I for one am eager to assent to the statement immediately preceding the last just quoted: 'If such abstractions are employed as principles of social policy, there may be a high price to pay in human suffering' (p. 10).

Nor shall I refrain from adding that, if there is such a high price to be paid, then it is my own most fervent albeit despairing hope that it may be paid by the élite making such frivolous and wanton calls for revolution, rather than by the vulgar with their 'predilections squalid and degraded' and their (of course advertiser-stimulated) 'desires ... for expensive material goods and pleasures' (p. 110).

Had Gibbs been prepared to do a bit of analytic work on his own collection of examples he would, I think, have found it unnecessary to multiply senses here. For all these particular specimens, although not by that token all other specimens, could be compassed within Berlin's definition of 'political liberty', or else within something very like it. The crux is that, given any definition on these lines, then the actual liberties secured to one individual or group are bound to be so secured at the price of possible liberties which might have been secured for others. It was Bentham again who most doggedly insisted upon the truth of this truism. 'Every law is an infraction of liberty', he said. For even when a law does secure some liberty for all of us, still it must at the same time prevent everyone from violating that liberty; the very laws which guarantee our liberties to cultivate our own gardens must do so by restricting everyone's liberty to vandalize the gardens of others.

This is a very simple principle. Yet it is one which you are sure to find very difficult to grasp if you want to insist that any freedom—or any true or real or perfect freedom—is always and in all circumstances and without qualification good. Once that self-imposed handicap is abandoned any paradoxes on page one are quickly resolved. There is no call to be surprised that two groups should be in conflict, and yet both sincerely profess to be fighting for liberty. The questions to ask are: 'Liberty in what direction?'; and 'Liberty for whom?' It will be time to think of multiplying senses, or to speak of intractable antinomies, when we find conflicts between groups demanding either the same liberties for the same people or equal liberties for all.

3. We have seen that in the second paragraph of his first chapter Gibbs begins by maintaining that '"freedom" has a number of meanings which, though distinct are . . . related to each other in specifiable ways' (p. 9). Then, before that paragraph is out, he starts to talk of 'a negation of true freedom' (p. 10). Later in the same chapter he lists these supposed or proposed meanings, specifying ways in which they are related. The first, which he calls prescriptive freedom, consists in what we have been calling legally guaranteed liberties: 'Prescriptive freedom is freedom from rules and rulers; still, where there is no authority and no law, there is no prescriptive freedom or bondage' (p. 13).

Gibbs next proceeds to 'distinguish and give appropriate designations to four kinds of non-prescriptive freedom attributable to persons' (p. 17). This is where he deploys most of his argument for the conclusion that 'A free society' is one in which people are *made* to do what is right and good, and *made* to like it, agreeing that it is right and good. The case thus developed is, I suggest, neither. Furthermore, although my own argument does not depend on this, I am inclined to think that only one of his proposed interpretations is indeed an established non-technical sense.

First, the scope of what Gibbs christens 'optative freedom' is precisely the scope of human action as such: 'Indeed', as he says himself, 'any act is free to that extent; there is no *acting* without the possibility of abstaining from acting. If a person has absolutely no choice about what he does— if he unavoidably breaks a window, for example, having been thrown against it by a gust of wind—then what takes place is just a happening, not strictly speaking a human act' (p. 18). Fine: I would not pretend to put it better myself. But whatever warrant can there be for introducing and labelling a fresh sense of 'free' appropriate always and only to action and such that all and only action can and must be free? What is wrong with saying, more simply and tersely, that this or that person was in this or that dimension an agent; without droning on about their being, therefore, necessarily and tautologically endowed with optative freedom?[6]

The second fresh coinage is 'conative freedom'. This time the description which Gibbs provides is not so satisfactory. But when we take this with his illustrations it becomes obvious: both that he has in mind the altogether familiar distinction between acting under compulsion and acting freely, acting of one's own free will; and that conative freedom is what one has in this second case. His own account runs: 'If someone does something out of fear, unwillingly, reluctantly, under duress, or *faute de mieux*, he does not do it of his own free will. Yet the act is voluntary; it does not take place without reference to the agent's will; he is not moved willy-nilly. As I said earlier, "free will" is a synonym for optative freedom' (p. 20, italics and punctuation original).

This is unsatisfactory, first, because it does not actually mention compulsion. It is, next, even more unsatisfactory in applying the word 'voluntary' to what is presented as, though not in so many words said to be, done under compulsion. Did not Austin teach us that in ordinary, untechnical usage the voluntary is opposed neither to the non-voluntary nor to the involuntary but to the compulsory? But it is most unsatisfactory of all in complacently (albeit correctly) conceding that 'free will' is a synonym for 'optative freedom' immediately after the former expression has been wantonly misemployed to pick out what Gibbs calls not optative but conative freedom. It is indeed the regrettable truth, which two pages earlier Gibbs was observing without regret, that many philosophers have regularly, albeit without realizing what they were doing, conscripted that expression to do supplementary service as a technicality. Yet it would be so much better—by instead simply talking about being an agent—to speak with the vulgar.

---

[6] Here however Gibbs keeps the best of company. For in the great chapter 'Of Power' in his *Essay concerning Human Understanding*, Locke gives an ostensive definition of what he wrongly describes not as an agent simply but a free agent: 'Everyone, I think, finds . . . a Power to begin or forbear, continue or put an end to several Actions in himself . . . We have instances enough, and often more than enough in our own bodies. A Man's Heart beats, and the Blood circulates, which 'tis not in his Power . . . to stop; and therefore in respect of these Motions, where rest depends not on his choice . . . he is not a *free Agent*. Convulsive Motions agitate his legs, so that though he *wills* it never so much, he cannot . . . stop their Motion (as in that odd Disease called *Chorea Sancti Viti*,) but he is perpetually dancing: He is . . . under as much Necessity of moving as a Stone that falls or a Tennis-ball struck with a Racket' (II (xxi) 7 and 11: italics and everything else original).

We have already approached the third Gibbs coinage in connection with the choice of apples. Here the free agent is taken to be free in precisely the same sense as before: he is not, that is to say, acting under compulsion. But, whereas in a case of the previous kind that agent may be confronted with only one single positively attractive option, in this kind there have to be at least two. The rationale runs: 'To have a choice, in the full sense, is to be able to choose between agreeable alternatives. I shall refer to this henceforward as *elective freedom*' (p. 21, italics original).

Certainly it is true that we do often say in cases of the second sort that the compelled (but not the free) agent had no choice, and could not have done otherwise. It is also very important to notice, as Gibbs does, that even in those compulsion cases, it is true to say that in other and most fundamental senses, there was a choice, and that something else could have been done. Yet none of this constitutes a reason for saying that in cases of the third kind the agent is free in another sense of 'freedom'; much less for saying—as we saw earlier that Gibbs does go on to say— that he only has a real choice, being truly free in yet another sense, when the options available, and in particular the option actually chosen, not merely seem to be but are good.

Thus Gibbs under this third heading is already beginning to confound freedom to choose between alternatives with the actual achievement of approved ends. It is a kind of confusion lamentably common in our time. It can be seen, for instance, though it is in fact rarely noticed, in those sociologists and educationists who systematically collapse the distinction between opportunity and outcome.[7] But it is with his fourth supposed kind of freedom that Gibbs really goes to town. This discussion is a prime manifestation of the author's resolve to mix up questions of meaning with questions of value. Thus he begins: 'The value of freedom depends on that of the goods which it is the power of achieving' (p. 22). Maybe it does. But this is no way to start detecting a further sense of the word 'free'.

Gibbs continues: 'The most precious freedom of all is the power of avoiding the greatest evils and achieving the greatest goods ... The most appropriate epithet for this sovereign freedom would be "eudai-monic" ... I shall use the term *natural freedom*, since this is the power of attaining and enjoying the cardinal goods appropriate to our nature' (p. 22, italics original). Gibbs thus indicates why what he has in mind should be accepted as precious. But how does it become a kind of freedom? 'To furnish a person with natural freedom', he goes on, 'would be to liberate him not just in this or that respect but completely ... Thus, whereas every other kind of freedom consists in *being able* to avoid evil and to do good, natural freedom consists primarily in *actually* being immune

---

[7] See, for a collection of choice specimens. *The Politics of Procrustes*, Chapter II, Sections 4–5.

from the worst evils and *actually* achieving the supreme goods' (p. 22, italics original).

'Yes indeed', you say, 'that is indeed the crucial move. But what is its warrant?' You have a good question, and one deserving a better answer than it gets. For Gibbs provides only his own version of that most notorious conversation-stopper of decadent Scholasticism, 'Aristotle hath said it'. It reads: 'Aristotle defines *eudaimonia* as "activity of soul in accordance with perfect virtue" (*Nicomachean Ethics* 1102a, 5): activity, not mere potentiality; practice of the good life, not simply possession of the capacity to live well. It involves *willingness* to use and extend one's human talents and powers' (p. 22, italics original). But what is needed here Aristotle hath not even said. This is his definition of nothing else but 'eudaimonia'. Certainly Gibbs would do a little better by calling his 'natural freedom' eudaimonic. But the real scandal is not adjectival but substantive. It is to commend what precisely is not as not merely a, but the, highest kind of freedom.[8]

III

That would have been a satisfactory punch line with which to conclude. But I do want first to rebut two objections, made against Mill and against Hume, both of which objections are tokens of types important to all who would provide a role for Guardians.

(a) Gibbs has a lot to say about 'The Romantic Libertarianism of John Stuart Mill'. 'Philosophers Now' are licensed to treat Mill with some respect because, unlike crude fellows who rail at all his works as 'nothing more than an exposition of the individualistic ideology of *laissez faire* economics . . . Marx himself said "It would be very wrong to class (Mill)

---

[8] In discussion both before, on and after the occasion of the reading of the first two parts of this paper at the Royal Institute of Philosophy, Gibbs protested that I have misrepresented the position of *Freedom and Liberation*. I can only respond by insisting that further rereadings leave me still equally persuaded that I have not: the other passages to which he would draw attention do not affect the point to which I take such strong exception. I had hoped to make the nature of that point clearer to him by comparing and contrasting: on the one hand, his own exercise of redefining (the highest kind of) freedom, as being made to act only in approved ways; with, on the other hand, the attempt of the Platonic Socrates to assimilate virtues to skills. For, whereas the former are dispositions to act in one sort of way and no other, the latter, as the critics always insist, are powers to act in different and even opposite ways. But Gibbs has reminded me of his contribution to the Symposium 'Virtue and Reason' at the 1974 Joint Session, which actually defended, albeit in a much qualified form, precisely that assimilation I see as preposterous (*PASS* XLVIII, 23–41).

with the herd of vulgar economic apologists" (*Capital* I, VI, xxiv, 5) . . . Mill was not a conscious or unconscious spokesman for capitalism' (p. 85).

May I not here ask out loud—just once—why we are thus and commonly required to reject unheard anyone who has any remarks to offer in favour of that form of economic organization which has in the last two centuries unleashed an altogether unprecedented increase in the forces of production; raising vast masses of people, and promising to raise more, from that abysmal poverty which was previously the almost universal human condition?[9] It is a question to be pressed the harder, since we are also nowadays generally required to attend respectfully, and as to disinterested friends of the human race, to spokespersons for the socialist alternative—the system of those wonderful people who created *The Gulag Archipelago*, and who now toil without rest to extend their tyranny over the whole world.

Be all that as it may. Certainly Gibbs applies some very harsh words to Mill, who is at one point denounced because 'He makes no attempt to give this fatuous and fantastic claim the support it calls for' (p. 90). Where, then, is the object of such contempt? What Gibbs says is that 'he says, apparently with conviction, that grown persons are always the best judges of what is in their own interest'. But what, immediately after this, Mill is quoted as saying is something else: 'With respect to his own feelings and circumstances, the most ordinary man and woman has means of knowledge immeasurably surpassing those that can be possessed by anyone else'. And this is by no means so silly as what Gibbs says he says.

The point is that, whereas there may be room for Guardians better able than we to determine our true needs and true interests, we are all our own best experts on what we like and dislike, what we want and how we feel. This is why the National Union of Teachers, opposing the giving of education vouchers to parents, to enable us to choose the kind of education which we *want*, boasts that its members are alone qualified to determine and to cater for the educational *needs* of children. It is also why democracy in the new, authoritarian or Eastern version refers not to the actual wishes but the supposed interests of the recognized people; whereas authentic or Western democracy is a matter of what, for better or for worse, electors do freely choose.

(b) The second, eminently rebuttable objection is against Hume. Gibbs has it in for any ought/is distinction: 'Liberal ideologists frequently invoke the positivist doctrine of a fact-value dichotomy, in support of libertarian social policies' (p. 115). So Hume has to be seen off. Seen off he is, in very short order. 'Hume claims', Gibbs reports, 'that morality cannot be derived from matters of fact, because it is impossible to move validly

---

[9] Nor can it be said too often, especially in contexts like the present, that in no socialist country are even the most fundamental civil liberties guaranteed and respected; and that in some though not in all the countries called capitalist citizens enjoy a range of liberties which, Gibbs suggests, is without precedent.

from "is" to "ought". The argument is misconceived. If the difference between "is" and "ought" were to lend support for the theory of a dichotomy between facts and values, it would have to be the case that all factual statements were "is"-statements and all value standards "ought"-statements. But some "is-statements—for example, "Fornication is disgraceful"—are value statements' (p. 116).

Oh dear! Oh dear! Certainly Benjamin Gibbs is not the first nor even perhaps by now the latest critic to be tripped up by the ironic Hume; and to be found in consequence sprawling flat on his face. I wonder whether he still thinks that that recently so much quoted passage is to be interpreted—as the French would say; if only they spoke English—at the foot of the letter? Does one really have to say again that Hume's contentions concerned a distinction which too frequently is not made; yet which, he thought, always could be and should be? He is not maintaining that, notwithstanding that this distinction regularly and most fastidiously is made, it was for Hume to recognize for the first time that it is 'of the last importance'. Had Hume in truth held the view so confidently refuted by Gibbs, then Hume's position might well have been described as—to coin a phrase—fatuous and fantastic,[10]

---

[10] Two other scholarly corrections, less relevant to my main theme, may be administered in the discreet privacy of a final footnote. First, Kant cannot have forsaken any of the ideas of the *Groundwork* in the *Critique of Pure Reason*: these works were first published in, respectively, 1785 and 1781 (p. 52). Second, and much more important, it is false to say 'that doctrines of predestination . . . usually say only that God has predetermined human *destinies*, not that he has predetermined every human choice and deed' (p. 28, italics original). In fact, as is required by the theist commitment to God as the constant and necessary sustaining cause of everything in the Universe, all the classical theologians seem to be on the record as supporting the stronger doctrine. For a collection of proof texts from Luther and Calvin, Aquinas and Augustine, see my *God and Philosophy* (London: Hutchinson, 1966), Sections 2.34ff. and 5.19; also *The Presumption of Atheism* (London: Pemberton Elek, 1976), 93ff.

Taking Liberties with Freedom: a Reply to Professor Flew[1]

BENJAMIN GIBBS

Professor Flew interprets my book *Freedom and Liberation* as a defence of a sort of radical authoritarianism disguised as a theory of freedom. He supposes me to be looking for a 'Guardian élite', a group of 'new philosopher kings who will . . . create, and impose their own values upon, what Gibbs wants to honour as "a free society"'. In the title of his lecture Flew suggests that the message of the book might accurately be summed up in the Orwellian slogan 'Freedom is Slavery'.

All this is gross, grotesque misrepresentation. Anyone whose curiosity is aroused by Flew's diatribe enough to induce him or her to read *Freedom and Liberation*[2] with a reasonable degree of attention will discover the contents to be (disappointingly, perhaps) less sensational and alarming but also, I think, more consistent, coherent and persuasive than Flew makes out. The book owes little to the Jacobins blacklisted in his lecture. Its sources are traditional, indeed classical: Plato (as Flew sees and states clearly enough), Aristotle, and their tradition through Aquinas and Locke to Burke, Mill and T. H. Green. It was partly because of my debt to these latter thinkers that I felt able to say that my theory of freedom 'might be described, not entirely inaptly, as a form of liberalism'.

Certainly, however, there are numerous real, substantial differences between my position and Flew's. We disagree in many of our judgments and sympathies and in our conceptions of philosophical method. I lack the space to consider all these differences at length. In this present response I shall concentrate on showing that Flew's criticism persistently mistakes the plain literal sense of what I say in the book.

I

It is an essential part of my thesis in *F&L* that 'freedom', 'liberty', 'libera-

[1] I should like to express my gratitude to Professor Flew for providing me with a typescript of his lecture in advance of its delivery, and for keeping me informed of subsequent revisions. I should like to thank also the Director of the Royal Institute of Philosophy, Professor Phillips Griffiths, for inviting me to reply both in person and in print.

[2] I shall refer to it as *F&L*. The present distributor (Harvester Press) has no connection with the original publishers.

tion' and cognate terms mean different things in different contexts. Freedom may be thought of, for example, as a status created by conventions such as laws and customs, and the institutions which establish and uphold them; or it may be thought of rather as a product of natural capacities and circumstances. Again, freedom may be understood minimally and neutrally, as, say, the power to form and execute intentions (the traditional conception of 'free will'): or it may be understood more positively, as a power (legal or natural or both) to avoid what is (either objectively or in the eyes of the subject or both) bad and achieve what is good; and thus an agent may be described as less or more free in proportion to the extent of his power over certain goods and evils. There is no single correct concept of freedom, no unique unambiguous definition which will fit all the senses 'freedom' may carry in our discourse. But of course a condition which is legitimately called 'freedom' may be accounted an inferior and imperfect kind of freedom beside some other—in the same way as one of two constitutions correctly designated as 'democratic' may be less unqualifiedly democratic than the other. A freedom which consists merely in the capacity to opt for a course of action, or in the tacit permission to do anything not forbidden by the law, will be judged indeterminate, or rudimentary and incomplete, by comparison with a freedom defined in terms of having access to specific goods and immunity from specific evils. Thus I wrote: 'There is no single correct concept of freedom . . . Freedom, like good, is multiplex . . . We are prone to misconceive and misrepresent this perplexingly polymorphous notion, to abstract from it something thin and stunted which we take to be the real essence of freedom. If such abstractions are employed as principles of social policy, there may be a high price to pay in human suffering. What is brought into being may be a negation of true freedom' (F&L 9–10).

Flew thinks he discerns a contradiction here. 'Whatever can this "negation of true freedom" be', he retorts, 'if it is not the negation of that allegedly non-subsistent "single correct concept of freedom"?' Well, what I had in mind was this. If we try to convey the essence of freedom in a single formula, we find ourselves specifying the lowest common denominator in a limited range of kinds of freedom. For example, we might define freedom simply as 'being able to do as one likes'. This would be a fair specification of what I call 'conative freedom', which is an element in several familiar conceptions of freedom. But the definition will not apply to any kind of prescriptive freedom (the freedom established by social convention), because prescriptive liberties and natural powers are radically different. Moreover, conative freedom is compatible with many kinds of servitude. Perfect conative freedom might exist in a community of contented 'junkies', who had access to unlimited supplies of their favourite drugs. But it would be paradoxical to describe their degraded, less than fully human condition as one of perfect freedom.

Obviously these people do exactly as they like, yet in a fundamental, not simply metaphorical way they are in a state of bondage. Their condition is 'a negation of true freedom'. By 'true freedom' here and in the passage from *F&L* quoted above I mean perfect freedom, freedom unmixed with servitude, freedom from the worst human evils and command of the greatest human goods—in short, what I call 'natural freedom', the liberation and fulfilment of our truly human potentialities and inclinations. This 'natural freedom' is, I allow and indeed insist, not the only condition that can correctly be called freedom; but it alone is complete and unqualified and in that way true freedom. Flew will think, perhaps rightly, that he detects a whiff of Platonism in all this;[3] but I think it stays close to common usage and common sense.

Since part of my thesis is that 'freedom' means different things in different contexts, I myself, in writing *F&L*, did not hesitate to use the term and its cognates to mean different things in different contexts, relying in each case on the context—together, sometimes, with explicit qualifications—to make my meaning clear. In order to get me pigeonholed with his customary opponents, Flew has to resort to the trick of quoting words and sentences without reference to their contexts and attendant qualifications, and imputing to them a meaning quite different from what was intended. This enables him speedily, but unfairly, to convict me of inconsistency, confusion and turpitude.

To avoid wearying whatever audience Flew and I may have, I shall refrain from cataloguing all the many instances of Flew's trimming and twisting my words to suit his polemical ends. I shall select a range of examples, proceeding from minor to more flagrant and serious misrepresentations.

First: I drew a distinction between (i) the potentiality for human action, 'free will' or, as I call it, 'optative freedom', which exists even when one's scope for acting is restricted to worthless or unpleasant alternatives, and (ii) 'conative freedom', which is being able to act in a way that commends itself to one's desires and inclinations. In *F&L* I explained conative freedom thus:

> There is a sense in which a person has freedom of action only if he is in a position to do what seems good to him, what he finds agreeable, pleasing or worthwhile. I shall call this *conative freedom*. To have conative freedom is, roughly, to be able to do what one likes; what one wants for its own sake, not merely because it is the least repellent option (*F&L* 19).

In his criticism of my 'conative freedom' Flew ignores this passage.

[3] I think the conflict between my 'Platonism' and Flew's empiricism underlies some of the deeper differences between us.

Instead he quotes an incidental, supplementary paragraph from the next page, introducing it as Gibbs's 'own account' of conative freedom. Is it? This is the paragraph (in full; Flew's quotation omits the first two sentences):

> When an agent exercises conative freedom he is said to act 'of his own free will'. This would not usually be said in cases where optative freedom, merely, is exercised. If someone does something out of fear, unwillingly, reluctantly, under duress or *faute de mieux*, he does not do it of his own free will. Yet the act is voluntary; it does not take place without reference to the agent's will; he is not moved willy-nilly. As I said earlier, 'free will' is a synonym for optative freedom (*F&L* 20).

Surely it is obvious from both its contents and its location that *this* is not intended as the determinative account of conative freedom. It is a subsidiary paragraph dealing mainly with optative freedom, which it contrasts with conative freedom. Flew accuses me of 'conceding that "free will" is a synonym for "optative freedom" immediately after the former expression has been wantonly misemployed to pick out what Gibbs calls not optative but conative freedom'. But Flew has read the paragraph carelessly. It does *not* employ the phrase 'free will' to pick out conative freedom; rather, it separates the substantive phrase 'free will' from the adverbial phrase 'of one's own free will', as usually employed. Setting out the point rather laboriously, the paragraph states that (i) in ordinary usage 'free will' is a synonym for optative freedom; but on the other hand (ii) it would not usually be said of someone that he acts 'of his own free will' in cases where optative freedom, merely, is exercised. Saying 'He does it of his own free will' suggests the more full-blooded conative freedom— that he does it willingly, gladly, because he likes it, etc. Whether or not this is a correct analysis of ordinary usage, it does not involve the confusion alleged by Flew.

Flew tries more than once to saddle me with the doctrine—which I denied and argued against repeatedly—that some or other use of 'freedom' or 'liberty', etc., is the one and only correct use; in particular, that freedom must be 'always and in all circumstances and without qualification good'. Flew quotes the following sentence from the section on 'elective freedom':

> When a person can select any of several apparently flawless apples he *thinks* he has a free choice, but he will not think so if some of the apples are discovered to be rotten (*F&L* 21).

On the strength of this, Flew interprets me as implying the unqualified (and therefore false) assertion that someone who has the misfortune to choose rotten apples cannot be said to have chosen them freely and without coercion. But this is sheer distortion, founded upon selective quotation. My use of the phrase 'free choice' in the sentence Flew quotes is not presented there or anywhere as the standard or only legitimate use. It occurs within the section on 'elective freedom', by which I mean: being in a position to choose between agreeable alternatives; and it occurs in the course of elucidating a particular, secondary use of the phrase 'free choice'. The section on elective freedom begins as follows:

> A person who has optative freedom or conative freedom may be said to have a (free) choice. Sometimes, however, the meaning of saying that someone has a choice is that more than one apparent good is accessible to him (*F&L* 20).

Surely it is impossible to say more plainly than this that the phrase 'free choice' has more than one sense, the sense specified in the first sentence as well as that specified in the second. As for the apple example, it is introduced (a page later, at the end of the section) explicitly and only to illustrate a sub-distinction, between specious elective freedom (where the subject has a number of apparently good options) and real elective freedom (where the options really are good). The apple-chooser can be said to lack a free choice, in the sense (only) that the apples offered to him are not really desirable. He does have a free choice in that the apples all *appear* to him to be desirable; and this (specious) elective freedom *entails* conative freedom—he is able to do what he finds agreeable (without, of course, being coerced). So on my account of the matter as much as on Flew's, there is a clear sense in which someone who, through ignorance or misjudgment, makes an unfortunate choice, does make a choice and is not coerced.

Flew is mistaken, incidentally, when he says that already under the heading of 'elective freedom' I am 'beginning to confound freedom to choose between alternatives with the actual achievement of approved ends'. For even real elective freedom is defined as being *able* or *in a position* to select from a range of desirable options, which does not amount to 'actual achievement of approved ends'. Even natural freedom, which (alone) does involve actual attainment of good, involves also the possession of powers, rights and opportunities.

In another attempt to show that, according to me, liberty is only liberty when it is 'a good thing', Flew says (referring to *F&L* 136–137): 'He asserts, it seems without a qualm: "Liberty is simply the area within which individual conduct *should* be free from legal and bureaucratic coercion"'. By way of refutation, Flew quotes Bentham: 'Is not liberty to do evil, liberty?' Now in fact I did *not* imply, either in the passage to which Flew refers (and in which he introduces a misleading stress on the verb 'should') or elsewhere, that there is no such thing as liberty to do evil. Of course there is such a thing as liberty in e.g. Bentham's sense—being legally permitted to do as one pleases, whether it be for good or otherwise—which is legitimately called 'liberty' notwithstanding the fact that it may be dangerous for its possessor or for others or both. But this indeterminate prescriptive liberty is not what is being discussed in the sentence quoted by Flew. I was there discussing the idea of *civil* liberty, and trying to distinguish it both from abstract, Benthamite liberty and from an omnibus conception of freedom as embracing every important human good. Certainly there is a difference between Flew's position and mine if he, like Bentham, conceives civil liberty simply as undifferentiated freedom from rules and rulers, a legal-cum-social status involving no essential relation to human welfare. For on my account of the matter, *civil* liberty—as distinct from liberty in the abstract—is a limited, specific freedom or set of freedoms designed to safeguard specific areas of human welfare. A tyrant might allow his subjects an area of irresponsibility in the ordering of their conduct, e.g. by not stipulating their mode of dress, the times at which they are to rise and retire, what they are to eat, etc., while at the same time forbidding them to discuss political topics and suppressing every manifestation of opposition to his rule. Then, as I say in *F&L* (p. 13), the people would have a kind of prescriptive freedom, but not the kind that is real civil liberty. On the same page as that on which the sentence quoted by Flew occurs (p. 136), there is a list of some of the specific rights in which, according to my analysis, authentic civil liberty consists: freedom from arbitrary arrest and detention, freedom from liability to taxation without representation in the legislature, and generally, the right to take part in the election and dismissal of government officers; freedom of association and discussion, freedom of the press, etc.[4] But I distinguish these specific liberties from abstract, indeterminate, 'merely nominal' liberty, while at the same time resisting the assimilation of civil liberty to that freedom which comprehends every important element in human life. Here is part of the paragraph from which Flew lifted the sentence quoted above:

> Civil liberty is . . . just one element in the combination of goods required for a properly human existence. It is not identical with natural freedom,

---

[4] Flew wonders why it does not occur to me to doubt that persons he describes as my 'fellow revolutionaries' will agree that the traditional liberties are essential to justice and freedom; for, he says, this has been denied 'by every Jacobin from Robespierre and Saint-Just, through Lenin and Trotsky, right up to Castro and Ho Chi Minh'. But why does he take for granted that Gibbsians (none of whom I know, apart from myself) would sympathize with the policies of these 'Jacobins' (none of whom is mentioned in my book)? It would not be more ludicrous if I were to respond by arguing that the traditional liberties are in as much danger of being abrogated by Flew's fellow conservatives, on the ground that every reactionary from Critias and Diocletian to Philip II, Metternich, Franco and the Ayatollah Khomeini has imposed severe restrictions on the liberty of his subjects in the name of a higher freedom.

and not sufficient to assure us of it. Liberty is a juridical creation, which complete natural freedom is not and could not be ... Nor is liberty necessarily deficient in a commonwealth that chooses not to use every means available to it to protect its people from injury. Liberty is simply the area within which individual conduct should be free from legal and bureaucratic coercion. A society may guarantee its members this, while defecting in its duty to ensure that as many of them as possible are provided with the ability and opportunity to make good use of their liberty (*F&L* 136–137).

I should have expected that the sentiments expressed in that paragraph (except perhaps the last sentence) would commend themselves to a philosopher of anti-socialist persuasions. But Flew cannot see the wood for one of its constituent trees. His perception of what he reads seems to be guided by a passion to discover fallacies on which to exercise his talent for vituperation.

Flew is particularly distressed by my choice of the epithet 'natural freedom' to designate a condition which, as I myself point out, either is or closely resembles Aristotelian *eudaimonia*. Here is part of what I say in *F&L*:

Natural freedom is neither the original nor the logically primary concept; yet it is freedom in the fullest, least qualified sense. Every other kind of freedom is a semblance of it or a means to it. To furnish a person with natural freedom would be to liberate him not just in this or that respect, but completely. Natural freedom is felicity, the perfection of nature (22).

I realize that this way of talking is bound to be controversial and demands explanation, and maybe qualification. I confess I did not find the phrase 'natural freedom' ready-made in ordinary discourse or in the writings of Aristotle, though I reckon it is more consonant with both than Flew supposes. Admittedly, Aristotle does not suggest that *eudaimonia* might be regarded as a kind of *eleutheria*; but he would have found no difficulty in understanding my reasons (which are stated in *F&L* more fully than Flew's account indicates and than I have space to reiterate here) for linking freedom, specified as 'natural', to human felicity. As for my assertion that perfect freedom requires actual immunity from the worst evils and actual achievement of the supreme goods, this does not rest on Aristotle's authority, but rather on the truism that *anything* which prevents a human being from making full use of his or her best aptitudes and opportunities constitutes an impediment to the full development of that person's nature. If I possess good abilities and opportunities, but through some defect of character (servility, indolence, alcoholism, addiction to gambling, or whatever) lack the motivation to exploit them, then my condition falls short of perfect freedom. As John Stuart Mill says, 'None but a person of confirmed virtue is completely free'. It should be noted, however, that I do not define natural freedom entirely in terms of activity and achievement; it does involve also the possession of powers, opportunities and rights—adequate civil liberty, and a fair measure of real elective freedom.[5]

II

Flew's principal and most serious accusation is conveyed in the very title of his lecture. But how are we to interpret the proposition 'Freedom is Slavery' which Flew attributes to me? That freedom as *Flew* understands it (Benthamite liberty) is slavery? Surely not: the most Flew could hope to establish is that I imply that Benthamite liberty is *compatible with* certain forms of slavery—economic bondage, etc. Presumably, then, the charge is rather that I meant to define either civil liberty, or natural freedom, or both, in terms of enslavement to a 'Guardian élite' or group of 'philosopher kings' comprising persons like-minded with myself. Flew admits I do not employ these Platonistic phrases, but he is confident that his introduction of them is 'appropriate and fair'. He admits I argue that the originating and sustaining causes of natural freedom are corporate entities—law, the courts and other social institutions, custom and traditional culture—rather than individual political leaders; but he dismisses this as 'inconsistent backsliding'. Where, then, does he suppose me to have revealed my real, ominous intentions?

Quite early in his lecture Flew assembles in a single paragraph three quotations, which seem to be his main evidence for, and together might seem to vindicate, his interpretation of my book. He has already, at this stage, announced the dawning of his 'certain conviction' that *F&L* is a 'tract against freedom'. 'It is now no surprise', he goes on, 'to find poor Mill again being hauled over the coals, this time for not owning up to having realized that "freedom in the sense of personal autonomy is a very different thing from being allowed to do what one desires".' Now when that sentence of mine is quoted in isolation—or rather, in the unnatural context of Flew's rhetoric—one might suppose its implication to be that personal autonomy can be divorced from, or even is incompatible with, being allowed to do what one desires. Here is Gibbs insinuating that personal autonomy can co-exist with, or is identical with, blind obedience to the new philosopher kings: so it might seem. But now allow me to put that

[5] If anyone is inclined to take seriously Flew's jovial insinuation that I would like to ban performances of *Madame Butterfly*, forbid the public sale of keg beer, and force philosophers to take strenuous physical exercise, I would beg him or her to look at what I actually wrote (Flew gives references).

sentence back in its proper home. I was there discussing a question that agitated John Stuart Mill: what is wrong with voluntary contracts of slavery? As I put it in *F&L*, 'Some people would welcome the chance to give up a freedom which involves rights and responsibilities they find onerous, in exchange for a different freedom in the guaranteed security of submission to a benevolent master' (92). If a person willingly espouses a condition of slavery he forfeits his liberty, in the sense that he loses a particular civil and moral status; but his liberty in Mill's terms (being able to do as he desires) is in no way infringed. Mill feels (rightly, in my view, though maybe not in Flew's) that there is something wrong with the moral state of such a person, and in his ideal community Mill (rightly, in my view, though maybe not in Flew's) will permit no one to sell himself or herself as a slave. But his reasoning to this end is—so I argue— unsatisfactory, controvertible on Mill's own principle of utility and Mill's own principle of liberty. Now here is the paragraph which terminates in the sentence excerpted by Flew:

> Slavery is intolerable, not because it is incompatible with liberty to do what one desires, but because it is incompatible with autonomy and natural freedom. The slave is not in command of his own person, as a man should be. Mill surely understands this; why does he not say it? He could not have said it without becoming aware of the inadequacy of his official conception of liberty. For freedom in the sense of personal autonomy is a very different thing from being allowed to do what one desires (93).

Of course my assertion that there is a distinction between autonomy and merely being allowed to do what one desires stands in need of argument, and elsewhere in the book it gets it.[6] Not everyone will agree with my criticism of Mill, perhaps. But anyone can see that the sentence quoted by Flew does not have the sinister meaning he imputes to it.

The second quotation Flew adduces in support of his exegesis is this: 'Moral freedom involves conformance, not so much between what one is and what one wants to be, as between what one is and what one *ought* to be' (*F&L* 105–106). I suppose Flew thinks this sentence can be taken to imply that a person's freedom is not necessarily infringed when he is forced to conform to moral standards different from his own. Now first, if the sentence were so taken, the implication is one that might be defended by some philosophers of the liberal tradition. It was not Rousseau, or Hegel, but Montesquieu who said: 'Liberty does not consist in an un- limited freedom to do what one pleases . . . In societies directed by laws, liberty can consist only in the power of doing what we ought to will, and

6 A fuller discussion of the concept of autonomy is undertaken in my later article 'Autonomy and Authority in Education', *Journal of Philosophy of Education* **13** (1979).

in not being constrained to do what we ought not to will.' And this dictum is reminiscent of (may have been derived from?) the famous section 57 of Locke's *Second Treatise*: 'That ill deserves the name of confinement which hedges us in only from bogs and precipices ... Liberty is not, as we are told, a liberty for every man to do what he lists.' But in any case, defensible as such claims may be, they are not entailed by *my* sentence; which is not concerned with any kind of civil liberty, but (again) with *moral* liberty or personal autonomy: the quality of self-mastery and self-understanding. Flew takes the sentence from a passage which criticizes John Stuart Mill's subjectivist analysis of moral virtue in *A System of Logic*. Here is part of the passage, terminating in the sentence on which Flew fastens:

> Mill implies that virtue is conformance of character to an ideal chosen by the subject. Suppose the subject chooses casually or unwisely; suppose he want to be like Alcibiades, the Marquis de Sade, or Hitler. Less fancifully, suppose him to be your typical smug pillar of commercial society, always chasing wealth and influence and material success, yet completely self-satisfied, blind to his own ignobility. Such a person is so enslaved to his habits and temptations that he cannot recognize his own cupidity for what it is. Moral freedom surely involves conformance, not so much between what one is and what one wants to be, as between what one is and what one *ought* to be (*F&L* 105–106).

One does not have to agree with this argument to see that it entails nothing whatever about the relation between individual liberty and the pressures which may be exerted by society and the state.

The third quotation used by Flew (from *F&L* 109) is one on which he rests a lot of weight. He exploits it not just once but three times, apparently convinced that here, if anywhere, my authoritarian colours are openly displayed. First he quotes as follows:

> A free society is not simply one that *makes* its people do what is right and good. It is a society that ... *makes* them do what is right and good by *making* them desire to do it understanding that it is right and good.

Already in this first quotation of the passage Flew has altered the flavour, if not the sense, of the original, by introducing stresses on certain words and removing stresses from others, and by omitting an important clause from the second sentence. When I give you the original version, I think you will agree that Flew's tamperings make a difference. But first consider his second quotation of the passage, which is so truncated as quite to invert its meaning. He now alleges that Gibbs permits nothing to detract from his bold conviction 'that a truly free society is "one that makes its people do what is right and good"'; as if *this*, without supplementation or qualification, were my official definition of a truly free society, and as if

I had never penned the sentence immediately preceding it, earlier quoted but now ignored by Flew: 'A free society is *not* simply one that makes its people do what is right and good'. By the time Flew gets to his third use of the same passage, he is no longer content to cull and clip my words: he substitutes words of his own. He now says my conclusion in *F&L* is that '"a free society" is one in which people are *made* to do what is right and good, and *made* to like it, agreeing that it is right and good'. In this manner Gibbs is shown to hold that freedom requires compulsion, indoctrination and very likely brainwashing of the citizens!

I hope it is already obvious that there is something wrong with this portrayal of my intentions. But if you will be patient enough to let me quote the offending passage yet once more, this time unedited and unadulterated, and restored to part of the context in which I set it, you will realize at once that the real meaning of the passage is directly *opposite* to that imputed to it by Flew. First, it rejects the idea that no real infringement of liberty is involved in forcing people to do what is right:

> People cannot be said to have liberty when their most cherished desires and ambitions are thwarted, when 'penalties of law and opinion' goad them into sullen conformity, against their consciences, with the officially promulgated conception of Law and Order. Maybe their consciences *are* deceived; maybe, if they knew better, they would have different desires and ambitions. But there may be no real possibility of getting them to know better. An erroneous conscience may be *de facto* incorrigible. In that case, surely, we should acknowledge that liberty *is* infringed by the use of force, even if the infringement be legitimate. A free society is not simply one that makes its people do what is right and good. It is a society that respects the human nature of its members, that makes them do what is right and good by making them *desire* to do it *understanding* that it is right and good. Freedom consists not merely in having one's conduct directed rightly, as the conduct of a marionette might be, but in having one's inclinations, and thence one's conduct, directed rightly. As Mill says, 'It is the privilege and proper condition of a human being, arrived at the maturity of his faculties, to use and interpret experience in his own way'.

And the passage continues with a warning that this point can easily be parodied and perverted:

> Forcing people into a mode of existence which they recognize to be mean and crippling is, in a way, a less hideous form of authoritarianism than *inveigling* people into the same mode of existence—manipulating minds, inculcating false opinions and corrupting the conscience, so that the victims willingly embrace what in itself is base and hateful (all from p. 109).

Again, more needs to be said and is said in *F&L* about all this; but I think enough has been said here to show that Flew has misinterpreted the passage utterly, without evident reason or excuse.

I should stop; an apologia is better kept brief. I hope to have persuaded anyone who may have become interested in this controversy but who has not read *Freedom and Liberation* that there is no way of reconstructing the argument of the book from Flew's summary of it. Meanwhile, I am left puzzled by the extent and degree of Flew's misinterpretations. What can it be that moves him to *raid* a book so brazenly, hunting out phrases and sentences which, when detached from their context and suitably reconstrued, merely provide convenient formulations of ideas inimical to his own prejudices? The only explanation that occurs to me is expressed nicely in Edmund Burke's *Appeal From the New to the Old Whigs*: 'It is in the nature of things, that they who are in the centre of a circle should appear directly opposed to those who view them from any part of the circumference'.

How Free: Computing Personal Liberty

HILLEL STEINER

Judgments about the extent to which an individual is free are easily among the more intractable of the various raw materials which present themselves for philosophical processing. On the one hand, few of us have any qualms about making statements to the effect that Blue is more free than Red. Explicitly or otherwise, such claims are the commonplaces of most history textbooks and of much that passes before us in the news media. And yet, good evidence for the presence of a philosophical puzzle here is to be found in the familiar hesitation we experience when we first reflect on the grounds for such claims. Is it really the case that the average Russian is less free than an Englishman in a dole queue? Are we quite certain that a dirt farmer in the Appalachians enjoys greater personal liberty than the inmate of a well-appointed modern prison? Were citizens of classical Athens more free, or less free, than their counterparts in today's welfare states?

Fashioning a criterion which will yield a set of satisfying answers to these questions is a task traditionally beset by a multitude of difficulties, among which two deserve particular mention. In the first place, there is still widespread disagreement about the meaning of the word 'freedom' or 'liberty'. Nor is this disagreement esoterically confined to the ranks of political philosophers, since ordinary language can readily be seen to sustain many uses of these and related terms, resting on different and opposed conditions for their application. But second, and even where divergent meanings are apparently absent, there is sometimes disagreement—though, more often, embarrassed demurral—over how to measure freedom and unfreedom, that is, how to *count* acknowledged instances of freedom and unfreedom. What I hope to show in this paper is that there is a plausible solution to the second of these difficulties, and that some of the objections levelled at it are misdirected inasmuch as they arise out of differences over the meaning of 'freedom' and not out of any mensural inadequacy in the proposal itself.[1] Duelling with intuitions until a mortal paradox is inflicted is enjoyable but, in the end, unsatisfying—especially when unnecessary.

The solution I have in mind is crude and simple, and runs as follows.

[1] An (imperfect) analogy to this kind of objection is that which takes exception to the capacity of a ruler to measure length, on the grounds that it is scaled in inches rather than centimetres.

Take a list of actions L_1 and discover which of them Red is respectively free and unfree to do. Let F_r and U_r respectively stand for the total numbers of Red's free and unfree actions. To ascertain how free Red is, we need only establish the value of

$$\frac{F_r}{F_r + U_r}.$$

Some objections to this formula are less interesting than others. One might object that had a different list than L_1 been used, say L_2, we might have come up with a different answer to the question of how free Red is. This objection is true, but easily accommodated. For we can simply add all the items appearing only in L_2 to L_1, and perform the same operation. The formula itself remains unimpaired. And it similarly withstands the criticism that the actions which a person is free or unfree to do may be infinitely numerous. For, aside from conceptual differences over what counts as an instance of freedom or unfreedom, there can never be a reason for rejecting any proposed addition to the list. A doctor does not reserve judgment on whether a patient is healthy merely on the grounds that the latter may be afflicted with a disease as yet unknown to medical science. And one is correspondingly unwarranted in refraining from extent-of-freedom judgments because there may be some unknown actions which Red is free or unfree to do. At the very least one is entitled to say that, with respect to those listed actions, Red is free to the computed extent.

A third possible objection to this method of measuring a person's liberty is directed against the structure of the formula itself, rather than the identifiability of its variables. Why, in trying to assess how free Red is, should we take into account those actions which Red is *un*free to do? Why not confine our calculation to summing those actions which he is free to do? It is an implication of this objection that a modern solitary Robinson Crusoe, equipped with a fair share of current scientific and technological knowledge, would be a great deal more free than Defoe's hero, in the same material circumstances. And more generally, it seems to be a widely held view that members of modern industrial societies are *ipso facto* more free than their counterparts in earlier or more primitive societies. That is, because technological development and increased production have enlarged the number of actions which it is possible for us to do, we must generally be more free than persons lacking these possibilities. Even an inmate of a modern prison—to say nothing of his unimprisoned fellow citizens—may be able unobstructedly to do many more actions than the most free member of a less advanced society.

The problem with this objection is that it confuses liberty with ability. If this is a proper conception of liberty at all, it is certainly not the one which concerns us as political philosophers. Liberty is a social relation, a relation between persons. The restraints imposed upon us by nature, and our struggles and successes in overcoming them, are subjects deserving of our closest attention. But it is not to physicists, doctors or engineers whom we turn in seeking answers to the question of 'How free?' For while it is undoubtedly true that the average member of an advanced society is able to do, and unrestrained from doing, many more actions than his counterparts in less advanced societies, it is equally true that he is able to do, but restrained from doing, many more actions than they. That is, there are many more actions which he is *unfree* to do. Simply to ignore them in estimating the extent of a person's liberty, is to misconstrue the object of such an exercise.

An apparently more interesting objection is sometimes prompted by the familiar problems of act-individuation. As is well enough appreciated, any piece of outward bodily behaviour can be described in a variety of ways, and these variations occur across a number of different dimensions. Since the items entered in the proposed formula's list are definite descriptions of acts, reluctance to accept the formula as an appropriate measure of liberty may be motivated by an apprehension that the compilation of such a list must—because of act-individuation problems—involve either arbitrary omissions or numerous instances of double-counting. Consider the following example, in which a dozen alternative descriptions are offered of a shooting:[2]

1. He tensed his forefinger.
2. He pressed a piece of metal.
3. He released a spring.
4. He pulled the trigger of a gun.
5. He fired a gun.
6. He fired a bullet.
7. He shot a bullet at a man.
8. He shot a bullet towards a man.
9. He shot a man.
10. He killed a man.
11. He committed judicial murder.
12. He saved four lives.

Needless to say, this inventory could be considerably extended. But the question is: should this be a matter for concern and a reason for rejecting the formula? I suggest that what we have here is an objection which is of the same kind as the second one discussed above. There is no reason why *all* these descriptions cannot be entered in our list. The various dimensions in which different act-descriptions subsist—and which discriminate between basic and non-basic acts and between intended and unintended

[2] The example is taken from Eric D'Arcy, *Human Acts* (Oxford: Oxford University Press, 1963), 3.

consequences—constitute no effective obstacle in this respect, inasmuch as inclusiveness along these lines at once rules out the possibility of arbitrary omissions and poses no danger of otiose double-counting. Each of the twelve act-descriptions recorded above is only contingently related to the rest and, therefore, each refers to an event which could have occurred even if the others had not. It is consequently perfectly intelligible to ask, in the case of each of them, whether the actor was free to do the action. And there is no reason why the answers to any pair of these twelve questions need have been the same.

Consider, next, the objection that this formula fails to measure the extent to which Red is free because, in simply adding up the numbers of actions he is free and unfree to do, it fails to take account of the extent to which he is free or unfree to do *each* of them. This objection suggests that we can speak, not only of the extent to which a person is free with respect to a list of several actions, but also with respect to a single action. Thus it is sometimes suggested that I am more free to see Walt Disney's film *Sleeping Beauty* than to see Sam Peckinpah's *Straw Dogs*, because the latter is banned in Manchester but not its environs, while the former is not banned at all. This objection fails inasmuch as it is based on an imprecision of language of a kind that is, admittedly, common enough in our everyday discourse. 'Seeing *Straw Dogs*', or for that matter 'Seeing *Straw Dogs* in Manchester', is not the name of a single action but rather of a *class* of actions. There are many single actions which would count as members of this class. Of course, I am unfree to do any of the single actions which comprise the class of actions called 'Seeing *Straw Dogs* in Manchester'. And I am thus also unfree to do a certain proportion of the single actions comprising the class of actions called 'Seeing *Straw Dogs*'. These classes amount to nothing more than lists of single actions and, as such, constitute sub-lists within the more extensive list which the formula invites us to compile. It is true that, in talking about the extent of a person's liberty, we are often thinking less about single actions than about classes of actions. But we should still wish to be able to distinguish—in terms of differing amounts of freedom—between the position where one is restrained from seeing *Straw Dogs* in Manchester and the position where one is restrained from seeing *Straw Dogs* in Manchester more than once. In the former case one is more unfree than in the latter. And we can only say this if, in making extent-of-freedom judgments, what we are counting are single actions.

Another objection to the formula similarly locates its inadequacy in its neglect of the variable extent to which persons are free or unfree to do the actions they are free or unfree to do. But this variation is held to consist in the variability of the *cost* or *difficulty* of doing an action. A British passport holder, it is said, is less free to enter the United States (at least, through an official entry-point) than a Canadian passport holder, because the former but not the latter requires a visa to do so. It is easy enough to see that this example poses no problem, for the use of the formula as a measure of liberty, if what it alludes to is merely the fact that applications for visas can be rejected. For our list of free and unfree actions can readily include not only entering the United States but also securing a visa to do so. The problem it more perspicaciously attempts to raise resides in the fact that securing a visa is an action which takes time, trouble and resources, even when that action is unthreatened with failure. So the point here is that, for the British passport holder, more actions must be done to do the action of entering the United States than is the case for the Canadian passport holder. And this, it is held, entails that the former is less free than the latter in respect of the action of entering the United States. Again however, the basis of this objection warrants closer scrutiny.

Here we must pause to notice an important distinction. It is often the case that, in order to do an action, a sequence of prior actions must be done: to do E, it may be necessary that one previously do A, B, C, and D, and that they be done in that order. However, the sense in which this prior sequence is necessary can vary. Clearly it is not a *causal* condition of a British passport holder's entering the United States that he secure a visa. It is not impossible for him to enter—even through an official entry-point—without a visa, since it is not impossible for the officials at that entry-point to allow him to enter without a visa. Compare this with the case of an imprisoned person attending the opera. It is a causal condition of his attending the opera that he leave his cell. And it is impossible for his gaoler both to allow him to attend the opera and to restrain him from leaving his cell. Hence, in the first case, we cannot say that it is the visa-issuing officials who make a British passport holder unfree to enter the United States by making him unfree to secure a visa. But we can say that it is the gaoler who makes the prisoner unfree to attend the opera by making him unfree to leave his cell. Where the sequence of actions, required to be done prior to the doing of E, is causally necessary, making a person unfree to do D implies making him unfree to do E; and making him unfree to do A implies making him unfree to do B, C, D, and E. But where the relation of necessity between each pair of consecutive actions in the sequence is not a causal relation, making a person unfree to do an earlier action in the sequence does not imply making him unfree to do any of the subsequent actions. And therefore his unfreedom to do any of them must be due to other restraints. Of course, the actions which must be done in order to do another action need not always be done in a particular sequence. Nor is it the case that, where such previously required actions must be done in a particular sequence, the relation of necessity between every pair of consecutive actions must either be causal throughout the sequence or non-causal throughout the sequence. The relation between submitting a visa application and, say, posting a completed visa application form is one of causal necessity, whereas that between securing a visa and submitting a visa application is not.

The cost or difficulty of doing an action arises from the fact that its performance requires the doing of other actions. If one is free to do each of those other actions, there appear to be no grounds for claiming that one is less than entirely free to do that action itself unless, of course, one is specifically restrained from doing *it*—in which case, one is entirely unfree to do it. And if one is unfree to do one of those prior actions, one is either (still) entirely free to do the action itself (if the relation between those two actions is one of non-causal necessity), or entirely unfree to do the action itself (if the relation between the two actions is one of causal necessity). Since the burden of the present objection is to suggest that the action itself can be one which we are less free to do, without being entirely unfree to do it, this objection fails.

We could perhaps reformulate the objection and say that the British passport holder's allegedly lesser freedom to enter the United States is not a consequence of his being less free to do any of the actions requisitely anterior to entry, but rather is a consequence of there being more such requisitely anterior actions: the greater cost or difficulty of doing an action reduces one's freedom to do it, not because it entails prior actions which one is less free to do, but because it entails a greater number of prior actions. There is an obvious sense in which this is true, but it too fails as an objection to the use of the formula for measuring the extent of a person's liberty. A clear and direct analogy is a hurdle-race. Suppose that the 500-yard track contains five hurdles, and that the action under consideration is crossing the finish-line 60 seconds after the starting-gun. And suppose that I am able to do this action. Now suppose that the organizers of the race add two more hurdles and, as a result, it now takes me 65 seconds to cross the finish-line. The organizers have thus rendered me not merely less free, but entirely unfree, to do the action of crossing the finish-line in 60 seconds. And how have they done this? They have done it by making it impossible for me (making me entirely unfree) to do an action—say, crossing the 450-yard mark in 55 seconds—requisitely anterior to the action of crossing the finish-line in 60 seconds. Increasing the cost or difficulty of doing an action, by increasing the number of requisitely anterior actions—in this case, increasing the number of hurdle-jumps— either leaves one entirely free to do that action or renders one entirely unfree to do it. And it achieves this latter effect by rendering one entirely unfree to do an action anterior to it.

The notion of degrees of freedom to do an action is superfluous, misleading and descriptively imprecise. Why then do we commonly say that British passport holders are less free than their Canadian counterparts (though not unfree) to enter the United States? I suggest that, like much else in ordinary parlance, this locution is an ellipitical abbreviation of a probabilistic judgment. Its meaning is more accurately conveyed in saying that British passport holders are less probably free than Canadians to do the action in question. This perfectly sensible statistical judgment reflects the fact that there is a wider range of possible reasons why any British passport holder will be unfree to secure a visa—and hence, will probably be unfree to enter the United States—than is the case for any Canadian passport holder. It is true that more hurdles make success less probable, but only because more hurdles probably make at least one of the actions required for success impossible. A list of actions which have and have not been made impossible for one to do, such as that proposed in the formula, can adequately take account of this truth.

The final objection to be considered is perhaps the most commonsensical of those examined so far, inasmuch as it takes exception to what many would regard as the most counter-intuitive aspect of using the formula to compute personal liberty. Isaiah Berlin suggests an expansive approach to any such computation:

> The extent of my freedom seems to depend on (a) how many possibilities are open to me (although the method of counting these can never be more than impressionistic. Possibilities of action are not discrete entities like apples, which can be exhaustively enumerated); (b) how easy or difficult each of these possibilities is to actualize; (c) how important in my plan of life, given my character and circumstances, these possibilities are when compared with each other; (d) how far they are closed and opened by deliberate human acts; (e) what value not merely the agent, but the general sentiment of the society in which he lives, puts on the various possibilities. All these magnitudes must be 'integrated', and a conclusion, necessarily never precise, or indisputable, drawn from this process.[3]

My argument, as developed above, asserts the computational relevance of (a) while rejecting that of (b) and (d). Should the magnitudes referred to in (c) and (e)—and which I shall conjunctively label 'valuational magnitudes'—figure in our assessment of the extent of a person's liberty?

Evidently, our first reflections on this question strongly incline us to the view that the significance of the actions which we are or are not free to do must enter into our estimations of how free we are.

When two or more properties or 'respects' are subject to precise mathematical comparison, they will always have some quantitative element in common. The difficulty in striking resultant totals of 'on balance freedom' derives from the fact that the relation among the various 'areas' in which people are said to be free is not so much like the relation

[3] Isaiah Berlin, *Four Essays on Liberty* (Oxford: Oxford University Press, 1969, 130.

between the height, breadth, and depth of a physical object as it is like the relation between the gasoline economy, styling, and comfort of an automobile. . . . What we more likely mean when we say that one subject is freer on balance than another is that his freedom is greater in the more valuable, important, or significant dimensions, where the 'value' of a dimension is determined by some independent standard.[4]

Can it seriously be maintained that the action of twiddling one's thumbs and the action of casting a ballot in an unrigged election should be accorded equal weight—should each be counted as one action—in measuring an individual's liberty? Charles Taylor attacks the 'crude' and 'tough-minded' negative conception of liberty underlying such a proposal, and suggests that 'it has no place for the notion of significance' and 'will allow only for purely quantitative judgments'. This conception is said to license the 'diabolical defence of Albania' against the charge of being a less free society than Britain, since the presence of severe restraints on religious practice in the former—and their absence in the latter—could thereby be forensically countered by pointing to the considerably fewer traffic restrictions in the former than in the latter.[5]

For the moment, at least, we can leave aside questions like whether the harassed London commuter, diabolical or not, would necessarily be disposed to accept this judgment of relative significance. The question we should first address is whether the use of the formula to compute personal liberty necessarily excludes the integration of valuational magnitudes in performing this computation. Is the formula ineluctably tied to the tough-minded negative conception of liberty? Or can it accommodate the measurement of what Taylor considers to be a more discriminating negative conception of liberty—one which assigns varying degrees of significance to restrained actions—and which, as he rightly argues, is thus not so readily distinguishable from many positive conceptions of liberty?

Now, in principle, there is no reason why the formula cannot be used to measure the extent of a person's liberty so conceived. Where previously each action was given the numerical value of unity in calculating the sums represented by F_r and U_r, under the proposed dispensation each action would be assigned the numerical value of its significance and the calculation could proceed in the same manner. Clearly the significance of various actions does vary and, although the basis for assigning numerical values to these variations may be unavoidably conventional, such assignability is a necessary condition of comparing the relative amounts of liberty enjoyed by any two persons who—like an Albanian and a Briton—are free or unfree

[4] Joel Feinberg, *Social Philosophy* (Englewood Cliffs: Prentice-Hall, 1973), 18–19.
[5] Charles Taylor, 'What's Wrong with Negative Liberty', *The Idea of Freedom: Essays in Honour of Isaiah Berlin*, Alan Ryan (ed.) (Oxford: Oxford University Press, 1979), 183.

to do different sets of actions. Taylor's previously cited criticism of the crude negative conception is thus somewhat overstated, since even a conception of liberty which *does* give place to the notion of significance must permit the latter's quantification if it is to allow its users to make the kind of comparative judgment he makes. That said, however, it is also the case that computing a person's liberty in this way is not without its logical difficulties, nor is it devoid of strongly counter-intuitive consequences.

Proposals that valuational magnitudes be integrated into the measurement of personal liberty are typically underspecified. On the face of it, we might imagine that the actions which we are free or unfree to do vary not only in their significance, but also that these variations can be either negative or positive. If saving another person's life is a highly significant act, it seems reasonable to think that the act of taking another's life is not perspicuously graded as 'insignificant' but rather (infelicitously) as 'anti-significant'. On one interpretation of the integration proposal, then, all acts on our list would be assigned positive or negative numbers representing the valuation of their significance or anti-significance. Suppose our list thus contains the following six actions and their respective valuations: A $(+10)$, B $(+8)$, C $(+6)$, X (-9), Y (-7), Z (-5). And suppose that Red is free to do A, B, X, and unfree to do C, Y, Z. Applying the formula to compute the extent of Red's liberty, we get the following result:

$$\frac{F_r}{F_r + U_r} = \frac{A + B + X}{(A + B + X) + (C + Y + Z)} = \frac{9}{3} = 3.$$

The extent of Red's liberty is 3. But observe that computing Red's liberty in this fashion leads to a contradiction. For suppose that the restraint on his doing Y were removed, and that he was thus free to do Y. The formula gives us the following result for his state of ostensibly increased liberty:

$$\frac{F_r}{F_r + r} = \frac{A + B + X + Y}{(A + B + X + Y) + (C + Z)} = \frac{2}{3}.$$

That is, Red's newly acquired liberty to do Y would entail a *decrease* in his freedom.

To avoid such contradictions, while still integrating valuational magnitudes into computations of personal liberty, it is thus necessary to exclude the use of negative numbers from our valuational assignments to listed actions. But how can this be done? For as was just noted, whatever positive value we assign to an act of life-saving, it would not make sense that an act of life-taking be assigned merely a lower positive value. If it were, this would have the utterly absurd consequence that a sufficiently large number of life-taking acts would be equal or greater in value than one life-saving act. If any acts have positive value, it is necessarily true that there are acts to which negative values attach.

Hence, to expunge negative valuations from our computation in order to avoid the contradictions they entail, it is necessary to make a move which is indeed a commonplace in most accounts of the *positive* conception of liberty. That is, we need to remove all negatively valued actions from our list of actions which Red is free or unfree to do. For Red, acts X, Y, Z, being acts which are negatively valued, are ones which he cannot be said to be either free or unfree to do. The boldness of this move deserves attention, for it constitutes a complete shift in the conception of the liberty we are measuring. The fact that Red is unrestrained from doing X and restrained from doing Y and Z no longer implies, as it previously did, that he is free to do X and unfree to do Y and Z. Accordingly, whereas on the crude and tough-minded negative conception, which admits of no valuational weightings in computing personal liberty, the answer to the question 'How free is Red?' is secured thus,

$$\frac{F_r}{F_r + U_r} = \frac{A + B + X}{(A + B + X) + (C + Y + Z)} = \frac{3}{6} = \frac{1}{2}$$

on the positive conception of liberty, the extent of Red's freedom is given thus,

$$\frac{F_r}{F_r + U_r} = \frac{A + B}{(A + B) + C} = \frac{18}{24} = \frac{3}{4}.$$

The difference between these two results does, in fact, reflect the difference commonly found between positive liberty theorists and their negative liberty counterparts, inasmuch as the latter typically charge the former with exaggerating the extent to which individuals are free in some kinds of society where state restraints on action are relatively numerous. Conversely, and as the formula would show, positive theorists find other sorts of society to be ones allowing individuals much less freedom than they are held to enjoy by negative libertarians. Thus, if Red were restrained from doing A and B, and not restrained from doing C, X, Y, Z, the extent of his negative liberty would be represented by 2/3 while his positive liberty would amount only to 1/4.

Taylor's argument is therefore correct in its suggestion that the integration of valuational magnitudes into the computation of an individual's liberty shortens the distance alleged to exist between 'more discriminating' negative conceptions and the positive conception of liberty. Indeed, as has been shown, it eliminates that distance altogether. For since no such integration can consistently be performed with respect to negatively valued acts, computations incorporating valuational magnitudes can be computations only of an individual's positive liberty: only positively valued acts can count as ones which we are free and unfree to do. Computations of an individual's negative liberty exclude valuational magnitudes, and the numerical weighting assigned to each act which we are negatively free or unfree to do must therefore be unity. The only consistent conception of negative liberty is thus the crude and tough-minded one.

I take it, then, that the foregoing argument serves to vindicate a claim registered at the outset of this paper: namely, that objections to the use of the formula, as a way of measuring personal liberty, are misdirected inasmuch as they arise out of differences over the meaning of 'freedom' and not out of any mensural inadequacy in the formula itself. The formula is perfectly capable of determining the extent of a person's liberty, whether negatively or positively conceived.

Nor is it among the principal aims of this paper to explore more than briefly the propriety of using the positive conception as a characterization of personal liberty, since this matter has been extensively canvassed elsewhere with varying degrees of success.[6] Among the many considerations adduced for doubting its propriety, three have been particularly prominent. First, there is something more than a little anomalous about inferring ostensibly factual descriptions of persons—as free or unfree or more free or less free—from inherently contestable act-valuations. As was previously remarked, there *can* be intelligible differences of opinion concerning what Taylor considers to be a diabolical defence of Albanian freedom. The fact that we are all firmly convinced that the average Albanian is far less free than the average Briton, is not due to any judgment on our part about the comparative significance of (restrictions on) acts of driving uninterruptedly and acts of religious observance. It rests, rather, on our amply warranted belief that the average Albanian is subject to many more restrictions than only those on religious observance, and many more than prevail in Britain. Indeed, and as I earlier suggested, were these the only restrictions to which average members of these societies are respectively subjected, we might well feel less convinced of Albanians' greater unfreedom. A second and somewhat related consideration is the peculiarity of the positive libertarian implication that a re-valuation of an act can, in itself, alter the extent of a person's liberty, even though there has been no change in his relation to other persons. Third, it seems odd to be logically permitted to deny that a person is unfree to do an act which others restrain him from doing, or to deny that he was free to do an act which he in fact did.

However, it must be conceded that these charges of absurdity themselves

[6] In addition to Berlin's seminal contribution on this subject, one might consult: J. P. Day, 'On Liberty and the Real Will', *Philosophy* **XLV** (1970), 177–192, and 'Threats, Offers, Law, Opinion and Liberty', *American Philosophical Quarterly* **14** (1977), 257–271; Felix E. Oppenheim, *Dimensions of Freedom* (New York: St. Martin's Press, 1961), and *Political Concepts: A Reconstruction* (Chicago: University of Chicago Press, forthcoming), Ch. 3 and 5; Hillel Steiner, 'Individual Liberty', *Proceedings of the Aristotelian Society* **LXXV** (1974–75), 33–50.

rest to a greater or lesser extent on features of our ordinary usage which, being fraught with ambiguity and inconsistency, cannot be regarded as absolutely authoritative in these matters. Moreover, and contrary to what Berlin and other negative libertarians have said, the grounds for rejecting the positive conception can be neither moral nor epistemological. That is, neither the fact that ascriptions of freedom positively conceived have been used to justify morally intolerable arrangements, nor the fact that such ascriptions presuppose elusive ontological entities like 'autonomous selves', can be grounds for holding such ascriptions to be improper uses of the concept of liberty. The reasons for their impropriety must be logical ones.

One such reason is as follows. The common starting point of negative and positive accounts of liberty—the reason why they at least purport to be talking about the same thing—is their shared view that Red is unfree if his acting is restrained, but not restrained by Red. A characteristic positive libertarian claim is that 'Red is not unfree because Red governs Red's acting'. Such claims are not intended to suggest that there are no restraints on Red's acting. Rather, they deny Red's unfreedom on the grounds that the source of such restraints is Red himself. Thus the condition required for Red to be unfree is held not to be satisfied by the presence of such restraints. Z, being a negatively valued action, is one which Red would choose not to do and would restrain himself from doing. Any restraint against his doing Z is self-imposed and does not render him unfree.

What is wrong with this argument is that it contains a false premise. The premise is the assertion that Red is the source of the restraint on Red's doing Z. The reason why (i) 'Red restrains Red's doing Z' does not entail (ii) 'Red is not unfree to do Z', is that the referent of 'Red' in (i) is not the referent of 'Red's' in (i), nor is it the referent of 'Red' in (ii). The 'Red' of (i)—the thing doing the restraining—is an autonomous self. (Whether such things exist is beside the point.) The 'Red's' of (i) and the 'Red' of (ii)—the thing whose doing Z is restrained and who is none the less not unfree to do Z—is an acting person. If it were not an acting person, if it were also the same autonomous self, the claim that 'Red restrains Red's doing Z' would be either tautologous or, more likely, meaningless.[7] As it stands, however, the statement 'Red restrains Red's doing Z' is more accurately read as 'Q restrains Red's doing Z'. And since 'Red's' in (i) has the same referent as 'Red' in (ii), the latter statement does not follow from the former. For on the shared view of the

[7] It would be tautologous inasmuch as it would be asserting that 'This autonomous self restrains the doing of Z by this (same) autonomous self—an assertion the contradiction of which is unintelligible, since 'autonomous' means 'self-restraining' or 'self-governing'. But it is more likely that the statement is meaningless, since there is no clear sense in which autonomous selves—as distinct from acting persons—can be said to do acts or to be restrained from doing them.

condition for ascriptions of unfreedom, what is entailed by 'Q restrains Red's doing Z' is not 'Red is *not* unfree to do Z' but rather 'Red *is* unfree to do Z'.

Finally, and regardless of whether the preceding argument is correct, something can and should be said about the comparison of *societies* as more free or less free. For here again our intuitions and ordinary language rapidly give way to reflective uncertainty. On the one hand, it might seem plausible simply to say that Orange society is more free than Green society because the sum of all Orangian persons' liberty, positively or negatively conceived, is greater than the corresponding total for all Greenians. Our readiness to say this soon falters, however, when we recall that Orangians outnumber Greenians by about three to one. For while the difference in size between two cups does not prevent us from saying that one contains more water than the other, this latter differential does not, of itself, imply anything about which one of the two cups is more nearly full. And our views about inter-social comparisons of (the extent of) freedom at least partly reflect the same structure as our comparisons of the cups' fullness.

So our initial intuition might well be modified along the lines of saying that Orangian society is more free because the *average* amount of liberty enjoyed by its members (total amount of liberty divided by number of members) is also greater than for Greenian society. This does begin to look more acceptable, but it too ignores some well-entrenched features of our common usage. For there can be a great deal of difference between the average amount of liberty enjoyed by members of a society, and the amount of liberty enjoyed by an *average member* of that society. Thus we would not typically regard as irrelevant to the question of whether Orange is a more free society than Green, the fact that Green is governed by a highly totalitarian state, with the consequence that the amount of liberty enjoyed by each of a vast majority of its members is greatly exceeded by the amount of liberty enjoyed by each of a tiny minority of its members. In Orange, on the other hand, the average amount of liberty enjoyed by its members more closely approximates the amount of liberty enjoyed by its average members.

These considerations all point to Orange as being a more free society than Green. But what if it were Orange, rather than Green, that was the totalitarian society? Then, although the average amount of liberty enjoyed by an Orangian would still exceed that of a Greenian, the amount of liberty enjoyed by the average Greenian could nevertheless be greater than that of the average Orangian. Or it might not: the average Orangian might still be more free than the average Greenian. In either case, I think we may have reached the limit of the capacity of intuition and ordinary language to determine whether Orange is a more or less free society than Green. How do we proceed from here?

I do not propose to answer this question directly. Instead, I invite the following reflection. One thing we know for certain is that, if Red is unfree to do A, this is because there is an action S which would be done by another person Blue that would stop Red from doing A. Hence Red's unfreedom to do A implies Blue's freedom to do S. But how would S stop A? The answer, simply, is by *getting in its way*—by interrupting the sequence of events which collectively constitute the doing of A. Since an event is a displacement of a material body in a portion of physical space, the interruption of an event involves a different displacement than the one required for the completion of the sequence. To secure such a displacement, it is necessary to insert a different material body into that portion of physical space at the time when the other material body would have occupied it. S would stop A because its sequence of events *intersects* the sequence of events constituting A: that is, at least one of its events occupies the same spatio-temporal location as is required by an event in A, and thereby renders the latter's occurrence impossible.[8] It is impossible that both S and A occur. Thus if Red were free to do A, Blue would be unfree to do S.

This line of reasoning suggests that personal liberty is a pie of a fixed size. Every act which Red is unfree to do implies the existence of an act which Blue or someone else is free to do. An increase in Red's freedom entails an increase in the unfreedom of others. Red's freedom is inversely related to the freedom of others. Nor is this a very surprising finding. For it corresponds to (and perhaps explains) our impressionistic view that, in two otherwise similar societies, the difference between each member's average amount of liberty and each average member's amount of liberty will be much greater in the society ruled by a totalitarian minority.

A vitally important consideration in this respect is the fact that societies are not hermetically sealed entities, even though much discussion in political philosophy tends to speak of them as if they were. Their members interact, whether individually or in combinations, with members of other societies. And among the more prominent aspects of such commerce are actions which constitute restraints. Orange may, on one criterion or another, be a more free society than Green. But if some portion of its total liberty has been secured at the price of Greenians' unfreedom, we may wish to reserve the evaluative judgment which otherwise normally follows upon such a comparison. If the person stopping Greenian 1 from doing A is not Greenian 2 but rather Orangian 1, we may find ourselves less impressed by Orangian liberty.[9] On the other hand, this consideration need not affect our judgment, if it is our judgment, that Orange is the more

[8] Cf. Steiner, 'Individual Liberty', 44–50.

[9] Similarly, we might morally discount Yellow's being more generous than Pink, if Yellow is a thief who impoverished Pink. Cf. Immanuel Kant, *Lectures on Ethics* (New York: Harper and Row, 1963), 194–195.

free society. Orange may be a modern liberal democracy conducting a militarily sustained imperialistic policy with respect to Green, which is itself oppressively governed by a megalomaniac—Supergreen—and his vicious cohorts. While we can certainly say that the average amount of liberty enjoyed by each Greenian is diminished by Orangians, we cannot hold Orangians responsible to the same degree for the relatively low amount of liberty enjoyed by the average Greenian. Some of this unfreedom is due to Supergreen.

At this point, it may be helpful to formalize these reflections only slightly, in order to display more clearly the relations involved. For the sake of simplicity, I shall assume that Orange and Green are the only societies existing, and that no one exists outside these societies. Let TOL and TGL stand for the total amount of liberty in Orange and Green, respectively; ALO and ALG stand for the average liberty of Orangians and Greenians; LAO and LAG stand for the average Orangian's and the average Greenian's liberty; COL and CGL stand for the degree of concentration of liberty in Orange and Green; and NO and NG stand for the number of Orangians and Greenians. The following are among the more interesting inferable relations holding between these variables:

(1) TOL varies inversely with TGL;
(2) ALO (ALG) varies directly with TOL (TGL);
(3) ALO (ALG) varies inversely with NO (NG);
(4) ALO varies inversely with ALG;
(5) LAO (LAG) varies directly with TOL (TGL);
(6) LAO (LAG) varies inversely with COL (CGL);
(7) LAO (LAG) varies inversely with TGL (TOL);
(8) LAO varies inversely with LAG.

Now, of course, functional relations such as these tell us nothing about the reasons why the related variables have the values they do have: functional relations are not causal relations and furnish little basis for the ascription of responsibility and the according of approbation.[10]

Nevertheless, the reflective uncertainty to which we are often driven in our efforts to determine whether one of two societies is commendable as the more free is, I suggest, due to a vague suspicion that—whichever kind of variable we adopt as our criterion—there might be some reason to believe that its value in, say, Orange would not be as high as it is if its value in Green were not as low as it is. If Orange and Green were the only societies in existence, this would necessarily be true with respect to

[10] The only independent variables here are TOL (TGL), COL (CGL) and NO (NG). Hence only these are open to normative appraisal. Of these, the first two reflect distributive states-of-affairs and may, therefore, be subject to the same norm. While the third variable is also subject to normative appraisal, it is doubtful that the same norm can be applied to it.

TOL/TGL. But it would not necessarily be true with respect to LAO/LAG. For although some change in the ratio TOL/TGL can effect a change in LAO/LAG—although a less imperialistic policy on the part of Orange may increase the amount of liberty enjoyed by the average Greenian—it need not have this effect if Supergreen extends his despotic control over his subjects still further, i.e. if the value of CGL increases. Similarly, some hesitation in judging Orange commendably more free than Green, even though ALO/ALG is greater than 1, is held by many to be warranted by the fact that the size of this ratio is affected not only by the interaction between these two societies, but also by the size of their populations.

My own view, for what it is worth, is that in the face of these cross-cutting considerations, we tend to think that Orange is a more free society than Green if LAO/LAG is greater than 1, if the average Orangian is more free than the average Greenian. But we may be well advised to modify any consequent comparative moral judgment were we to suspect that this ratio would be smaller if TOL/TGL were smaller. That is, the distribution of liberty *within* Orange and Green seems an exclusively appropriate criterion for morally grading them, to the extent that the distribution of liberty *between* Orange and Green is morally acceptable. If TOL/TGL is morally right, then the comparative moral significance of LAO/LAG hangs entirely on that of CGL/COL.[11] Alternatively, and for those who quite plausibly regard the size of a society's population as irrelevant to determining the moral entitlements of its members to liberty,[12] it would be the rectitude of ALO/ALG—rather than simply TOL/TGL—that would constitute the necessary condition for treating CGL/COL as decisive in assessing the comparative moral significance of LAO/LAG. And needless to say, our moral comparisons of societies along these lines become indefinitely more complex when the number of interacting societies is greater than two.

The amount of freedom enjoyed by any one person depends upon the amount of unfreedom enjoyed by other persons, in his own and other societies. Isaiah Berlin rightly remarks that 'Freedom for the pike is death for the minnows'.[13] The universal quest for greater personal liberty

[11] This is not, however, to say that no comparative moral significance attaches to CGL/COL—and hence to LAO/LAG—when TOL/TGL is morally unacceptable. Orange's military imperialism does not excuse Supergreen's despotism.

[12] Indeed, few of us have any independent intuitions about *societies'* entitlements to liberty—independent, that is, of our views as to individual persons' entitlements.

[13] Berlin, *Four Essays*, 124. Interestingly, there is a momentary intimation of this same idea in Marx who writes: 'But does not freedom of the press exist in the land of censorship? ... True, in the land of censorship the state has no freedom of the press, but one organ of the state has it, viz. the *government* ...

is, indeed, a zero-sum game. Undue neglect of this fact has resulted in many players having their attention distracted from normative questions about the distribution of liberty.

Does not the censor exercise daily an unconditional freedom of the press, if not directly, then indirectly?'; 'Debates on Freedom of the Press (1842)', *Karl Marx/Frederick Engles Collected Works*, Vol. 1 (London: 1975), 155. I am grateful to G. A. Cohen for drawing this passage to my attention and, more generally, for an extended series of searching criticisms which compelled the systematization of the arguments advanced in this paper.

Liberty in a Culturally Plural Society

L. S. LUSTGARTEN

I want to begin this paper by recalling a once-lively school of English political and legal thinking which has fallen undeservedly into neglect. I refer to the pluralists, notably the lawyer F. W. Maitland, the religious scholar J. N. Figgis, and, early in their careers, the political theorists Harold Laski and G. D. H. Cole. All were influenced by the writings of the German legal scholar Otto von Gierke, which Maitland as editor and translator had first introduced into England.[1] The pluralists' concerns were at once political and legal; virtually alone among English writers in this century until the 1970s, their work avoided the barrenness that comes of treating political theory and jurisprudence as unrelated enterprises. I shall describe the problems that preoccupied them and some of their resultant theories, and also the way in which specifically legal doctrine was both a target of their criticism and an important element in their thinking.

From this point of departure, I shall examine what I regard, for reasons directly analogous to the pluralists' concerns, as one of the critical issues of liberty in contemporary Western states: the protection of the cultural freedom or rights[2] of ethnic minorities. I shall argue in general terms for wide-ranging recognition of cultural pluralism—acceptance by the majority of a society that cultural minority groups should be permitted to live according to their disparate norms. The multifarious specific issues which have raised this broader question will be illustrated by a selection of what seem the most important, put in the form of questions. Nearly all of them are drawn from cases which have come before the courts in Britain or the United States, and I shall argue that when, as is inevitable, these conflicts are transmuted into legal issues, they are seriously distorted by factors inherent in the legal process. Hence consideration of the question of principle must include analysis of the specifically legal doctrines and techniques required; in particular I shall consider whether ethnic minorities could be treated in the same manner as English law treats other forms of collectivity.

---

[1] Under the title of *Political Theories of the Middle Ages* (1900), the first fragment of Gierke's *Das Deutsche Genossenschaftsrecht* to appear in English.

[2] In this paper I shall use the term 'rights' to refer to claims that are vindicated through legal institutions, especially courts, whilst reserving 'freedom' or 'liberty' for appeals to political or moral principle.

I can do little more than state the basic precept, but in the first tentative steps toward constructing a theoretical framework to uphold cultural pluralism, I shall explore whether the conception of liberty as expounded by John Stuart Mill—and by implication the liberal tradition within which he is so important a figure—is in its implications supportive or hostile to it.

Finally, since acceptance of the general position would by itself say very little about the outcome of the large number of difficult specific applications, I shall conclude with an extended series of questions and observations, all of which would require an answer or fuller treatment—as in the concluding chapter of *On Liberty*—if the position taken here is to be at all persuasive. The present paper must be seen as merely a rough outline of what needs to be done.

I

The pluralists were opposed to what they diagnosed as a powerful historical movement: the eradication of all political and legal entities except the individual and the state—what Maitland called 'the pulverizing, macadamizing tendency'.[3] Gierke attributed it to the ascendancy of what he termed 'Natural Law', by which he meant the political theory of Liberalism with its concomitant individualism.[4] A prime example from English law is the *quo warranto* proceedings commenced by Charles II in 1682 to revoke the status of the City of London as a corporate body. His argument, echoing Hobbes, was that the King could not tolerate alternative centres of power that might interfere with the exercise of sovereignty in maintaining public order and controlling social conflict. He was successful in the courts, but the Glorious Revolution soon reversed the verdict as to the King, whilst beginning the process whereby Parliament succeeded to the identical role.[5] An even more spectacular example, offered by Maitland, is the decree issued by the Assembly of Revolutionary France in 1792, proscribing all corporative organizations except, apparently, business partnerships.[6]

The historical movement, traced to its material roots, was one of the truly fundamental changes brought about by the rise of a capitalist market economy. Various medieval institutions—cities, guilds, churches,

[3] F. W. Maitland, 'Moral Personality and Legal Personality', in *Collected Papers*, III, H. Fisher (ed.) (1911), 304–320.

[4] Hence the title of the next portion of Gierke's massive work to appear in English, translated and preceded by a long and excellent introduction by Sir Ernest Barker: O. von Gierke, *Natural Law and the Theory of Society* (1935). A good brief discussion of Gierke's analysis of liberalism may be found in Frug, 'The City as a Legal Concept', *Harv. L. Rev.* 93 (1980), 1057, 1086–1089.

[5] Frug, op. cit., 1090ff. See also J. Levin, *The Charter Controversy in the City of London, 1660–1688, and its Consequences* (1969).

[6] Op. cit., 312–333.

colleges, manors—which had been part political unit, part definer of personal identity and focus of allegiance, were weakened or destroyed by the growing power of the centralized state. One influential liberal response to the threat to personal liberty thus created was that exemplified by John Stuart Mill. Given the lack of mediating institutions to shield the individual from direct confrontation with the state apparatus,[7] liberalism attempted to build a wall around the individual, and defined his freedom as the space thereby delimited.[8] A related response, particularly characteristic of lawyers, is to impose ostensibly procedural restrictions on the manner in which the state may exercise its power over individuals, although there has been a pronounced political bias in the choice of the areas where these restrictions will be imposed.

The pluralists' response was quite different. It was to reject, on both descriptive and normative levels, the stark polarity expressed in Herbert Spencer's title *Man Versus the State.* Descriptively, a multitude of disparate 'fellowships'—Gierke's term for associations—were seen as the true locus of men's lives: 'Whatever man has accomplished is due to his association with other men.'[9] To this purported factual observation was added the further claim that groups had a psychological reality, less readily demonstrable by the canons of empiricism but recognized implicity in expressions like the 'will' or 'soul' of a people, the 'shame' of a nation, or class 'consciousness'. Hence the group itself had an existence independent of its individual members and—the normative corollary—its legal existence, its status as an independent legal personality, did not arise from the generosity of a gracious sovereign (the so-called Concession theory) but was rather the necessary and morally imperative recognition of an irrefutable fact. Indeed the state itself could be seen as no more than a specialized kind of group—of necessity more powerful than the rest, but entitled to no greater moral deference or consideration.[10] Gierke, and Figgis following,

---

[7] Mill of course was not concerned only with the pressures against individuality exerted by the state, but equally if not more so with those of what he termed 'public opinion'. This is a much more sophisticated appreciation of the obstacles to individual liberty than that evinced by most liberals, who have concentrated almost exclusively on the dangers of the state.

[8] Also central to liberalism, of course, has been the protection of private property. Exploration of the connection between this value and Mill's notion of self-regarding action, though an intriguing question, cannot be attempted here. It should be said too that in Mill at any rate the older notion of freedom as participation in self-governance was not completely abandoned; see e.g. A. Ryan, *J. S. Mill* (1974), 202–203.

[9] O. Gierke, *Associations and Law*, G. Heiman (trans.) (1977), 13.

[10] See D. Nicholls, *The Pluralist State* (1975), Ch. 3, especially pp. 43–47, and the essay by Harold Laski. 'The Pluralistic State', first published in 1919 and reprinted as Appendix B. of ibid.

indeed went further, claiming that groups had a real personality, with a moral status equivalent to that of individual humans.[11]

It is not necessary to follow him on to this terrain or, as Sir Ernest Barker put it, into the realm of 'billowy cloud and rolling nebulosities',[12] to appreciate the force of the argument. The reality of groups, whatever their ontological status, is to be respected for the same reason human beings command respect; the polity and its legal system cripple human endeavour if they outlaw, or fail to make proper arrangements for, the reality of co-operative action.

Two points about the pluralists' thought are particularly relevant. The first is that though most of them did not deny the authority of the state to regulate group activities to varying degrees, they did insist that the internal development and functioning of the group be left strictly alone.[13] (One may note a striking parallel to the Millian treatment of individuals.) They therefore failed to consider whether individuals within the group require protection from the majority, except to allow dissidents complete freedom to give up their membership.

Secondly, they seem to have ignored the question whether some outside force—the state, or other groups—might impose substantive limitations on a group's purposes or means of realizing them. In view of their awareness of the problem of the legal personality of trade unions, and the controversy surrounding the legality of their activities, this was a serious surprising flaw.

Gierke was not purely a scholar but equally a propagandist: he wished to ensure that the law of the new German Empire would recognize and give full freedom to association, and he thought this required extirpation of the influence of Roman law doctrines. In England the conflict was not so severe. As might be expected, the common law—i.e. judical decision— sedulously eschewed any theoretical analysis of how collections of persons engaged in a common endeavour could fit within a structure in which the complexities of human behaviour are stripped down to the stark individualism of the typical 'case': Person A *v.* Person B. None the less, it managed to treat medieval cities[14] and, for a time, universities, as legal persons.

Analogous treatment was then extended to large agglomerations of capital used in risk-taking enterprise (the limited liability corporation).

---

[11] For Gierke, see Barker's introduction, op. cit., ix–xxvii; J. N. Figgis, *Churches in the Modern State* (1913), 248ff.

[12] Barker, op. cit., xvii.

[13] E.g. Figgis, op. cit., 121–124. However, as Nicholls points out, op. cit., Ch. 5, there was considerable variation of opinion and emphasis among the various pluralists.

[14] Frug, op. cit., 1081–1090.

Furthermore—a factor to which Maitland attached particular importance[15] —it permitted, through the device of the trust, some very important institutions—e.g. the public schools—to function as legal actors without formal incorporation, and to ensure the concentration of wealth holding within a line of family descent for generations. To these one might add a sort of obverse example—the venerable and indispensible fiction that allowed the mantle of the Crown, which until 1947 was wholly immune from suit, to be stripped from at least some of its officials, who could then be sued in their so-called 'personal capacity'. This made possible, among other things, the great cases of the 1760s, in which John Wilkes and his printers recovered enormous damages for illegal searches ordered by the King's chief minister.[16] Whilst untidy, a system of law comprehending human persons, corporations, trusts and various other unincorporated associations (not to mention the state itself which, one readily forgets, is—once it ceased to be equivalent in political theory and reality to the person of the monarch—neither more nor less an abstraction than any other non-human entity), managed to avoid doing violence to certain important spheres of social reality. When it came to facilitating the conduct of business enterprise, and more generally to the management and transfer of property, legal classifications were well adapted to the desires and expectations of those engaged in such activities.

The doctrinal waters were not always smooth, however. I must glide quickly over a lengthy and controversial story, but the question whether a trade union was a legal person—and hence whether it could be sued by its own members or, even more critically, by employers against whom its members had taken, or threatened, industrial action—has been, at least formally, at the storm centre of the tangled history of judicial animus against those bodies.[17] It has also led judges and commentators to perform the most extraordinary analytical contortions,[18] and although for most practical purposes the matter has been settled by Parliament,[19] it has not wholly vanished. Recently a High Court judge held that a trade union could not maintain an action for libel, which may reflect as much the

---

[15] F. W. Maitland, 'Trust and Corporation', op. cit., 323–404.

[16] Notably, *Entick v. Carrington* (1765) 19 St. Tr. 1030, and *Wilkes v. Wood*, (1763) 19 St. Tr. 1153. A similar distinction is at the root of one of the most important doctrines in American constitutional law, which permits plaintiffs to protect their civil rights in the federal courts by suing officials rather than the state: *Ex parte Young* 209 U.S. 123 (1908).

[17] Most spectacularly in the celebrated *Taff Vale* case, [1901] A.C. 426.

[18] Notably in *Bonsor v. Musicians' Union* [1956] A.C. 104, and the comments of Lloyd (1956) 19 *M.L.R.* 221, and Wedderburn (1957) 20 *M.L.R.* 105.

[19] Trade Union and Labour Relations Act 1974, s. 2 which lays down that no trade union can be treated as a body corporate, but does have the capacity to make contracts, sue and be sued in its own name.

failure of the law of defamation to accord due recognition to the reality of group existence, as defects in labour law.[20] Of even greater relevance to the present topic was the inability of the law to respond sensitively to the needs of non-commercial groups. The most celebrated instance, and the one which galvanized the pluralists, particularly Figgis, to inquire into the deeper issues of political theory and jurisprudence, was the *Free Church of Scotland* case, decided by the House of Lords in 1904.[21]

The facts were straightforward. In 1843 there occurred an event known as the Disruption, in which a substantial minority left the established Scottish Church to form the Free Church. The new organization set out its precepts in a series of documents, which were re-affirmed in subsequent 'formularies'. Long after the death of its founding leaders, and probably nearly all its original members, the Assembly of the Free Church voted to merge with yet another Church, which involved modification of some of its original tenets. The merger was approved by a majority of better than twenty to one, but the opponents, appositely called the 'Wee Frees', challenged its legality. Eventually the case reached the House of Lords, where the majority identified, or rather equated, the Free Church with the doctrines thus enunciated. They concluded that the modification of doctrine entailed in the merger had so radically altered the character of the Free Church that it had ceased to be the body for which solicitation of support had been made, and awarded all the Church's substantial property to the dissenters.[22] The Law Lords treated the statements of precepts as a deed of trust, with the consequence that the purpose as established by the founders could never be altered without violation of the trust. Maitland aptly described this judgment as 'the dead hand [falling] with a resounding slap upon the living body'.[23] By insisting that those who wished to remain within the Church adhere to the original doctrines, presumably unto eternity, the court seemed to deny the social reality of change that may occur in the nature and values of groups. Figgis perceived an even more dangerous implication: denial of power to groups to control their own evolution without the approval of the state.[24]

II

Those who accept the pluralists' perception of the importance of group

[20] *E.E.T.P.U. v. Times Newspapers Ltd.* [1980] 1 All E.R. 1097. A registered trade union can, however, bring such an action.

[21] *General Assembly of the Free Church of Scotland v. Overtoun* [1904] A.C. 515.

[22] After an outbreak of rioting, the effect of the decision was reversed by Parliament in the Churches (Scotland) Act 1905.

[23] 'Moral Personality and Legal Personality', op. cit., 319.

[24] Figgis, op. cit., Ch. 1.

activity, with their more controversial corollary that protection of group rights is essential if liberty is to be meaningful, must come to grips in contemporary conditions with a phenomenon quite beyond their ken. Their concern was with the freedom of voluntary associations, groups which the individual could join to achieve a shared purpose, and from which he could readily withdraw. Churches apart, all these groups—trade unions, corporations, worker-run industries,[25] even social clubs—are directed to the achievement of some material interest. The pluralists shared with liberalism, and with the law, an inability to find a place for a qualitatively different form of sodality: groups of persons distinguished by language, ethnic or racial origin, or religion. Especially where—as is often though not always the case—these characteristics are coincident, they form the deepest roots of personality identity and produce a distinctive way of life which sharply sets apart group members from outsiders. The 'generic and diffuse core' of this personal identity may be called culture; in its collective dimension, which emphasizes its ascriptive elements and its transmission through generations it is often known as ethnicity.[26] Such groups lack economic goals, indeed ultimately they may have no instrumental purposes at all; to borrow a duality from the psychologist Erich Fromm, they are concerned not to have, but to be.[27]

It is tempting to explain the pluralists' lack of awareness of ethnic groups as a result of the dominance of the view, taken as a central assumption by John Stuart Mill, that a viable polity must contain a culturally homogeneous population.[28] Certainly Gierke, a fierce German nationalist and exponent of the so-called 'historical school' of law, was concerned only with the realization of a distinctively Germanic legal system. The English pluralists, working at a time when the Irish Question came close to tearing British politics apart, and having seen the failure of Gladstone's disestablishment of the Irish Church to solve the issue, may perhaps have concluded that cultural or national divisions, as distinct from merely religious ones, were intractable. We in the 1980s have no such excuse. I cannot explore the sociological background in adequate depth, so I shall simply call attention to one of the most important social changes that has occurred in Western Europe since the war: every reasonably populous state now has ethnic minorities of considerable size within its borders. The permanent settlement, not merely migration, of workers—and their families—from Third World and poorer European countries, and the

[25] G. D. H. Cole's distinctive contribution to pluralist theory was his advocacy of participation in industry in a series of books written during and just after World War I, notably *Self-Government in Industry* (1917) and *Guild Socialism Restated* (1920).

[26] See further N. Glazer and D. Moynihan (eds), *Ethnicity* (1975), *passim*.

[27] E. Fromm, *To Have or To Be* (1978).

[28] J. S. Mill, *Considerations on Representative Government* (1958 edn.) 230–233.

resurgence of long-quiescent or defeated indigenous groups, has combined to bring this about. In my view this change is irreversible. Western Europe now shares with the United States, Canada, Australia, the Soviet Union and most of the larger Third World states, what has become the dominant characteristic of twentieth-century states: ethnic pluralism within the framework of a united polity. The working theoretical model of the state—this is as true of international law as of political theory— remains, however, what it was for Mill.[29] Political theory and jurisprudence are thus largely unprepared to answer what has become one of the most pressing issues of liberty in these times: how, within the over-arching political unity, are conflicts engendered by the co-existence of diverse and at times opposed, cultural values and ways of life to be resolved? The easy, if often bloody, answer that equates ethnic and cultural differences with nationality and prescribes secession or self-determination as the solution, is not available to a first-generation German of Turkish origin, or the British-born child of Punjabi Sikhs living in Coventry, and indeed is not of much assistance to Bretons or Basques. Even limited self-government as the United Kingdom has practised it for centuries with the Scots—which has permitted survival of a separate legal system— cannot be adapted to treatment of minorities geographically and physically dispersed. This is equally true of proposals for devolution, which rose and fell so rapidly in the 1970s.

III

Let me simply put a series of questions, all based upon cases which have found their way into the Law Reports in England and the United States over the past decade, or which have been discussed within a legal framework: should single sex schools, generally being abandoned, be retained in deference to Muslim parents' religious views about the separation of boys and girls after the onset of puberty? Should those pupils who, under legal compulsion, attend mixed schools be excused from PE classes?[30] Should objections to mixed-sex education not based on religious grounds be treated differently? Must a Sikh whose religion requires him to wear a beard, be denied employment under the hygiene requirements in certain

[29] A point made very fully in two articles by an American political scientist, Vernon Van Dyke, 'Justice as Fairness: for Groups?', *Am. Pol. Sci. Rev.* **69** (1975), 607, and 'The Individual, the State and Ethnic Communities in Political Theory', *World Politics* **29** (1977), 341.

[30] See the sensitive discussion of these questions in a pamphlet published by the Yorkshire Community Relations Committee, *The Education of Muslim Girls* (1975).

factories or, indeed, entire industries?[31] Similarly, must he be forced to choose between wearing a crash helmet and removing his turban, giving up that form of cheap transport, or suffering criminal prosecution?[32] Should educational authorities be required to provide bilingual and/or bicultural education for ethnic minorities?[33] Are ethnic or racial minorities entitled to be represented in seats in the legislature, employment, or admission to educational institutions in rough proportion to their numbers in the general population?[34] Should a follower of Mesmer, whose religious scruples forbid him to give blood, be regarded as having a 'reasonable excuse' under the Road Traffic Act 1972 when prosecuted for failing to produce a specimen of blood on request?[35] What are the implications of the request of the Union of Muslim Organizations at a conference some years ago that the United Kingdom authorities recognize the applicability of Muslim personal law to British adherents of that faith? If, as seems plausible, this would entail legal recognition of the validity of polygamous marriage and divorce by *talaq*, is it therefore to be rejected? Given that blasphemy remains a crime in English law, should it be extended to outlaw statements offensive to non-Christian belief in a society containing at least two million adherents of other faiths?[36] Is a community of persons—the Old Order Amish—who share not merely common doctrine but an entire way of life premised upon the religious injunction to 'be not conformed to this world', entitled to withdraw its children from compulsory state education after a certain minimum period, to avoid their 'contamination' by outside influences?[37] Ought a devout Muslim schoolteacher, who interprets his religion to command attendance at a mosque on Friday during an hour of the school day, be required to accept part-time status, or should his assignments be altered to take account of his devotions?[38] Should a Nigerian immigrant who made incisions on her two sons' cheeks

---

[31] *Panesar v. Nestlé Co. Ltd.* [1980] I.R.L.R. 60.

[32] Sikhs finally achieved exemption from the crash helmets requirement by the Motor-Cycle Crash-Helmets (Religious Exemption) Act 1976.

[33] See Comment, 'Cultural Pluralism', *Harv. Civ. Rights–Civ. Libs. L. Rev.* **13** (1978), 133, 146–168.

[34] On political representation for ethnic minorities, see Van Dyke, op. cit., and C. Palley, *Constitutional Law and Minorities* (1978). Employment and university admissions are of course at the centre of the celebrated 'reverse discrimination' question, on which see L. Lustgarten, *Legal Control of Racial Discrimination* (1980), 14–25, and sources cited therein.

[35] *R. v. John* [1974] 2 All E.R. 561.

[36] This was the view of Lord Scarman in the *Gay News* case, *R. v. Lemon* [1979] A.C. 617, though it was not shared by the other judges who held the defendant rightly convicted.

[37] *Wisconsin v. Yoder*, 406 U.S. 205 (1972).

[38] *Ahmad v. ILEA* [1978] 1 All E.R. 574.

as part of a ceremony to solemnize their tribal identification, be permitted to plead tribal customs as a defence to a charge of assault occasioning actual bodily harm? If not, what should be the appropriate sentence of the court?[39]

Now there is a common thread running through these apparently disparate matters. In different contexts, each raises the question of how 'deviant' group practices or institutions are to be treated by the majority. If the practice is of sufficient importance, the maintenance and perpetuation of the minority group's existence may be threatened. At the very least, institutional arrangements (e.g. the Monday to Friday work and school week) established unreflectingly before the arrival of a new group, may significant restrict their full economic participation. The fact that a specific issue, if it arises as a question of law, is cast in terms of a claim of legal right by an individual may seriously obscure what is ultimately involved. The legal process has a genius for individuation and simplification, which though it may serve some very important social values[40] is positively unhelpful in the present context, for it conceals that fact that the individual litigant may be standing surrogate for the way of life of a community. I cannot here do justice to this very important point, but it must surely make a substantial difference whether the case of the Muslim schoolteacher is seen *primarily* as a question of a breach of the contract of employment, or as one of adjusting institutional arrangements in light of the emergence of large numbers of people whose devotional practices do not fit conveniently with traditional arrangements.[41] Equally it makes a critical difference whether one regards discrimination law as an attempt to secure fair treatment of individuals or social equality for groups.[42]

There is a more subtle point. If I may borrow a term with very different connotations, the methodological individualism of law distorts the issues in another way: it elevates certain values—those which comport with the ideology of individualist liberalism—over those which do not. Freedom of belief, even where as in Britain it is not explicitly protected by a constitutional or broad statutory provision, is given great respect by the courts; the practice of religion (and, even more, a secular value structure), much less so. Implicit in the distinction is the notion that religion as doctrine can be separated from religion as a way of life: the divorce between

---

[39] *R. v. Adesanya*, *The Times* 16–17 July 1974, discussed by Poulter (1975) 24 *I.C.L.Q.* 136.

[40] Tay, 'Law, the Citizen and the State' in E. Kamenka *et al.* (eds), *Law and Society: The Crises in Legal Ideals* (1978).

[41] This difference of perspective was crucial in the divergence of opinion in the Court of Appeal in the *Ahmad* case, supra. n. 38. Orr L.J. took the former view, Scarman L.J. the latter.

[42] In reality the issue is by no means as sharply polarized, or as clear-cut, as the text suggests. See further L. Lustgarten, op. cit., Ch. 1.

belief and culture. This may be a fundamental, indeed logically necessary assumption of a society which is individualistic, orientated towards material gain, and which perceives truth through what it calls the scientific method. But it is precisely this assumption which is rejected by ancient religions like Islam, or minority sects like the Old Order Amish. It expresses the logic of individualism, which exalts conscience and intellect and deprecates collective identity and loyalty unless centred upon the state. In a secular context, the parallel is to the denial of high value, at least when compared to administrative convenience and the purported need for uniformity of laws, to differences of language, morals or what, somewhat misleadingly, may be called custom.

I certainly do not mean to suggest that the separation of belief and culture was wholly undesirable. It seems to have emerged as a coherent conception in the political struggles following the Reformation, and made possible the toleration of doctrinal differences, and hence a considerable measure of liberty for those outside the Established Church. I know too little of the history of that period to say whether this liberty was purchased at the cost of devaluing the importance of controversial beliefs as a main-spring of action, but it is obvious enough that at some point curbs on action in the name of social order turn freedom of belief into triviality and quaintness, a matter for the antiquarian. The presence of ethnic minorities which are also cultural minorities revives and gives urgency to the question at the heart of *On Liberty*: can people live, and not merely believe, as they wish?

IV

I should like to put forward a general precept, neither as simple nor as wide-ranging as Mill's, but directed solely to the kinds of issues canvassed herein. It is that ethnic minorities shall be permitted unrestricted freedom to follow their own customs and religious practices, be governed by their personal law, and receive education in their language and cultural tradition. This is subject to but two limitations. The first is that a practice may rightly be outlawed where it results in severe physical abuse or worse.

The second is that institutional accommodation to different patterns of life among minorities is required unless it can be shown to be wholly impracticable. Both these exceptions are designed to encompass a small number of extreme cases, and are deliberately expressed in restrictive language. With the first, I have in mind the custom of suttee and the practice of female circumcision; I certainly do not mean to proscribe polygamy provided the marriage is not brought about by threat of physical force. Additionally, and in order to assist in the effective protection of these liberties, I would propose that ethnic minorities as such be recognized as independent legal entities.

A fully elaborated defence of this position would require a theory of liberty which, whilst not jettisoning Mill's great contribution to protection of the lone or abstract individual, would present an equally powerful case grounded in the worth of pluralism. It must also pay greater attention than political theory normally does to the legal mechanisms, doctrinal and institutional, required to translate principles into effective rights. It is important to emphasize, however, that *On Liberty* is not the place to look for inspiration for such an endeavour; quite the reverse. Mill's most cherished value was individuality, both intrinsically and instrumentally as a means of fostering moral and technological progress; and he despised actions based upon inherited custom.[43] The animating spirit which must be invoked is rather that of Johan Herder, whose outlook has been thus described:

> Valuing the plurality of cultures and languages, the subtle ecological variety and nuance of human practices, distinctly for themselves, for their existent idiosyncracy . . . he refused to see hierarchy within the realm of cultures and insisted that as structures of lived sentiment, they must instead be accorded intrinsic value other than appraisal sternly from the bastion of a single culture.[44]

What is required, in short, is a conception of liberty equally sensitive to the concerns of the pluralists as to those of Mill, combined with an understanding of the dimensions of human identity and action that both failed to appreciate.

This is, however, not the place to attempt to construct and defend such a theory, which would require an essay as long as Mill's. All I can do here is indicate, by means of series of questions, what problems any such theory must address. I would, however, like to preface this compilation with two brief observations meant to draw attention to significant differences between the approach taken by Mill, and by contemporary liberalism which he continues so deeply to influence, and that which a theory of liberty encompassing cultural pluralism must adopt.

In one vital respect, Mill's doctrine is if anything an obstacle rather than a foundation of the required theory. One may accept, as his most trenchant critics like Stephen and Devlin do not, that there is a sphere of activity that may properly be called 'self-regarding'. However, under any plausible conception cultural rights would extend far beyond it. As the examples given earlier make plain, recognition of cultural rights would involve major changes in education; in substanstive law governing significant aspects of people's lives—notably marriage and divorce, the status

---

[43] This antipathy is expressed very strongly throughout Ch. 3 of *On Liberty*.
[44] J. Dunn, *Western Political Theory in the Face of the Future* (1979) 76. For an extended treatment of Herder, see I. Berlin, *Vico and Herder* (1976).

of children, and inheritance; and in the administrative arrangements now controlling much of the day-to-day functioning of industry and government. The critical question then becomes whether a society can tolerate behaviour based upon radically divergent clusters of values, not merely—as in the controversy over 'permissive' sexual legislation—differences limited to one relatively narrow area of deviant behaviour. This is perhaps another way of saying that the libertarian space created by Millian liberalism, though invaluable, is a small one. And those who believe that Mill's principle marks the outer limits of the permissible space, and who have been accustomed to see it attacked as too wide, will instinctively oppose the claims urged in the name of cultural pluralism.

The second point is that the nature of some of the rights involved is very different from rights as understood by Mill. His was of course the position of negative liberty; his concern, to prevent external interferences in what the individual chose to do with the use of his own resources, moral and material. Yet in the critically important sphere of education, the concrete manifestation of cultural pluralism is as a claim upon public resources, as for example in the provision of bilingual and bicultural education. Indeed, I would argue that this point far transcends the specific rights under discussion here. The massively extended scope of state activity since the Victorian era, often as an effective near-monopoly supplier, in my view requires that a realistic conception of liberty—of any kind—must incorporate claims upon public resources as a central element.

V

1. I have argued that ethnic groups with distinct patterns of behaviour and belief should receive certain protections and legal status. Which and what kinds of groups should be thus treated? Should the same treatment be extended to a racial group, which may require vigilant legal protection because of widespread discrimination, but which does not differ significantly from the majority in fundamental matters like language, religion, or personal law? (I have in mind here the various Asian groups compared with West Indians.) It should be noted that in the United States, where the question of group rights has received some attention, racial rather than cultural minorities have been the focus.[45] However, rights for racial groups require quite different justification—grounded in compensatory justice, and concerned with the distribution of resources and opportunities—from that proposed in this paper. A related and converse question is why col-

[45] In addition to the writings of Van Dyke cited earlier, see especially Fiss, 'Groups and the Equal Protection Clause', *Phil. & Pub. Affair.* **5** (1976), 107 and B. Bittker, *The Case for Black Reparations* (1973).

lectively based actions should receive greater respect than individual non-conformity, or non-conformity based upon a mere religion whose adherents are otherwise largely indistinguishable from the dominant group. Is this due to fears for public order and the cost of its maintenance, the moral weight of numbers, or the suspicion that a long-established culture is far less likely to be simply absurd than the odd individual? Should the very age of an alternative mode of life command respect? Does cultural pluralism based upon ethnicity overcome the Devlin position about the need for a shared morality precisely because of the width and visibility of the gap between majority and minority, whereas the person who opposes the majority so to speak from within is much more of a threat?

2. To what extent, i.e. in what spheres, should ethnic minorities have rights? I would argue that the constitutional and political arrangements for representation of groups, found in states as otherwise unlike one another as Belgium and Fiji, are not appropriate in Britain, but this view reflects my assessment of their likely practical value, which may be quite mistaken and in any case is not a judgment of principle.

3. The question of how conflicts between majorities and minorities within groups are to be treated must tread the fine line between undesirable interference and protecting individuals. To take analogies from developed areas of law, the problem resembles not so much expulsion or discipline, as with trade unions and their members, as abuse of interests of bene-ficiaries and shareholders by trustees or directors of limited companies. The *Free Church of Scotland* case is a tailor-made example: would critics of the decision have felt differently if the abandonment of some of the organization's fundamental doctrines had been approved by a majority of three to two, rather than upwards of twenty to one? One can envisage a wide range of matters—the substantive meaning of a particular law, the content of education, the degree of deviation from some ordained norm required by practical circumstances—on which opinion may be bitterly divided. The essence or indeed existence of a cultural practice may itself become problematical. Whose view are those outside the group to accept as authoritative, particularly if it appears in the case of a group which is part of a world-wide community that practices are changing elsewhere? Cultural pluralism is not meant to be a mechanism of ossifica-tion.

4. An even more difficult problem of internal conflict is that raised most clearly by the Amish case, though it also complicates the controversy over single-sex schools. To what extent should parents' views of the proper way of life not only govern their children's behaviour until they leave

home, but effectively foreclose their ability to participate in the wider society, or at any rate, opt out of the group? It is apparent that the Amish child withdrawn from school at the age of fourteen will find it exceedingly difficult to make up for the lost years if he wishes to pursue a technically skilled occupation requiring advanced and lengthy study; and he will certainly be at a severe disadvantage in competition with everyone else.[46] A single-sex school for Muslim girls would probably be pervaded with an ethos opposed to further education and independent careers for the pupils, whatever the formal instruction provided. Yet all parents retain a significant measure of control and influence over children; do parents who refuse to support their children at school after sixteen, or who actively or tacitly discourage their girls from any ambition other than early marriage and child-rearing, really have a substantially different impact on the 'life chances' of their children than did the Amish parents?

5. Many people would consider that the acceptance of cultural pluralism is in Britain a political question, to be decided in each particular instance on grounds of public policy, not a matter of rights based upon the application of principle. Concretely this means that such issues are not for the courts and further, unless one hopelessly idealizes the political process, that they will be decided on the basis of the balance of forces among pressure groups. On the simplest level, this conception of a political issue ignores the fact that political or moral principles, like Mill's, can themselves change that balance if a sufficient number of persons find them persuasive. For example it is very doubtful that if Mill had not written, the Wolfenden Report would have taken the position it did, or that the liberalization of various sumptuary laws would have proceeded as rapidly as it did, even granted that the late 1960s were for other reasons a particularly propitious time for reform. Furthermore, as the earlier catalogue of questions illustrates, issues of this kind frequently come before the courts. They arise in the context of a clash of legal principles or commands. A teacher does indeed work under a contract of employment, but Parliament has also inserted into that contract protection against any form of deprivation of benefit or opportunity because of his religious beliefs and observance, or absence thereof.[47] In the case of the Muslim schoolteacher, the Court of Appeal had to determine whether his claim to take time off fell within this provision, and two of the three judges treated policy questions concerning cultural pluralism as central to the construction of the statute.[48] Moreover, the European Court of

[46] This was the ground of the thoughtful and cogent dissent of Douglas J. in the *Yoder* case, supra, 406 U.S. 205, 241ff.

[47] Education Act 1944, s. 30.

[48] Lord Denning M.R. who rejected cultural pluralism and joined Orr L.J. to make the majority (see n. 41) against Scarman L.J.

Human Rights, which must be growing tired of the number of cases emanating from this country, will be evaluating the outcomes of our political process in light of Art. 9 of the European Convention on Human Rights, which protects both freedom of belief and freedom to 'manifest' one's religion. The Convention occupies a peculiar position in UK municipal law,[49] but its presence will I think ensure that conflicts over cultural pluralism, like others formerly regarded as purely political, will increasingly find their way into a judicial forum, here and in Strasbourg. These issues are as much questions of legal doctrine as of political theory.

6. On the practical level, what specifically legal techniques and institutions can contribute to the support of cultural pluralism? Would recognition of parallel legal systems be desirable? It is certainly possible, as the experience of the British Empire abundantly demonstrates, for different ethnic groups to be subject to different personal laws,[50] which may be applied in separate courts. Closer to home, well into the last century the stannary courts of the West Country exercised jurisdiction of a range of subjects and persons far removed from mining operations, and created and applied a substantive law quite different from that found in the common law courts.[51] In the sphere of public law, where the ordinary courts cannot be displaced, what would be the implications of treating the ethnic group as a legal person? Who would speak for it and how would the spokesman be chosen? Before the idea is dismissed as unworkable or absurd, it should be appreciated that even the class action device commonly used in North America, which enables an individual litigant to represent 'all others similarly situated', would be insufficient to convey the full collective dimension of the issues under discussion. It cannot be used in criminal matters, where the court is concerned solely with the guilt of named defendants. More fundamentally, the technique is most frequently used to join the claims of persons who share nothing except a common dispute with a particular defendant. This is a radically different structure from a continuing body whose existence transcends its members at any given point in time, and which may have interests which are more related to the future than to the past. The pluralists perceived an awkward but important truth about the nature of group existence; it is up to us to alter legal and political institutions in recognition of that perception.

---

[49] To oversimplify, it is not part of UK municipal law and cannot be used by a British court to invalidate an Act of Parliament, but the courts will use it as an aid to construction of a statute in ambiguous cases.

[50] M. B. Hooker, *Legal Pluralism* (1975), Ch. II and III.

[51] R. Pennington, *Stannary Law* (1973), *passim*.

VI

One final matter requires emphasis. Respect for cultural diversity is desirable in part because it is a mark of respect for the diginity of persons whose values differ from one's own. It is not meant to enforce difference among people of different cultural background; its ultimate negation would be to impose a series of status classifications on all inhibitants of a society. Thus if any individual chooses to assimilate into the wider culture, to embrace its norms and reject all ties to a minority group, that decision should command the same respect as that of someone who lives by traditional norms. If a sufficient number of people vote with their feet in this way, the group may reassess its practices, or may indeed disintegrate. That is as may be. What is valuable is not simply pluralism for its own sake, but pluralism meaningful in people's lives.

Liberty and Compulsory Education

PETER GARDNER

1. Introducton

Although it is primarily concerned with the value of liberty and the justification of compulsory education, what lies behind much of this paper is the question 'Why treat children like children?' The fact is that we do not regard children as having the same rights, privileges and liberties as adults, and children may not be thought of as deserving the same degree of respect or consideration as their seniors. In the past this has led to some horrific states of affairs,[1] and while matters have undoubtedly improved, it is still the case that most people accept what Graham Haydon describes as 'the assumption that one thing can go for children and quite another for adults'.[2] One likely consequence of this, and an important example of the different treatment reserved for children is compulsory education. Illiterate and innumerate adults are not compelled to practise their letters or play with counters or watch prescribed television programmes. Even when, to quote Mill, we have an adult 'who shows rashness, obstinacy and self-conceit—who cannot live within moderate means—who cannot restrain himself from hurtful indulgencies—who pursues animal pleasures at the expense of those of feeling and intellect',[3] we do not subject him to character-building games or uplifting scripture readings, or initiate him into the mysteries of home economics, or read Shakespeare at him. But we compulsorily do all of this and more to children. Moreover, compulsory education, as we have it, is not something from which the young can gain remission. The law that requires 'every child of compulsory school age . . . to receive an efficient full-time education suitable to his age, ability, and aptitude'[4] effectively defines an approach where what counts is the arbitrariness of chronology, not standards or excellence.

[1] See, for example, Lloyd de Mause, 'The Evolution of Childhood', in *The History of Childhood* Lloyd de Mause (ed.), (London: Souvenir Press, 1976).

[2] G. Haydon, 'Political Theory and the Child; Problems in the Individualist Tradition', *Political Studies* **27**, No. 3 (1979), 413.

[3] J. S. Mill, 'On Liberty', in *Utilitarianism, Liberty and Representative Government* (London: Dent, 1910), 134.

[4] *The Education Act*, 1944, Section 36.

Given this state of affairs, cannot we repeat Mill's observation, originally made about the subjection of women, and say that those who support such treatment of children have 'the double presumption against them that they are opposing freedom and recommending partiality'?[5] Mill also observed that where a practice 'is supported . . . by universal usage, and . . . by so great a preponderance of popular sentiment'[6] argument may prove ineffective. Still, let us travel in hope; not all the ground need be stony.

2. The Liberation Argument

The basic argument of this paper, which I will call the libertarian argument, is that compulsory education needs justifying precisely because it is compulsory. Obviously having compulsory education as a social institution affects the freedom of various people, such as, for instance, parents and rate payers. Yet, it is simply with those subject to compulsory education that the libertarian argument is concerned, and since almost all of these are young, I will refer to them without, I trust, giving too much offence, as children. Thus, what the libertarian argument involves is a principle of liberty which is held to apply to children and the premise that compulsory education is an encroachment on the freedom of children. What this argument can be taken as resting on is the view that freedom is valuable in itself, a view which has many supporters. It underpins both Benn and Weinstein's claim that 'Since freedom is a principle, whatever interferes with it demands to be justified'[7] and J. P. White's assertion that 'Any infringement of liberty is *prima facie* morally unjustifiable'.[8] It would also seem to support Dworkin's principle of the least restrictive alternative according to which we should, whenever possible, aim to achieve our desired ends without restricting freedom, irrespective of cost, inconvenience and other countervailing factors,[9] and when Mill maintains 'all restraint, *qua* restraint, is an evil', he, too, may appear to be of the opinion that freedom is valuable in itself. But appearances can be deceptive, for Mill immediately goes on to say of some restraints that they 'are wrong solely because they do not really produce the results it is desired to pro-

[5] J. S. Mill, 'The Subjection of Women', in *Three Essays: On Liberty, Representative Government, The Subjection of Women* (London: Oxford University Press, 1975), 429.

[6] Ibid.

[7] S. I. Benn and W. L. Weinstein, 'Being Free to Act and Being a Free Man', *Mind* **80** (1971), 200.

[8] J. P. White, *Towards a Compulsory Curriculum* (London: Routledge and Kegan Paul, 1973), 5.

[9] G. Dworkin, 'Paternalism', *The Monist* **56** (1972), 84.

duce by them',[10] which is why, no matter how convoluted the reasoning required, Mill's remark on the evil of restraint is best interpreted as representing a teleological stance.

Returning to the libertarian case, we may observe that to accept the basic argument is to adopt a position which has curricular implications, just as, analogously, attempts to justify punishment have implications for our penal institutions. However, in keeping with what was said earlier, to consider education and the curriculum from this point of view is to adopt a far from common position. Remarks such as 'the march towards freedom has caught up with education',[11] even when made about America, are best treated as educational slogans, rather than descriptions.[12] In this country the recent 'Great Debate' on the curriculum and the lack of libertarian contributions to this debate about what children should be compelled to do probably reflected our degree of concern for the liberty of the child. Nevertheless, those who give little thought or attribute little value to the freedom of children could be said to be operating along the right lines. The fact of the matter is that popular sentiment in this area can find a variety of philosophical allies. Consequently, while the libertarian argument looks simple and, I hope persuasive, it could face a variety of attacks, and even some of its supporters may do little to advance the libertarian cause. In what follows I will explore and question some of this opposition as well as some of the support which the libertarian might be better off without.

3. The Freedom of Children

If the Cartesian thesis that animals are automata were sound, much moral disapproval of hunting would be groundless, just as, if children, *qua* children, are incapable of being free, the libertarian case would be unfounded. However, while the Cartesian thesis is difficult to support, an attack on the libertarian case based on a denial of children's freedom can be easily mounted. What is needed is some definition which posits a moderately demanding condition as necessary for freedom or for 'true' freedom as some prefer to call it. (I say 'moderately demanding', because were it too demanding, adults might take offence.) Couple this definition with the proposition that children cannot satisfy the condition in question, and one can argue: children lack the wherewithal to be free, *ergo*, compulsory education cannot constitute an infringement of their freedom. More-

---

[10] J. S. Mill (1910), 150–151.

[11] C. Bereiter, 'Moral Alternatives to Education', *Interchange* 3, No. 1 (1972), 27.

[12] Concerning the nature of educational slogans see I. Scheffler, *The Language of Education* (Springfield: Charles Thomas, 1960), Ch. 2.

over, with the addition of some premise about the value of freedom, one has an argument for compulsory education. The adult version of this argument, which concerns forcing men to be free, might be thought to lack respectability. The children's variation can, surprisingly, still sound persuasive.

Various theorists might be appealed to for support for the argument that children lack freedom. Locke, for example, maintains that man's freedom 'is grounded on his having reason' so that to 'turn . . . (someone) loose . . . before he has the reason to guide him, is not allowing him . . . to be free',[13] and this he believes gives parents authority to govern their children or to appoint tutors over them.[14] The contemporary educational philosopher G. H. Bantock pursues a similar, if more academic, line. Dissatisfied with negative definitions, Bantock believes that 'true' freedom 'springs . . . from allowing one's desires to be sifted by reason', 'from the observation of the moral law' and 'from . . . submission to the authority inherent in the various bodies of human learning',[15] and that the teacher's job is to develop 'true' freedom.[16] The Kantian view that morality is a condition of freedom has also received recent support from Charles Taylor, who insists that 'moral discrimination'[17] is one of the conditions necessary for freedom. Taylor's other conditions include 'self-understanding' and 'self-control'.[18] In so far as intellectual development is necessary for satisfying the conditions we have listed, the writers we have mentioned have an ally in John Kleinig according to whom 'A young child left to itself is not free. To be free one must first have developed physically and intellectually.'[19]

Many other positive accounts of freedom could be presented here, but lest I leave the impression that such accounts need be individualistic if they are to be used against the libertarian, let us consider a more communal view. It is T. H. Green's oft-quoted claim that true freedom is 'the liberation of the powers of all men equally for contributions to a common good'.[20] Clearly such an account could be employed to support

[13] J. Locke, 'The Second Treatise of Government', in *Two Treatises of Government* (London: New English Library, 1960), 352.

[14] See J. Locke, op. cit., 352, 356.

[15] G. H. Bantock, *Education and Values* (London: Faber and Faber, 1965), 98, 100.

[16] G. H. Bantock (1965), 100.

[17] Charles Taylor, 'What's Wrong with Negative Liberty', in *The Idea of Freedom*, Alan Ryan (ed.) (London: Oxford University Press, 1979), 179.

[18] Ibid.

[19] J. Kleinig, 'Mill, Children, and Rights', *Educational Philosophy and Theory* **8**, No. 1 (1975), 12.

[20] T. H. Green, 'Lecture on Liberal Legislation and Freedom of Contract' in *Works of Thomas Hill Green*, III, *Miscellaries and Memoir*, R. L. Nettleship (ed.) (London: Longmans, Green, 1888), 372.

both the proposition that children lack 'true' freedom and a wide-ranging compulsory education designed to liberate those powers which, in someone's judgment, will contribute towards the common good.[21] Equally, the preceding individualistic accounts of freedom have their curricular implications. Suppose, for instance, moral discrimination and self-control are necessary for freedom. A curriculum planner who valued freedom might then prescribe studying the lives of the saints and early morning runs, or, if more progressive, a Humanities Curriculum Project and Outward Bound courses. Still, compared with this specificity, some of the conditions that have been mentioned afford, if not *cartes blanches*, at least considerable scope for the curriculum planner—and all in the name of freedom![22]

In response to the argument that children are not free the libertarian can employ at least three defences. Firstly, he can say that what he is facing here are defective accounts of childhood, and if we take a child to be someone of compulsory school age, then many children will satisfy the conditions mentioned providing the standards are not set too high. Secondly, arguing *ad hominem*, it could be pointed out that if failure to satisfy those conditions were grounds for compulsion, many adults would be in for a rude enlightening. Thirdly, and more importantly for this paper, the libertarian can argue that he is being opposed by defective accounts of freedom. However, in the light of contemporary triadic analyses of freedom,[23] it is difficult to sustain the argument that since negative definitions tell us what freedom really is, the previous positive definitions are wrong. It would be equally difficult to argue that satisfying the recommendations mentioned earlier will not increase freedom in some ways, for, undoubtedly, subjecting a person to the discipline of various bodies of human learning may enable him to think in ways that were new to him, just as developing a person's physique could make him free to do things that would otherwise have been impossible. Yet, I take it that those who advanced the previous accounts would not be content simply to be associated with such uninteresting theses; for they are seeking to tell us what

[21] See D. K. Jones, *The Making of the Education System, 1851–81* (London: Routledge and Kegan Paul, 1977), 81–82.

[22] Sir Isaiah Berlin observed of another positive account of freedom from T. H. Green that 'many a tyrant could use this formula to justify his worst acts of oppression' ('Two Concepts of Liberty', in *Four Essays on Liberty*, (Oxford: Oxford University Press, 1969), fn. 1, p. 133). Perhaps 'tyrannical schoolmaster' could be substituted for 'tyrant'.

[23] See, for example, Felix Oppenheim, *Dimensions of Freedom* (New York: St Martin's Press, 1961); G. MacCullum, 'Negative and Positive Freedom', *Philosophical Review* **76** (1967); and J. Feinberg, 'The Idea of a Free Man' in *Educational Judgements*, J. F. Doyle (ed.) (London: Routledge and Kegan Paul, 1973).

freedom truly is, and this is where they fall down. The amoral, the un-tutored, those with underdeveloped physiques and intellects and those whose powers have not been liberated for the common good, can be free from many constraints and impediments, and free to do many things. If we value freedom, rather than some ideal of how we would like people to use their freedom, we forget this at our peril.

It could nevertheless be claimed that parts of the preceding accounts should not be dismissed so hastily, in that being able to reason and to sift desires, and being in control of oneself constitute an important dimen-sion of individual freedom, a dimension which is lacking or diminished in the lives of the heteronomous and anomic and the indoctrinated and brainwashed. It could also be claimed that the importance of this dimension is reflected in our dissatisfaction with Hobbes' definition of freedom as 'the absence of external impediments',[24] and in our preferring Locke's definition in which he talks of 'the power a man has to do or forbear . . . as he (the agent) himself wills it'.[25]

I do not wish to deny the significance of these claims. What they suggest is that personal autonomy is an important and necessary part of individual freedom,[26] and in so far as the preceding accounts endorse this, they deserve support. But this is not to say that the previous criticism cannot be repeated: the amoral and the untutored, for example, as well as those with under-developed physiques and intellects, can still be very autonomous. As for trying to use the relationship between freedom and autonomy to argue that children lack freedom and, therefore, compulsory education cannot impinge on their freedom, this contradicts the observed facts. As many a schoolteacher will testify, pupils are often more autonomous than their parents. Of course, autonomy being a matter of degree, one could stipulate that only those who are markedly autonomous deserve to be classified as truly free, but even such stringency would lead to some school children being classified as truly free, just as it would assuredly lead to many adults being classified as unfree,[27] which is why this approach would lack appeal as an argument for compulsory education.

Still, granted that the concept of liberty is applicable to children, it might be argued that with the right approach, a child-centred approach,

[24] T. Hobbes, *Leviathan* (London: Dent, 1914), 66.

[25] J. Locke, *Locke's Essay on Human Understanding, Bks II and IV*, M. W. Calkins (ed.) (Leipzig: Felix Meiner, 1913), Bk II, Ch. XXI, Sec. 15.

[26] See W. E. Connolly, *The Terms of Political Discourse* (Lexington: D. C. Heath, 1974), Ch. 4.

[27] Spencer asked, 'When does the child become a man?' and concluded, ' . . . that whichever qualification is chosen, will class many as men who are not at present considered as such; whilst it will reject from the list, others who are now by universal consent included in it' (H. Spencer, *Social Statics* (Farnborough: Gregg International Publishers, 1970) 173). Also see below.

compulsory education need not constitute an interference with a child's freedom. Bearing in mind the previous analogy, this argument might be likened to the hunter's retort that his quarry enjoy being chased, and is, I suspect, hardly more convincing. If we characterize a child-centred approach as one in which what the pupil is interested in doing is the primary determinant in the learning process, then this way of proceeding may enable the teacher to avoid many of the anxieties and confrontations that arise when he is directing operations.[28] But the question we have to attend to is whether, by adopting this approach, those responsible for the compulsory education of pupils can avoid the charge of restricting freedom.

At least two points are at issue here. The first concerns the acceptability of defining freedom in terms of want-satisfaction. If this is acceptable, then, with an extreme child-centred approach, there could be compulsory education without encroachment. Now whatever practical problems this defence faces, it is, I believe, *pace* Rousseau and Russell,[29] founded on a definition which is unsatisfactory in various ways. For one thing, as Russell himself observes, it implies that minimizing wants and modifying desires constitute an increase in freedom.[30] Unfortunately Russell does not treat this as a *reductio ad absurdum* of his position. Of course, were such a definition acceptable, teachers skilled in manipulating desires could face the libertarian with a clear conscience, and this must surely make us suspicious of the definition in question. There again where this definition fails is that it overlooks the fact that to bar routes to possible, not just preferred, alternatives is to interfere with freedom.[31] Even if within a

[28] The following remarks, from which I have borrowed the expression 'primary determinant', and which were made with American teachers in mind, are by Bereiter: 'Currently teachers are very drawn to "informal" education, as inspired by the English infant school ... Here is an approach in which the child's own interests are supposed to be the primary determinant of what he learns and how. Thus it would seem that over and above whatever this approach has to offer children, it should get teachers off the hook morally. It should enable them to quit imposing goals on children' (C. Bereiter, *op. cit.*, 26).

[29] According to Rousseau, 'That man is truly free who desires what he is able to perform, and does what he desires' (J. J. Rousseau, *Emile* (London: Dent, 1974), 48). According to Russell, "Freedom" in its most abstract sense means the absence of external obstacles to the realization of desires' (B. Russell, *Sceptical Essays* (London: George Allen and Unwin, 1928), 169).

[30] B. Russell, op. cit., 169–170.

[31] As Benn and Weinstein observe, 'The range of alternatives open to me does not depend on my preference for one rather than another; consequently, to eliminate an otherwise available alternative ... is just as much an interference with freedom, whether or not I should have chosen it had it been available. To abridge the possibility of choice is to abridge freedom' (S. I. Benn and W. L. Weinstein, op. cit., 205).

compulsory system pupils have their so-called 'free-days' and their elective curricula and want the options offered, some options such as that of opting out of the whole enterprise and the range of alternatives for which this is necessary, are not available,[32] hence, the system interferes with freedom.

The second point also concerns a definition of freedom. Those who believe that freedom consists of not feeling coerced or aggrieved by those agents and agencies that affect one's life,[33] might also argue that with a child-centred approach, compulsory education need not constitute an encroachment on the freedom of pupils. According to this argument where a pupil's preferences are efficacious, he may not feel unfree or any grievance towards those responsible for his compulsory education,[34] and, so, he may not be unfree. But this approach to freedom is too subjective by far; the pupil who does not feel constrained or resentful about having to do maths or attend assembly is, nevertheless, not free to do other things. We might also inquire why the pupil does not feel constrained, especially if we have in mind Rousseau's advice to the teacher to let the pupil 'always think that he is master while you are really master'.[35] Suppose this advice were followed. That a pupil never experienced the pressure of coercion or feelings of resentment would be an irrelevance in discussing his freedom or, rather, his lack of it, and the pupil's feeling of being in control, of being able to do those things as he himself wills them, would be a dangerous illusion. As Rousseau sinisterly observed: 'There is no subjection so complete as that which preserves the forms of freedom; it is thus that the will itself is taken captive'.[36]

To summarize, the libertarian case might be opposed on the grounds that the concept of liberty should not be applied to children and that compulsory education need not interfere with a child's freedom. Such opposition may be found wanting in so far as it involves inadequate views of the young and of the practicalities of teaching, though without inquiring into these areas the libertarian can defend his position by showing that the attacks we have considered rely upon defective accounts of freedom.

4. Principles and Applicability

If, then, we are correct in talking of the freedom of children, and if com-

[32] As J. P. White has noted, 'in a voluntary system (of education), opting out of the whole programme is itself an option' (J. P. White, op. cit., 69–70).

[33] See B. Barry, *Political Argument* (London: Routledge and Kegan Paul, 1965), 137, 139.

[34] See ibid.

[35] J. J. Rousseau, op. cit., 84.

[36] Ibid.

pulsory education does encroach on that freedom, we can next turn to the need for justification. In maintaining that compulsory education needs justifying the libertarian is appealing to a principle of liberty applicable to children, and on this matter his position might be thought to differ from those held by such supposed champions of freedom as Humboldt and Mill, both of whom can be seen as presenting another way of attacking the libertarian case. This attack does not consist of support for the thesis that children lack freedom,[37] but, rather, of the qualification that our regard for individual freedom should not extend to children. Humboldt, for example, while concerned to preserve freedom for most adults and, in this connection, to limit state interference,[38] recommends that lunatics, idiots and minors be treated as exceptions.[39] Similarly, although Mill says that 'the sole end for which mankind are warranted, individually or collectively, in interfering with the liberty of action of any of their number, is self-protection' and 'to prevent harm to others',[40] he emphasizes that this, his harm principle, 'is meant to apply only to human beings in the maturity of their faculties ... not ... (to) children, or ... young persons below the age which the law may fix as that of manhood or womanhood' or 'barbarians' or, or so it seems, those who are incapable 'of being improved by free and equal discussion'.[41]

But why should Humboldt and Mill oppose freedom and recommend what looks like partiality? It is tempting to reply: because neither values freedom as an end, but only as a means, and both believe that the end they regard as desirable is best achieved by qualifying their principles of liberty so as to exclude children. This, I am aware, is a contentious answer. It involves, for instance, an interpretation of Mill which could be contested on several grounds, one being that he makes remarks, one of which we considered earlier, that are those we would expect from someone who values freedom for its own sake. Yet, we have to take stock of the fact that the remark we quoted and his harm principle occur in *On Liberty*, the avowed purpose of which is to demonstrate the importance of human

[37] Thus W. von Humboldt wants youngsters to be allowed more freedom as they grow older (see von Humboldt, W. (1969). *The Limits of State Act on.* (London: Cambridge University Press), p. 125, while Mill says that his principle does not apply to children, since paternalism, despotism and compulsion may be in order when we are dealing with the young and with barbarians. (See J. S. Mill (1910), p. 73), which we may take as indicating that neither writer thinks that children lack freedom.

[38] See, for example, von Humboldt, W., op. cit., Chs. III and IV.

[39] See op. cit., Ch. XIX.

[40] J. S. Mill, op. cit., 72–73.

[41] Op. cit., 73.

development and diversity, for which freedom looks like a means.[42] In addition, in *On Liberty* Mill proclaims that 'utility is the ultimate appeal on all ethical questions',[43] and often his defences of freedom are consequentialist, being along the lines that we should not interfere with individual liberty because 'each is the best judge and guardian of his interests'[44] and that, in any case, and this is something we have already touched upon, when we do interfere, we usually get things wrong.[45]

Still, even if Humboldt and Mill unlike the libertarian, adopt a teleological attitude towards freedom, and because of this wish to exclude the young from their regard for freedom, it would be wrong to labour these differences without indicating ways in which the libertarian might be sympathetic to several of the views of those who look like his opponents. One reason, and a crucial reason for the possibility of such sympathy, is that to regard freedom as valuable in itself is not to be committed to regarding it as the only thing worth valuing for its own sake. In this connection it is worth paying attention to Hayeck's view that 'Liberty does not mean all good things or the absence of all evils . . . to be free may mean . . . freedom to make costly mistakes, or to run mortal risks'.[46] However, regarding more than one thing as a desirable end can result in having to resolve conflicts. If one values freedom highly, one will ensure that if, in any resolution, freedom is to be sacrificed, it will not be sacrificed cheaply. From this point of view the libertarian might take some comfort from the fact that both Humboldt and Mill, even if they do not regard freedom itself as part of the moral currency, are far from inclined to sell freedom short when what is at stake is the freedom of most adults. Humboldt, for instance, is in favour of restricting state interference to areas concerned with 'the negative welfare of citizens'.[47] In similar vein in

---

[42] According to Mill *On Liberty* is 'a kind of philosophic text-book of a single truth . . . the importance, to man and society, of a large variety in types of character, and of giving full freedom to human nature to expand itself in innumerable and conflicting directions' (J. S. Mill, *Autobiography*, J. Stillinger (ed.) (London: Oxford University Press, 1971), 150), and the opening quotation in the essay is von Humboldt's view that 'The grand, leading principle towards which every argument unfolded in these pages directly converges, is the absolute and essential importance of human development in its richest diversity' (J. S. Mill (1910), 62). cf J. S. Mill, (1971), 151–152.

[43] J. S. Mill, (1910), 74.

[44] See, for example, op. cit., 75, and J. S. Mill, 'Representative Government', loc cit., 208–210. See also H. J. McCloskey, 'Mill's Liberalism', *Philosophical Quarterly* 13 (1963).

[45] See, for example, J. S. Mill, op. cit., 140, 150–151.

[46] F. A. Hayeck, *The Constitution of Liberty* (London: Routledge and Kegan Paul,), 1960, 18.

[47] See, for example, W. von Humboldt, op. cit., Ch. III and IV.

Mill's harm principle the grounds for legitimate interference are described in what we might call negative terms, such as the prevention of harm to others, not in positive terms, such as doing good for others or maximizing their interests. In fact there may be a danger of talking of negative and positive terms here; it could encourage the mistaken idea that these are different ways of talking about the same thing, the point at issue being that preventing harm coming to people is a sufficient but not a necessary condition of doing them some good.[48] It is after all one thing to prevent an adolescent from mugging the elderly and quite another to train him to be their servant. Failure to appreciate the general distinction involved in this type of example could lead to a gross undervaluing of freedom and to a system of compulsory education which treated the child as raw material to be used for the common good.[49]

Another feature of Mill's harm principle which may appeal to the libertarian is that the prevention of harm to others is not presented as a sufficient condition of rightful interference. Mill actually says that we must not suppose that what 'can alone justify ... interference, ... always does justify such interference'.[50] His defence of this view, as we might expect, is consequentialist,[51] but it is a view that the libertarian could also defend. If restraint and harm are both evil, it does not follow that avoiding the latter is always the best way of resolving conflicts.

Of course, the libertarian need not agree with every feature of Mill's principle. In particular he need not subscribe to its opposition to paternalistic interference in the lives of adults, for there could be situations where the cost to the agent is so great that, despite valuing freedom highly, the libertarian could recommend interference. But, as revealed by his treatment of the example of the unsafe bridge, Mill is not opposed to certain, admittedly limited, types of paternalistic interference in the lives of adults.[52] Nevertheless, it is surely his views on paternalism which most clearly mark the difference in his approach to the liberty of adults and the young, which brings us back to the attack on the libertarian case we mentioned earlier; for if it is suggested that we should follow writers like Humboldt and Mill and not apply our principle of liberty to children, what is meant, I take it, is not that the protection of others should never

---

[48] This point underpins Houlgate's observation: 'not being harmed is assuredly a benefit, but there are some benefits we can achieve for a child over and above his not being harmed' (L. D. Houlgate, 'Children, Paternalism and Rights to Liberty', in (eds) O. O'Neill and W. Ruddick, *Having Children*, (New York: Oxford University Press, 1979), 257).

[49] See part 4, below.

[50] J. S. Mill, op. cit., 150.

[51] See ibid. and see also D. G. Brown, 'Mill on Liberty and Morality', *Philosophical Review* **81** (1972), 139–140.

[52] See J. S. Mill, op. cit., 151–152.

constitute grounds for interfering with the liberty of the young; it is rather that we should practise paternalism on the young, but not on adults save in extreme cases.

The apparent partiality involved in this attack might be defended by an appeal to some teleological thesis structured round the view that such discrimination is the best way to promote particular types of happiness or individuality or human development. In keeping with this suggestion Francis Schrag has recently presented what he takes to be part of Mill's case for prescribing paternalistic interference in the lives of the young. It is that as far as children are concerned 'the chances of their achieving happiness if left to pursue their own good in their own way are slim. They must submit for a time to the paternalistic rule of others.[53] Whether Mill is best treated as a hedonist need not detain us. Instead, let us note that this type of case for discrimination prompts questions about how the appropriate distinction is to be drawn. Spencer put the matter succinctly: 'if it be asserted that the law of equal freedom applies only to adults . . . we are immediately met by the question—When does the child become a man?'[54] Amongst the various criteria Mill presents is, as we have seen, 'the age the law may fix', a criterion to which Humboldt, albeit reluctantly, lends support'[55] But, then, as Spencer less succinctly observed, in reply to his question, 'None will have the folly to quote the arbitrary dictum of the statute book as an answer. The appeal is to an authority above that of legislative enactments—demands on what these are to be founded— on what attribute of manhood recognition of the law of equal freedom depends.'[56] Yet, to look behind some age fixed by law is to appreciate the unsatisfactoriness of using age as a measure, for whatever desirable end one may be trying to promote, to advocate that a certain age be treated as a kind of paternalistic ceiling, save for exceptional cases, is to encounter the objection that some less crude qualification or test could be employed. In reply it might be claimed that this type of objection looks powerful because we are thinking of individual cases, whereas Humboldt and Mill are concerned with rules,[57] and, by their lights, a society which follows their recommendations would be better than any alternative, though such

[53] F. Schrag, 'The Child in the Moral Order', *Philosophy* **52** (1977), 174.

[54] H. Spencer, op. cit., **175**.

[55] Humboldt in fact says of a criterion concerned with 'the maturity of the body', where 'maturity' is understood chronologically, that it is 'indefinite and, strictly speaking, incorrect', though he still supports it (W. von Humboldt, op cit., **122**).

[56] H. Spencer, op. cit.

[57] While the question of Mill's rule utilitarianism has been much explored, little attention, so far as I am aware, has been directed towards his views on the treatment of the young with a view to deciding whether such views are those of a rule utilitarian.

a reply, I believe, has little force; apart from the inadequacies in rule utilitarianism itself,[58] it is surely neither beyond the wisdom of its supporters to devise a less crude rule than the one under consideration, nor beyond societal practicalities for people to abide by it.

At this point a defender of Mill would observe that Mill also presents having mature faculties as a criterion for drawing the relevant line of demarcation,[59] and that, were this criterion to be treated evaluatively rather than chronologically, Mill might avoid the charges of arbitrariness and of using a measure which is not well suited to his purpose. Mill, we can note, might also end up agreeing with J. F. Stephen that someone 'may be more mature at fifteen than another at thirty'.[60] How to test for such maturity is undoubtedly a problem, but I am sure whatever tests we might suggest are not ones that Mill would employ. As far as he is concerned the rash, the obstinate, the self-conceited adult who cannot live within moderate means or restrain himself from hurtful indulgencies, who is 'incapable of self-government',[61] who is drunken, incontinent and unclean,[62] is not to be subject to the treatment he recommends for children because such a person is 'of ripe years'.[63] Is this one more case of reluctance to oppose universal usage and popular sentiment? Possibly someone might draw attention to the fact that Mill does advance another criterion when he says, 'Liberty as a principle, has no application to any state of things anterior to the time when mankind have become capable of being improved by free and equal discussion'.[64] Like Stephen I am not sure what Mill means by an equal discussion. Maybe he is seeking to exclude guidance which relies on authority and status. As for a criterion concerned with a person's capability of being improved by free discussion, again I find myself in sympathy with Stephen who suggests that this is open to two interpretations: interpreted loosely it would mean that hardly anyone is to be excluded from Mill's principle since 'The wildest savages, the most immature youths, capable of some sort of education, are cable of being improved by free discussion upon a great variety of subjects';[65] interpreted narrowly almost everyone is to be excluded, especially those who are obstinate and cannot restrain themselves from hurtful indulgencies.[66] Clearly neither interpretation is acceptable to Mill, but, then, this approach

[58] See, for example, J. J. C. Smart, *Philosophical Quarterly* **6** (1956), 344–354.
[59] See J. S. Mill, op. cit., 73.
[60] J. F. Stephen, *Liberty, Equality, Fraternity* (London: Cambridge University Press, 1967), 68–69.
[61] J. S. Mill, op. cit., 137.
[62] Ibid.
[63] J. S. Mill, op. cit., 133.
[64] J. S. Mill, op. cit., 73.
[65] J. F. Stephen, op. cit., 69.
[66] Ibid.

to paternalism will be quite unacceptable to the libertarian, for a ground for interference concerned with self-improvement by discussion and an objective such as self-improvement, though offering considerable scope to the curriculum planner, are so imprecise and wide-ranging that they pose a very real threat to freedom.

We began this latest part of our inquiry by considering an attack against the libertarian based on the suggestion that, like Humboldt and Mill, we should subscribe to a principle of liberty, but exclude those below a certain age from its concern. What lies behind this suggestion is not that the young are to be immune from interference for the protection of others, but that paternalism is to be practised on them but not, or only minimally, on adults. Faced with such a proposal the libertarian can draw some comfort from the fact that the young are not simply to be trained and manipulated for the good of others. To adopt such a strategy would be a gross under-valuing of freedom. Faced with the same proposal the curriculum planner can organize his courses accordingly. Were his objectives to be limited to the protection of others, his curriculum would be minimal—adherence to Mill's harm principle need not only lead to a minimal state. Given that the curriculum planner should also be paternalistic, his horizons are, as it were, widened, his curriculum is expanded, and pupils' freedom is encroached upon even further. What such arrangements appear to rely upon is a consequentialist evaluation of freedom and partiality. This is not to say that there might not be areas of agreement between the libertarian and the teleologist, but then the main difference between them is of particu-lar importance in this context. To the libertarian compulsory education is evil in itself; whatever its benefits, he will always be under a *prima facie* obligation to do away with it. This way of thinking will be foreign to the teleologist, and reveals what many will take to be a major flaw in the teleological approach, namely, a lack of concern for freedom itself. If, in addition, the teleologist discriminates against children then, as we have seen, his case will look both arbitrary and difficult to reconcile with his own ethical stance.

5. Liberty and the Curriculum

Suppose, then, we decide to apply a principle of liberty to children based on a libertarian evaluation of freedom. Such an attitude will have its curricular implications, though before these can be drawn we need a clearer idea of the principle we are supporting, and here we should bear in mind that to value freedom for its own sake will be to accept that all restraints are evil in themselves and to ensure that there will be no restraint when there exists a less evil way of achieving the desired end. There again, to value freedom highly will be to ensure that it is never sold short, which may mean recognizing that freedom should only be interfered with when there is no better way of preventing some greater evil. This type of evaluation may call to mind Mill's example of the unsafe bridge where there is no other way to prevent great harm befalling the agent than by seizing him.[67] In such a case freedom is not sold short, for the agent is not constrained just for the sake of his own good, but to prevent great and certain danger, and there is no better way of achieving the desired end because in this particular example constraint is necessary to achieve the desired end. Now the view that restraints should be necessary is central to Dworkin's principle of the least restrictive alternative according to which we should never restrict freedom when alternative routes to desired ends are available.[68] However, to subscribe to Dworkin's principle involves accepting that amongst possible routes, those involving restricting freedom are always the most evil, and in so far as this overvalues freedom and undervalues other goods such as justice, for Dworkin would always have us sacrifice justice in any decision between an unjust and a restrictive route, this principle is unacceptable. We may also observe that if something taken as an end can weigh against freedom, then it can surely do the same when taken as a means, though, apparently, this is something that Dworkin is not prepared to concede.[69] Nevertheless underlying the principle of the least restrictive alternative we may detect a principle that deserves our support. We may call it the principle of the least evil alternative, and it is that we should always select the least evil route or procedure towards achieving the desired end. The view that there should be no restraint when there exists some less evil or better way of achieving the desired end is in keeping with this principle.

Turning to what the desired end or ends should be and how they affect education, we can note that one of the few recent writers to concern himself with this matter is J. P. White, and if we consider what White has to say we may be better able to appreciate further features of the principle of liberty we want to support and some of its curricular implications.

Operating from the libertarian base that any infringement of freedom is *prima facie* morally wrong,[70] White observes that sometimes we restrict freedom to prevent agents from harming themselves and sometimes we restrain to prevent harm coming to others. Since he sums this up by saying, 'Considerations of a person's own good as well as that of others may justify interference',[71] we may suspect that White is mistakenly equating

---

[67] See J. S. Mill, op. cit., 151–152.

[68] See G. Dworkin, op. cit., 84.

[69] I am grateful to Professors A. Phillips Griffiths and J. F. Lively for discussing this matter with me.

[70] J. P. White, op. cit., 5.

[71] J. P. White, op. cit., 6.

preventing harm with doing good. Our suspicions are confirmed when he maintains, 'Applying this to education, it would be right to constrain a child to learn such and such only if (a) he is likely to be harmed if he does not do so, or (b) other people are likely to be harmed . . . To put the same point positively: a curriculum course is justified under (a) if it is good for the pupil. It is justified under (b) if it is good for others . . . '[72] White's recommendations might be challenged, of course, not just on the ground that he equates preventing harm with doing good, but also because he moves from likely harm to good, not likely good mark you, but good, and because, unlike Mill, he finally presents his grounds as sufficient for justifiable interference, and thereby overlooks the question of whether a less evil route is available. All of which may lead one to conclude that White's support for the libertarian position may do little to advance the libertarian cause. In addition White might be opposed by those who see it as fallacious to separate the child's good from that of society. Such opposition, for instance, would come from Devlin and Warnock, for in an attack on those who feel that society's needs and interests should not determine what children must study, Devlin and Warnock maintain, 'What children need and what society needs are two interlocking concepts'.[73] But White, I suggest, should not be worried about opposition from this quarter. The case that Devlin and Warnock mount involves contingent falsehoods, which hardly bodes well for their attempt to confirm its analyticity.

What, then, of the objection that White wrongly equates preventing harm with doing good? And what of an important rider to this equation and to his concern for sufficient conditions, that such an approach would justify encroachment just for the good of others and thereby undervalue individual freedom? To reply that we should remember that White is considering children and education, not adults, could take us back to some of the arguments we have explored and found wanting, and even though it might explain his lack of regard for freedom, it is clear that this is not a reply that White would support.[74] Suppose, therefore, we let these objections stand. We will be rejecting the idea that individuals should be constrained just for the good of others and those approaches

[72] Ibid.

[73] T. Devlin and M. Warnock, *What Must We Teach?* (London: Temple Smith, 1977), 65.

[74] White in fact says, 'It is a feature of our present chaotic thinking about educational matters that this fundamental point about justification (i.e. the justification of infringements of freedom), which we are quick to apply to the encroachments of the tax man or the government planner, is not one which we readily apply to school curricula' (J. P. White, op. cit., 5). It is difficult to see how anyone could adopt this stance and yet recommend that children be treated as exceptions.

to the curriculum that are based on this idea. Admittedly finding overt approaches of this kind is not too easy, for the appeal is often the economy, to the need for technologists and so on. However, on meeting such arguments we should look beyond the stated aim—for no one is going to say that these aims are good in themselves—and endeavour to see whether the appeal is simply to the good of others. Should it turn out that their *rationale* also concerns the prevention of harm to others we still need to be on our guard, and we need inquire not just whether the envisaged encroachment constitutes the least evil route to the desired effect, but also whether the desired effect justifies the envisaged encroachment. This latter question will be difficult to answer, but one way of trying to illuminate the problem would be to tackle the further question: are you prepared to recommend similar compulsion for adults in the event that they lack what is being considered as desirable to compulsorily cultivate in the young?

Of course, to equate preventing harm with doing good and to couple this with a concern for sufficient conditions means that White's approach would justify all manner of paternalistic interferences as well. Mill no doubt erred in his purported rejection of paternalism. White, it seems, has erred in the other direction.

Our consideration of White's attempt to justify compulsion has, then, brought to the fore the value of having a principle which one interprets strictly, and so avoids the slide from preventing harm to doing good, or in which some explicit attempt is made to preserve the important distinction involved here, for in so far as such a distinction can be drawn, this is a context where we should be mindful of it and, if necessary, put it to use. Our consideration of White's approach to liberty has also highlighted why we should be reluctant to specify sufficient conditions. We should, on the contrary, be on the look-out for routes and procedures that involve the least evil. It might even be felt, despite his avowed concern for freedom, that White's apparent lack of concern stems from his directing his attention towards the young. Now although we are not following such a path, and although the preceding arguments give some indication of a principle of liberty which we would be willing to apply both to adults and to children, we must avoid moving to some other extreme and thinking that because of the general application of our principle, we must eschew concern for differences between adults and young people. The fact of the matter is that there are, or may be, common but not universal differences which are worth attending to, particularly as far as education is concerned, two of which I want to consider.

To the person who lacks linguistic competence, government health warnings and much more besides will be ineffective, and to develop such competence is a way of preventing harm befalling him. As the very young are usually deficient in this competence, we have an argument for developing their linguistic skills, including literacy, but we should note that this is neither an argument that may just apply to the young nor, as it stands, is it an argument for compulsion, for there may be less evil routes to the desired end. In so far as it is an argument that has greater application to the young, this is simply because more young people lack the appropriate powers than do adults, and in so far as it is an argument concerned with achieving a certain level of competence, it is not an argument for the analysis of poetry or for writing free verse or for studying Shakespeare, unless, that is, these activities constitute the most desirable way of cultivating the skills in question, which is hardly likely.

Another argument based on a supposed difference between children and adults goes as follows: children are not autonomous adults, and given that autonomy is an important element of individual freedom, we should compulsorily educate the young for autonomy. This is the kind of argument a libertarian will take very seriously for the appeal is to freedom itself, though again it needs to be carefully explored. One reason for such care is, as I commented earlier, that some children may be more autonomous than some adults, and another is that this type of argument may lead to the demand for a wide-ranging compulsory curriculum, especially if it is joined with the thesis that in order to think autonomously about X, where 'X' can stand for space-flight, abortion, the music of Bob Dylan, nuclear weapons and so on, or in Y, where 'Y' can stand for atomic physics, history, micro-economics and so on, one needs to be informed and knowledgeable about X or have been initiated into Y.[75] Even if this thesis is true, we must guard against assuming that in order to be autonomous one needs to be able to think about a wide variety of topics or in a great number of areas. To elaborate on something suggested above, the essence of autonomy is self-leglislation and its range concerns the amount of his life over which the individual has control and for which he is responsible, which is why we can avoid the claim that a wide-ranging education is a necessary condition of being autonomous. As for whether some form of compulsory education can develop personal autonomy and is the least evil way of doing so or whether it is the least evil antidote to the heteronomous effect of other agencies,[76] the answers, I feel, are by no means certain, though just in case the answers are in the affirmative, we should perhaps

[75] R. F. Dearden who values personal autonomy highly sees a wide-ranging curriculum as important in its development. See R. F. Dearden, *The Philosophy of Primary Education* (London: Routledge and Kegan Paul, 1968).

[76] Dearden has noted, '. . . the granting of various freedoms (to a child) by a parent or teacher *might* simply have the result that his direction is replaced by that of some other agency still external to the child, such as the peer group, or 'pop culture' heroes' (R. F. Dearden, 'Autonomy and Education', in *Education and the Development of Reason*, R. F. Dearden, P. H. Hirst and R. S. Peters (eds), (London: Routledge and Kegan Paul, 1972), 451–542).

suggest that those agencies, such as certain religious movements, which will try to capture the mind of the child while he is still young, had best be excluded from such an education.

At this point someone might claim that my approach to education is too consequentialist and that, as a result, I have overlooked the crucial facts that education consists of initiation into and engagement in activities concerned with the pursuit of knowledge and truth, and that such activities are intrinsically valuable.[77] Now it might be true to say that what we are facing here is both a vision of the intrinsically valuable which lacks a solid theoretical base and public appeal, and a persuasive definition of 'education'.[78] It might also be true that an unfortunate consequence of such persuasion has been the discouragement of questions concerned with purpose in education and the encouragement of the belief that where learning is planned and undertaken for the sake of some consequential benefit, it is best labelled and deprecated as 'training'.[79] But even if we overlook these blemishes, we may still be reluctant to see this approach justifying compulsion. Firstly, because while valuing freedom is not incompatible with favouring some cases of paternalistic interference, if what has been said so far is satisfactory, there will be a reluctance to encroach just for the agent's good, and no one, I take it, is going to argue that a sticky end awaits those who have never thrilled to the joys of pure maths or been overcome by the delights of historical inquiry. Secondly, it may not be clear that such compulsion is necessary to achieve the desired end. And, thirdly, suppose we ask ourselves whether we would be justified compelling adults to engage in what is intrinsically valuable. If the answer is in the negative, and there is no good reason for discriminating against the young, then we should not avoid the conclusion of this argument.

If a picture of the curriculum has emerged from the previous considerations, it will be seen to be one concerned with autonomy and with the prevention of harm. With the latter as an objective one might recommend moral education, education about the environment and political education in order to prevent or guard against learners harming others and in an attempt to cultivate learners who will act to prevent harm, just as one might recommend health education to prevent individuals from harming themselves. Still, whatever courses are chosen, if they are to be compulsory, then such a way of proceeding must be the least evil of the available alternatives to the desired end and the end itself must be such as to justify such encroachment. Furthermore, in view of our regard for freedom, there must be care to ensure that learners are not compelled to

[77] This is very much the view of education and educational justification that has been associated with R. S. Peters. See, for example, R. S. Peters, *Ethics and Education* (London: George Allen and Unwin, 1966), especially Ch. I and V.

[78] See, for example, J. P. White, op. cit., 12–15.

[79] See, for example, R. S. Peters, op. cit., 32–35.

continue with courses when they have achieved the desired standard and that those who are incapable of reaching such standards are not subjected to pointless compulsion. In addition I would suggest that there is important work for educationalists and psychologists to do with regard to the question of whether compulsion may be avoided, my reasoning being that while some writers on education, such as A. S. Neill, operate with an optimistic psychology, believing that all children can and will learn what they should without compulsion,[80] other writers are much more pessimistic.[81] If we are to take freedom seriously, we will want to know how we may so arrange our educational practices that we can, with justification, employ the most optimistic of psychologies.

Upon seeing the implications of the preceding arguments some may well maintain that they are impractical. It would be tempting to reply that this is precisely what one would expect to hear when universal usage and popular sentiment are challenged. A more thoughtful reply would be that taking freedom seriously may well necessitate some fundamental changes in educational practice.

6. Conclusion

To adopt a libertarian attitude towards compulsory education is to face opposition from those who would say that we are wrong to apply the concept or a principle of freedom to children. It can also involve opposing those who subscribe to principles which undervalue liberty. Yet, the libertarian attitude, I believe, is to be encouraged because it inspires an approach to compulsory education in which there is concern to seek the least evil way of achieving ends, in which ends may have to be assessed in terms of compulsion, and in which the child is not arbitrarily treated as an exception or as something to be manipulated for some utilitarian purpose. What would ensue from such an approach would be minimalist and would be in contrast to the contemporary tendency, a tendency which seems both strongly paternalist and utilitarian, and which demands that children pursue an ever broader set of subjects for an ever longer length of time.

[80] Neill actually says, '. . . a child is innately wise and realistic. If left to himself without adult suggestion of any kind, he will develop as far as he is capable of developing' (A. S. Neill, *Summerhill* (Harmondsworth: Penguin, 1968), 20). Such optimism is frequently found in the history of education and is used by contemporary reformers. See R. Barrow, *Radical Education* (London: Martin Robertson, 1978).

[81] Dearden, for example, maintains, '. . . though interest as a motive is doubtless very desirable, it may reasonably be doubted whether everything of educational value ever could be learned under its steam alone' (R. F. Dearden, op. cit., 1968, 23).

Of course, I doubt whether the libertarian case will be efficacious. As Lord Devlin has pointed out 'The pressure of opinion that in the end makes and unmakes laws in not to be found in the mouths of those who talk most about morality and reform, but in the hearts of those who continue without much reflection to believe most of what they learnt from their fathers and to teach their children likewise'.[82] I suspect, though regret, that the ending of Devlin's remark might be changed slightly and still ring true. The ending I have in mind is as follows: who continue without much reflection to believe most in how they learnt and recommend that their children be taught likewise.

[82] P. Devlin, *The Enforcement of Morals* (London: Oxford University Press, 1965), 125–126.

The Free Man

DAVID E. COOPER

Not long after the historian, Seeley, had defined 'perfect liberty' as 'the absence of all government', Oscar Wilde wrote that a man can be totally free even in that granite embodiment of governmental constraint, prison. Ten years after Mill's famous defence of civil freedoms, *On Liberty*, Richard Wagner declaimed:

> I'll put up with everything—police, soldiers, muzzling of the press, limits on parliament . . . Freedom of the *spirit* is the only thing for men to be proud of and which raises them above animals.[1]

These remarks illustrate a broad contrast between those for whom freedom is a function of authority and power in society, and those for whom it is partly, largely, or even totally independent of, so to speak, the state of the commonwealth. Between those who view it, for example, in terms of absence of legal restraint and those who see it consisting in a state of mind, the fostering of which may have little to do with the ways of the political world. Let us label these contrasting perspectives the 'civil' and the 'private' respectively.

It would be wrong to assimilate this contrast to Berlin's familiar distinction between 'negative' and 'positive' conceptions of freedom;[2] for there are several thinkers in whom the two distinctions cut across one another. Giovanni Gentile, assassinated because of his admiration for Mussolini, held civil organization to be determinative of freedom; but not through the state's keeping a low, 'negative' profile: rather through totally assimilating individuals into its 'organic' structure, so that their 'real selves' might be 'realized'.[3] Dr Johnson, conversely, exhibits an attitude at once 'negative' and 'private':

> Sir, I would not give a guinea to live under one form of government rather than another . . . the danger of the abuse of power is nothing to a

[1] Seeley's comment is quoted by Bernard Bosanquet on p. 119 of his *The Philosophical Theory of the State* (Macmillan, 1958); Wilde's remark is from his essay 'The Soul of Man Under Socialism', included in *De Profundis and Other Writings* (Penguin, 1979), 29; and Wagner's outburst is recorded by his wife, Cosima, in her *Diaries* (Oxford University Press, 1979).

[2] *Two Concepts of Liberty* (Oxford University Press, 1958).

[3] See, for example, his *Genesis and Structure of Society* (Urbana: University of Illinois Press, 1960).

private man. What Frenchman is prevented from passing his life as he pleases?[4]

His point is that, while freedom is absence of external constraints, even those imposed by the harshest regime are relatively unimportant (for the 'private man' at least) since they do not touch the vast mass of those everyday activities which make up the bulk of a man's life.

A fusion of the 'positive' and 'private' approaches yields the kind of position which will be my main concern, and which I dub the 'Promethean'. On such a view, freedom does not primarily reside in the absence of external constraints; but nor is it to be found in some Gentile-like immersion of individual wills into that of the political whole. Why 'Promethean'? In Shelley's version, at least, Prometheus is the paradigm of the man who, enchained by the ruler of rulers, Zeus, yet remains defiantly free. And Goethe's Prometheus sees his captors, the immoral Gods—and not himself—as the ones who are unfree ('Ach, ich diene keine Vassallen').

I want, first, to sketch some main 'Promethean' lines of approach; second, to glance at some causes of the present desuetude of such an approach to freedom; third, to examine some objections frequently levelled against the very cogency of a 'Promethean' conception; and finally to consider the moral centrality of that conception.

A first 'Promethean' approach is the classical Stoic one. 'He is free', says Epictetus, 'who lives as he wishes to live ... whose desires attain their purpose';[5] hence a free man must have wishes and desires that have a good chance of being satisfied. But people grossly exaggerate the range of such wishes and desires: those directed towards material possessions—even towards one's own body—are subject to being thwarted by factors over which one has no real control. Only when our desires are directed towards our own thoughts and attitudes, towards the formation of our minds, is their satisfaction truly under our control. The laws of the land may leave the disposal of material possessions and our bodies in our own hands, but this can only tinker with the odds on our satisfying wishes focused upon such recalcitrant items. The only sure strategy is to limit our desires to those inner-directed ones whose satisfaction is, to a greater extent, under our control. The freedom enjoyed by the sage man who has retreated into this inner sanctum is one that civil arrangements can do relatively little to enhance or hinder. In some crucial respects, the same idea is, interestingly, echoed centuries later by Karl Marx: the 'fetish' for material wealth together with men's 'alienation' from the products of their labour conspire to create a society in which the satisfaction of powerful (albeit 'illusory') material wants is subject to laws over which men have no control.

[4] Quoted by Boswell in Ch. 26 of his *Life of Samuel Johnson*.
[5] 'Freedom as Self-mastery', in *Freedom*, Dewey and Gould (eds) (U.S.A: Macmillan, 1970).

A second approach stresses the role of self-regulation and self-discipline. In Thomas Mann's *Dr Faustus*, the composer-hero Leverkühn remarks:

> Law, every law, has a chilling effect, and music has so much warmth anyhow, stable warmth, cow-warmth . . . that she can stand all sorts of regulated cooling-off—she has even asked for it.

Later he refers to a man 'bound by self-imposed compulsion to order, hence free'.[6] Leverkühn is credited with the invention of the 12-tone system, and the point is well made that someone composing according to this, or another, system is not thought of as a less free musical agent than someone composing without method. To begin with he chooses the system to whose discipline he now submits; and even were it imposed upon him, the preference is for some system or other, in order to avoid that 'cow-warmth', that excess of emotionality which has free rein in the absence of method. The system, moreover, permits an indefinitely large number of choices, and indeed increases the scope of *significant* choice: for in the absence of system, what would turn on the choice between this and that note?

Writ large, the idea is close to the familiar one that freedom is incompatible with license. Minimizing the controls of law or convention might threaten freedom in a number of ways. First, men become victims of whim, caprice, and passion that could not hold such sway where there is regulation and constraint. Second, a man whose horizons of allowable behaviour are too far apart can be left floundering: his choices cannot be significant ones, or informed, but must be picked out of a hat. People complain sometimes about the restrictions a particular moral code imposes; but try to consider— it is not easy—the position of a person for whom the live options are not just those allowed in our (loosely structured) code, but also those provided in the Samurai code, that of the Icelandic sagas, and that of the Ayatollahs. He would be a moral cripple; for to have to select a framework of choice each time one faces a decision is to be immobilized. These points, it should be stressed, are quite separate from the familiar 'civil' theorist's criticism of license—to the effect that too much freedom for some will mean too little for those they are able to damage. For my points concern the freedom of those with the license, not the freedom of those who may suffer at their hands.

A third 'Promethean' approach focuses upon rationality. Goethe defined freedom as the possibility, under all circumstances, of doing what is rational.[7] Freedom has to do with acting as one wants; but if those wants are inconsistent, there is a sense in which one cannot act upon them—not with success anyway. Moreover, there is no freedom in acting compulsively, which—it is claimed—a man whose behaviour is plainly irrational

6 London: Penguin, 1968, 69, 188.
7 Quoted in W. Biedermann, *Goethes Gespräche*, Vol. 3.

must be doing; or must be doing, at any rate, if he is aware of the irrationality. And if he is unable to recognize the irrationality, there must be some obstacle to his understanding: he is deluded, self-deceived, or victim of indoctrination. How, then, could plainly irrational behaviour be free? It might even be argued that such a man does not want to do what he is doing; for this surely conflicts with a more fundamental and persistent desire of his—that his wants be satisfiable, sensible, and harmonious. Isaiah Berlin has condemned the 'monstrous impersonation' of equating what a man *would* choose (if he were more rational, or if . . .) with what he *does* choose.[8] But it is certainly intelligible to deny that a man really wants to do what it is his expressed desire to do—on the ground, for example, that he has no grasp of the situation, or that this desire conflicts with one we know to be important for him. Can't a man convince his friend that he is too fond of his travels, his work, and his privacy to really want to marry the girl he has proposed to? In an age that speaks easily of unconscious desires, of self-deception, of ideology, and of bad faith, the idea has surely been abandoned (if it was ever there) that wants are transparent to their owners.[9]

It is unimportant, for our purposes, whether the three approaches sketched are thought to exhibit distinct 'Promethean' conceptions of freedom, or to constitute strands in a composite portrait of the free man. If the latter, then the portrait which emerges is of a man who, in control of his material desires, resistant to whim and fashion, regulates his life through rationally adopted principles and plans.

Although the 'Promethean' conception was characterized in contrast to the 'civil' one, according to which freedom is actually understood in terms of civil arrangements (for example, in terms of the absence of certain types of external constraint), the 'Promethean' need not deny the existence of piecemeal, typically indirect, connections between freedom and the civil. What he will deny is that there are big, *a priori* assumptions or generalizations to make here. In particular, he will deny that there is a simple functional relationship between 'Promethean' and 'civil' freedom. The removal of some civil constraints will, the removal of others will not, have a positive effect on 'Promethean' freedom. Only such dubious assumptions as that the average man, left to himself, is a pretty rational sort of fellow, could support the idea that, as 'civil' freedom (of the sort envisaged by Mill) increases, so does 'Promethean' freedom. On the whole, the 'Promethean' will think that it is through education, culture, and most of all personal endeavour—rather than through legal and political arrangements—that his

---

[8] Op. cit., 18.

[9] See Charles Taylor, 'What's Wrong with Negative Liberty?', in *The Idea of Freedom*, A. Ryan (ed.) (Oxford University Press, 1979), for an elaboration of this point. The title of his essay reveals the use to which he puts the point.

freedom will be won. In this connection, he will stress the Johnsonian point that for the 'private man'—in societies at all like our own—there exists a large sphere of behaviour relatively immune to the impact of the legal and political in which, nevertheless, there is clear scope for the development and exercise of 'Promethean' freedom.

A moral conception may go out of favour because it is not cogent: more likely its fall from grace has little to do with this, and the 'Promethean' does well to identify some historical causes for his conception's present desuetude—or rather, as we shall see later, *apparent* desuetude—in order to defeat the presumption that this is evidence of that conception's poverty or lack of cogency. He may, for example, point to the importance of ours having become a very *public* world. Popular newspapers and television inform us about the public arena and parade its actors—politicians, industrial leaders, editors—before us. Unsurprisingly, those who operate the media and those with whom they predominantly deal will, when it comes to talk of freedom, occupy themselves with those freedoms in which they have a special interest: a vested interest, perhaps, or an interest *qua* public figures. Hence, perhaps, the powerful focus upon freedom of expression, or of political protest, or of association—all classic 'civil' freedoms. Unsurprisingly, too, this focus will mould the dominant, or at any rate manifest, conception of freedom. Freedoms like those mentioned will be seen as *the* freedoms which matter. But it does not follow that this focus reflects the real moral centrality of what has become the dominant, manifest conception. Newspapers have much more to say about defending newspapers' publications of exposés than they do about defending people against insidious advertising—and for obvious reasons which may have nothing to do with the relative moral importance of the two matters.

The 'Promethean' will also point out how the last century has confirmed a prediction of Nietzsche's: that as society becomes more democratic, more egalitarian, a premium will be put upon the *common* values, by which I mean those qualities or those arrangements which all, or very many, men can to a more or less equal degree exhibit or benefit from. Equality is not only become a value in itself, but is employed—at a second level, as it were—to grade other values. Physical courage, which is hard to come by for those who do not have it as a gift from nature, does not enjoy the status it once had; while industriousness—to the extent, at least, of putting in an honest day's work—has climbed the scale of values; to the point, it seems, that people feel a sense of shame when they are unable to exercise it. Now 'civil' freedom is something that all of us, to a more or less equal degree, and with little or no individual effort, enjoy. We are all equally free (and unfree) from the reach of the censor. In our society, broadly, a man must do something—commit a crime, say—in order to lose a 'civil' freedom, rather than do something to get one. 'Promethean' freedom, on the other hand, is a personal, and difficult, achievement (for those who are not naturally prone to it). It requires intelligence, self-discipline, self-honesty, and a distancing of oneself from one's possessions, even one's friends. Goethe speaks of a man being 'strong enough' for freedom. It is, as it were, an *élitist* virtue, against which the tide of our democratic, egalitarian times is bound to have run.

The 'Promethean' could mention other factors, but the main business is not sociology, and so I turn to the reasons his critics, especially those in the Millite tradition, have offered for thinking that the 'Promethean' conception is incoherent, or otherwise unacceptable. The reasons are of a conceptual kind and, generally, to the effect that the 'Promethean' is not really talking about freedom at all.

Mill begins *On Liberty* by distinguishing 'Liberty of the Will' from 'Civil, or Social Liberty'; and it is frequently said that those in the 'Promethean' tradition are really talking about the former, whilst imagining they are talking about freedom as a moral, social value. Considerations of self-discipline, or of the caprices of one's body, so it is argued, may well bear on the free will issue; but have no more to do with moral freedom than considerations of legal obligation or censorship have to do with freedom of the will. Wilde's remark that a man can be free even in prison gains its effect through equivocation: as a claim about the will's remaining free in prison, it may be true, but not otherwise.

The 'Promethean's' reply will be that, depending on what is taken as the free will issue, either he is not talking about that, or if he is then is also talking about moral freedom. Certainly he is not concerned with such issues as whether actions are physically caused or divinely pre-ordained: but the literature contains accounts of free will which, he can happily admit, do concern him—the idea, for example, that the will is free when not compelled, or that free choices are those which result from rational deliberation rather than impulse. Accounts like these bear directly on the issue of freedom as a moral value—for one may certainly strive for, or regard as desirable, freedom of the will in these senses. Moreover, with free will treated in these ways, the 'Promethean's' critic is also concerned; for he certainly discusses ways—threats of punishment, say—in which, in some sense, the will may be compelled. Free will, so treated, and moral freedom are no longer exclusive concerns. The 'Promethean' will, of course, take particular exception to the way Mill sets things up: for not only does he regard free will and moral freedom as exclusive concerns, but by labelling the latter 'civil, or social' freedom, begs all the questions. Play Mill's game and you are forced to talk either about a morally irrelevant free will issue or about civil freedoms: 'Promethean' freedom is defined out of existence.

With a second, rather dull objection, we can be brief. Governmental interference, or laws against expression of belief, and the like, are paradigmatic examples of what we can be said to be free from. Since being free is a matter of being free from this, that, and the other, it must be absurd to deny that freedom consists in being free from just the kind of things mentioned. The 'Promethean' certainly does not deny that we may properly speak of being free from such things; though he will quickly add that grammar puts few restrictions on what we may be said to be free from. Pangs of desire, or self-delusion, are certainly allowable. What is wrong with the objection is the idea that freedom is, simply, a matter of being free from lots of things. The prisoner, after all, is free from any number of things that the man on the outside is not—his wife's nagging, having to choose where to take a holiday, and worrying whether he might go to prison. Freedom, as a moral goal, is freedom from those things it is morally important to be free from. There is nothing in the objection to show that the 'civil' theorist's list of 'free froms' contains the most important items.

A complaint to be found in several of Berlin's writings is against the unfortunate tendency for a word laden with value to become radically extended by those who seek to curry favour for whatever it is they approve. The 'Promethean'—and other 'positive' theorists—are allegedly guilty of this. Perhaps he does draw attention towards things we should approve— self-discipline, harmony of purposes, and the like: but *these* are the terms in which he should describe them, and not with the aid of a term borrowed from another area. Otherwise, warns Berlin, the term 'freedom' becomes 'so vague and distended as to make it virtually useless'.[10] Nor is it clarity alone which demands we resist the extension, for once the term becomes thoroughly distended we shall soon find regimes of the most despotic kind being condoned with its help. Think of how Nazi students defended the sackings of Jewish professors by arguing that it could be no infringement of academic freedom to suppress teaching and thinking that, by Nazi lights, were irrational.

The charge that it is the 'Promethean' who has extended a value-laden term is, historically, a suspect one. As Burckhardt describes it, it is the creation of 'freedom of the personality' not civil freedoms within the *poleis* that occupied the Greek genius;[12] and we have already encountered the once well-entrenched Stoic conception. Again, it is a 'Promethean' note that is sounded in remarks on freedom by early Christians: 'A wise man', said St Ambrose, 'though he be a slave, is at liberty'.[12] and in the middle of the last century, Alexander Herzen, himself a crusader for 'civil' freedoms, could complain bitterly about how little 'civil' freedom meant to most people:

They are indifferent to individual freedom, liberty of speech: the masses love authority.[13]

[10] Op. cit., 44.
[11] *Griechische Kultur* (Berlin: Safari, 1958), Pt. 4, Ch. 15.
[12] Quoted in Berlin, op. cit., 20.
[13] Quoted in Berlin, *Russian Thinkers* (London: Pelican, 1968), 88.

Anyway, the relevance of the historical charge is obscure, as is that of the claim that today, at least, the standard application of 'freedom' is in the 'civil' arena. It has yet to be shown that the 'Promethean's' extension of the term's current use is not a perfectly proper one warranted by its meaning.

A number of points can be made about the charge that a 'Promethean' conception may somehow be used to condone Nazism and its ilk. First, this charge needs to be distinguished from the kind of charge, levelled by Thomas Mann and others, that as a matter of history, the concern of German intellectuals with the 'free personality' rather than the 'free citizen' eased the political path for Nazism; that an obsession with the 'Inner Reich' made the Third Reich possible.[14] Second, the 'Promethean', while denying any general functional relationship between 'civil' and 'Promethean' freedom, need not deny that a certain minimum of 'civil' freedom is a precondition of the emergence of 'Promethean' freedom. Third, there is no reason why he should be blind to cruelty and injustice, and not condemn despotism on these grounds, even if, perchance, freedom of the sort he stresses happened to flourish under it. Finally, he can challenge the relevance of an example like that of the Nazi students—a clear example of a *mis*application of the 'Promethean' idea. Reason was to be found, if anywhere, among the sacked professors, not among the sackers. Would the example retain its force had the professors been from Laputa? The example no more invalidates the 'Promethean' conception than examples of the misapplication of the 'civil' conception invalidate it. And there are plenty of such examples. Recently I came across a radical teacher's complaint that celibacy during school hours was an intolerable restriction on the sexual freedom of children; a state of affairs to be put right by schools providing the appropriate facilities.

It is just worth mentioning here a charge that is more a debating point than an argument: to the effect that it would exhibit the merest cruelty or *Schadenfreude* to tell the victim of political oppression that he may none the less be free—yet this is something the 'Promethean' is committed to telling him. Well, it would also be cruel to tell him that his wife is as pleased as punch about it, but that might be true. It is, of course, not what is said, but the saying of it, which is cruel—and to the saying of it, as distinct from the truth of what is said, the 'Promethean' is in no way committed. Nor, of course, is he committed to ignoring the obvious respects in which the man certainly is not free. Finally the charge, with equal lack of effect, could be turned against the 'civil' theorist: it would be merely cruel to tell a drug addict *in extremis* 'Still, you are free', on the grounds that he can still vote, or express his political views in a newspaper.

There remains a final objection, which is more powerful in that it threatens to provide what has so far been missing—namely, a *reason* for

[14] See J. P. Stern, *The Führer and his People*, (Glasgow: Fontana, 1975).

thinking that the 'Promethean' is not talking about freedom. A fair, if fairly unhelpful, characterization of the general notion of freedom is that one is free to the extent that one can do what one wants to do without constraint or hindrance, that—as Bosanquet puts it—one can 'determine oneself'. At first blush, this rubric will accommodate 'Promethean' as well as 'civil' freedom—for can't desires or illusions constrain and hinder, and get in the way of determining oneself? The objection, however, is that such talk can make literal sense only on a certain account of the self, of what a person is—an account, unfortunately, which is false. Given a proper account of the self, such talk must be seen as metaphorical. Only when a person is considered as something distinct from his desires, interests, or illusions could it make literal sense to speak of these as constraining him, or of his being free from them. On a more adequate conception of a person as a composite, a bundle, of *inter alia* his desires, motives, and the like, such talk makes no more literal sense than talk of an engine's being controlled by one of its component parts. True, we do not ordinarily quibble with being told that the boiler is run by the thermostat; but this cannot be literally true, since then the thermostat would have to be controlling itself, which is absurd.

One could, to be sure, debate whether the model of the self proposed by the objector is the more adequate; instead, I shall focus on the alleged consequences of accepting it. What, exactly, is meant to follow if 'Promethean' talk of freedom is metaphorical? Perhaps that he should not be talking in terms of freedom at all. This must mean more than that he should not use the word 'freedom'; for even the 'civil' theorist does not *have* to use it and might be advised, in contexts where sobriety is required, to eschew such an emotively charged word. 'But at least the "civil" theorist is justified in using it', someone will say, 'whereas the "Promethean" who uses it is not talking about freedom at all—any more than someone who refers to "the warmth of her smile" is talking about warmth.'

There is confusion here. When I refer to 'the warmth of her smile' I *am* referring to warmth, albeit of a non-kinetic variety. If a word has a reference in the language—literal *or* metaphorical—it must be possible to designate what it refers to by the word itself. 'The word "W" refers to W' is a semantic truism, and remains so when 'W' has metaphorical meaning.[15]

---

[15] Actually, a distinction is needed here between (i) a word's having a metaphorical sense in the language, and (ii) someone's using a word metaphorically. I may use 'pencil-sharpener' non-literally, e.g. to refer to an *avant-garde* sculpture, but (as far as I know) the expression has no metaphorical sense in English. It is only where (i) obtains that it will be true both that someone using 'W' metaphorically is talking about W (in a metaphorical sense) and that '"W" refers to W' remains a semantic truism when 'W' is occurring metaphorically. When I use 'pencil-sharpener' metaphorically, I am not talking about pencil-sharpeners—even in a metaphorical sense, since there isn't one.

This the critic may concede, but then insist that the 'Promethean' is still not referring to the same thing as the 'civil' theorist, but to something that can only be called 'freedom' in some derivative, secondary sense. If the point is that the freedoms talked of by the 'Promethean' are importantly different from those which concern the 'civil' theorist, this is not a point of objection, but something which the 'Promethean' wants to proclaim. If the point is that the 'Promethean' simply changes the subject, is not on the same topic, and is arguing at cross-purposes, this may only be so by inappropriately narrow criteria of sameness, of what the subject is. After all, he like the 'civil' theorist is concerned with those factors which may be incompatible with a man's executing, or even formulating, plans and purposes which are of significance in his life. This common area of concern, whatever the differences of terrain within it, might surely justify us in saying that both are on the same topic. Here the 'warmth' example can mislead, for it is indeed difficult to imagine likely cases where kinetic warmth and warmth of smiles would belong to the same topic of interest. But the example is not representative. Is someone in a discussion about the punishment of child molesters changing the subject when he draws attention to the 'punishment' meted out by fellow-prisoners? Is a teacher in a discussion about curricular arrangements going on to another topic when he starts talking about the 'hidden curriculum'? In many contexts, reference to punishment or the curriculum in these metaphorical senses may be just what is required by the topics of interest.

There is more confusion in the charge that 'Promethean' freedom, being metaphorical, can only be freedom in some derivative, secondary sense. Taken one way, the charge is truistic; unless his use of the term were semantically derived from 'freedom' in a literal sense, that use would not be a metaphorical one. But it cannot follow from this that what he expresses by the term can only have an interest or importance that is derived from, and secondary to, what is literally expressed by the term. It is quite possible that the order of both historical and moral importance should be the reverse of the semantic; quite possible, as Bosanquet argues, that concern for 'civil' freedoms emerged from a prior, and perhaps morally fundamental, concern with 'Promethean' freedoms.[16] (This is parallel to Nietzsche's suggestion that a concern with equalities in a literal sense—equality of wealth, say—derived from an earlier concern with equality in the eyes of God; a notion which, divorced from notions of measurement and quantity, would seem to require a non-literal interpretation of, equality'.[17]

[16] Op. cit.

[17] *Friedrich Nietzsche: Werke*, Vol. 4, K. Schlechta (ed.) (Berlin: Ullstein, 1977), 414. '"Equality of souls before God". In this is the prototype of all theories of equal rights ... Small wonder that men end up taking it seriously, taking it *practically*—that is, politically, democratically, socialistically ....'.

Finally, there is confusion again in the charge that the 'Promethean', since he is arguing at cross-purposes, can be saying nothing to impugn the 'civil' conception. Some 'Prometheans' may, in their more dramatic moments, say things like 'Freedom is not be found in civil liberties', but they need not be taken as denying that, in a literal sense, this is just where freedom is to be found. Their point is, rather, that 'civil' freedoms do not have sovereign weight, that they may be less morally fundamental than their 'Promethean' freedoms. It is no reply to simply reiterate what the literal sense is. That would be like trying to diminish the importance of the 'hidden curriculum' by reiterating that in a literal sense there is only the patent curriculum.

The 'Promethean', then, presents us with a genuine conception of freedom, so that the substantial moral issue may now be raised of its relative centrality *vis-à-vis* the 'civil' conception. In what follows, I assume that 'Promethean' freedom is a value—even if the value does not usually go by the name of freedom. It is not this assumption which is contentious, but the claim about its relative moral centrality. I have time only to indicate the general form which a debate about the issue must, I think, take; and to offer a suggestion as to its outcome.

In a good sense, it seems to me, 'Promethean' freedom has at least as much explanatory centrality as 'civil' freedom. Suppose we draw up a catalogue of those human characteristics generally reckoned to be virtuous or vicious—tolerance and intolerance, say, or temperance and greed. It is perfectly possible, no doubt, to partially explain many of the valuations in our catalogue in terms of the value of 'civil' freedom. The intolerant man and the greedy man are men who, given the muscle, will forcibly constrain other people, in order to impose their views or get what they covet. Equally, it seems, explanations could be offered in terms of 'Promethean' freedom. Nietzsche remarked of Goethe that he was tolerant, not out of weakness, but out of strength; not because he feared intolerance would bring re-prisals, but because, firm in his purposes, rational, self-disciplined, resistant to fashion and caprice and allurement, he had nothing to fear from the views of others.[18] The intolerant man 'doth protest too much', betraying the fear that he will not stand firm at the sound of those sirens whose voices he therefore insists on stilling. Intolerance appears as a symptom of the man without 'Promethean' freedom. And the man of greed is, of course, the Stoic paradigm of the man without such freedom—a paradigm vividly incarnate as Arthur Miller's Willy Loman—his direction controlled as it is by the carrots put in his path.

Both conceptions, then, can do an explanatory job; but the two kinds of explanation are very different and correspond, it seems, to me, to two fundamentally different modes of moral assessment. It is the difference

[18] *Götzen-Dämmerung, Werke,* Vol. 3, op. cit., 471.

between a mode which places at the centre a conception of how a man ought to be, of human virtues, of character—and one which does not, but which instead places at the centre demands on what roles and duties men should perform, or what the outcomes of their behaviour should be. Convenient labels for the two modes might be 'homocentric' and 'facto-centric' (Latin 'factum' = act, deed.) respectively. Utilitarianism, for example, is an instance of the 'factocentric' mode, since it is concerned with virtue and character in a purely derivative way: the desirable charac-ter, roughly speaking, is that of the man who is most likely to do things which maximize utility. The 'Promethean' conception is an important instance of the 'homocentric' mode; for it is how a man is, which is central, and what states of affairs he produces which is derivative, in importance. The 'civil' conception, on the other hand, typically looms large in the 'factocentric' mode. Those who argue for the importance of 'civil' freedom do so, standardly, on two kinds of ground: on broadly instrumental, especially utilitarian, grounds, or on the basis of their being rights—natural or contractual—to various 'civil' freedoms. Utilitarianism, we saw, has no logically central concern for how a man should be; nor does such a concern figure in the appeal to rights. No demand, therefore, is made on how a man should be: the demand, rather, is that, in various areas, a man should be left alone to become what he will.

Over a fairly wide range, no doubt, what has central value according to one mode of assessment will have derivative value according to the other. If conscientiousness is central for the 'homocentric' approach, and the performing of duties for the 'factocentric', the opposite is true of their derivative value: since performing duties is one good way of displaying conscientiousness and encouraging conscientiousness is one good way of getting duties performed. But there can be no *a priori* reason to suppose that the same list of values will figure in both modes; nor that those values which are mutual will receive anything like the same weighting.[19]

If we could consider the 'homocentric' mode of assessment to be the prime, or proper, one, we would then have good reason to look on 'Prom-ethean' freedom as the prime form of freedom—for it is reasonable to think that such freedom will enjoy an honoured place in any 'homocentric' evaluation. 'Civil' freedom will then have whatever value it has derivatively. By this I do not mean, or simply mean, that 'civil' freedoms are instru-mental in value—for that is happily conceded by many of its strongest supporters. The point is, rather, that the value of these freedoms will

[19] See A. O'Hear, 'Guilt and Shame', *Proceedings of the Aristotelian Society*, **77**, 1976, for an interesting discussion of two notions the contrast between which has much to do, in my terminology, with the different modes of assessment—'factocentric' and 'homocentric' respectively—in which they have central significance.

reside in the alleged contribution they make to 'Promethean' freedom; to conditions favourable for the emergence of men of 'Promethean' freedom. 'Civil' freedom then becomes thoroughly subordinate to 'Promethean'.

But can there be any reason to take the 'homocentric' mode of assessment as prime? It might be that we are beyond a point where reasons, that do not beg questions, can be offered. It might seem that moral reasons must be extracted from one or other of the modes of assessment, and hence cannot be used to support the modes themselves. If, for example, the 'factocentric' thinker were to complain about the inequalities that a society geared to produce men of 'Promethean' virtues might create, or if the 'homocentric' thinker were to complain of the cultural sterility that a utilitarian society might exhibit, then each is perhaps appealing to considerations that can have no force for his opponent.

One manoeuvre might be to try to show that the sense of the word 'moral' determines the primacy of one or other mode of assessment. 'Isn't it part of the very meaning of the term', the 'factocentric' theorist might argue, 'that morality aims at social harmony, well-being, and the like?' But not only is it unclear that his opponent could not make similar moves; not only is it unclear that such 'analyses' do more than record contemporary, perhaps passing, linguistic fashion—but it is difficult, anyway, to see how anything of great moment could be settled. The central issue of primacy would remain even if it were agreed that only one mode of assessment could, in all purity, lay claim to the term 'moral'.

More fruitful, it seems to me, would be an anthropological, perhaps phenomenological, look at how men, in live, concrete cases, do evaluate their fellow men and their actions. A superficial glance would suggest, perhaps, that recent history favours the 'factocentric' mode. Many contemporary men, asked out of the blue, or in the context of a philosophy or sociology seminar, will offer broadly instrumental, utilitarian accounts of their valuations. Tolerance, for example, or punishment, or civil liberties will be warranted or excused by their contribution to well-being. But I doubt that these, frequently glib, accounts are adequate to the feelings, reactions, and assessments that live cases elicit. I take one example to suggest that the 'homocentric' mode goes deep—deeper than is suggested by glib accounts given, so to speak, *in vitro*. It is but one example of moral judgments whose strength, even ferocity, cannot be accounted for on a 'factocentric' mode of assessment. The example is that of lying.

To be sure, one can easily think of broadly utilitarian reasons why lying should, in general, be undesirable; but these reasons do little, as I see it, to explain the peculiar horror with which people regard it, the lengths they will go to avoid it, or—more common, perhaps—to avoid admitting to themselves that this is what they are doing. Witness the extraordinary gymnastics people will go through to convince themselves that their lies are 'white' ones—and that, anyway, 'white lies' are not *really* lies. An explanation of all this requires a focus upon the relation between lying and a conception of how a person should be. It is not what lies do, but what liars are—and what they make out of other people—that attracts such censure. In particular, it is what lying signifies for 'Promethean' freedom—or rather its absence—that is crucial; and this in at least three ways.

The wife who has been lied to for years will not find this mitigated by the fact that they may have been 'happy years': for what is terrible is that her life has been a deception, lived under illusions, one which she might not have chosen had the truth been known to her. The discovery of the truth gives to her life a new freedom and scope—but perhaps too late. So, in the first place, the liar is a threat to the freedom of those his deceptions place in a false position. Second, lying like intolerance (as we saw earlier) can be a symptom of the person who is not free. A man should be honest out of strength, not out of the fear that his lies will be detected; just as the tolerant man should be tolerant out of strength. For such a man has nothing to fear from telling the truth about himself: he has no shame in actions which belong to his rationally adopted purposes, rather than issue from the drives, allurements, or illusions that could indeed occasion shame. The man whose actions issue from what he has disciplined himself to do cannot have the same reason to conceal them as the man for whom they are deviations from what he would want himself to do. Finally, there is that special form of lying, into which ordinary lying can slip, known as self-deception. The self-deceived man, of course, is a paradigm of the man without 'Promethean' freedom: one's life is not based upon rationally adopted purposes if it is based on misunderstandings about oneself. To undeceive a man is to lend him a freedom to consider those ways of living from which his self-deception debars him. Some of the finest novels—*The Magic Mountain* or *The Brothers Karamazov*—present a sense of the exhilarating, if giddy, freedom that a man may feel when his deceptions as to the kind of person he is fall away. (This is not the only connection between self-deception and freedom. We have learned from Sartre that a peculiarly important form of self-deception, 'bad faith', is precisely the denial that one is capable of freedom; the insistence that one is simply a victim—of one's desires, circumstances, or whatever.)

The example of lying is intended to indicate the deep role that 'Promethean' freedom, and hence a 'homocentric' mode of assessment, plays in our valuations—a role that is much deeper than could be gleaned from much of the fashionable theorizing about morality that is heard today. If such examples pile up, then an anthropology of our moral culture—or perhaps of any moral culture—must place the notion of 'Promethean' freedom at or close to the centre. It would be pleasant, naturally, to end on a note of compromise—albeit one which favours the 'Promethean' conception; and to see in 'civil' freedom an essential instrument for the furtherance of 'Promethean' freedom. But while there may be an area of 'civil' freedom without which 'Promethean' freedom, or any other human excellence, could not emerge, there is no general reason to suppose that the two freedoms must march in step; and none for thinking that a maximization of 'civil' freedom would provide the conditions most favourable for the flowering of 'Promethean' freedom.

Paternalism

JACK LIVELY

I

What I wish to do in this paper is to look at a part of John Stuart Mill's 'one very simple principle' for determining the limits of state intervention. This principle is, you will remember, that 'the only purpose for which power can be rightfully exercised over any member of a civilized community, against his will, is to prevent harm to others. His own good, either physical or moral, is not a sufficient warrant.'[1]

Although it is not the only criterion offered by Mill in *On Liberty* for determining the boundaries of state interference with individual behaviour, the rejection of paternalism seems at first sight the clearest, the least qualified and the least ambiguous. It is at the same time a position immediately attractive to the liberal conscience, for the paternalist principle, if consistently and extensively applied as a warrant for state intervention, would leave little or no freedom of individual action and virtually eliminate all individual responsibility for action. The nanny-state might provide all the loving care of the nursery, but it would require also the nursery's tight regulation of conduct. Yet, after examination, Mill's initial and apparently absolute rejection of state paternalism seems both inconsistent and less attractive, inconsistent because Mill himself in the course of his essay qualifies it considerably and less attractive because even the most fervent libertarian might acknowledge that there are at least some instances in which paternalist considerations could reasonably be presented as justifications for state intervention.

Mill's initial assertion that a person's own good is not a sufficient warrant for exercising power over him is subsequently qualified in a number of ways. In the first place, he excludes from this rule particular categories of persons—children and 'barbarians'—who can rightly be regulated for their own good. The reason Mill gives for this exclusion is that such persons have not yet become 'capable of being improved by free and equal discussion', and that therefore the principle of liberty is inapplicable to them.[2] Secondly, Mill points to particular circumstances in which paternalist intervention is allowable. In his example of the man about to cross an unsafe bridge, he allows the use of force to prevent what must be

---

[1] John Stuart Mill, 'Essay on Liberty', *Utilitarianism, Liberty and Representative Government* (London: Everyman, 1910), 73.

[2] Ibid., 73–74.

assumed to be self-harm. He insists of course that such paternalist licence can be granted only when there is insufficient time to allow for advice and information.³ Lastly, Mill insists that there are particular kinds of action harmful to persons which they should be prohibited from performing. He instances contracts of slavery, and argues that legal prohibition of such contracts, even if voluntarily entered into, is justifiable since they would involve the absolute abdication of liberty beyond the single contractual act. He allows that this argument is 'of far wider application', and we can see that, if the prevention of the restriction of future choices in action were good grounds for legal regulation, the scope for paternalist intervention would be wide indeed.⁴

Aside from these exceptions which Mill poses to his blanket rejection of paternalist intervention, it is difficult to see how his opposition to state paternalism can be reconciled with his general utilitarian commitments. At any rate, it is difficult if what is being claimed is that self-inflicted harms, as distinct from harms inflicted on others, should never be taken into account in any felicific calculus. For surely, from a utilitarian stand-point, a harm is a harm and is in principle to be avoided whoever inflicts it and whoever suffers from it. This is not to say that a utilitarian argument justifying severe restriction of paternalist intervention could not be mounted. It might be that, as a general rule, such intervention cannot achieve its objective of preventing persons harming themselves or that its costs will generally outweight its benefits. There may therefore be a purely utilitarian case for restricting severely such intervention. Mill hints at such arguments and they will be pursued further later in this paper. However, such a utilitarian case would provide no support for the claim that the paternalist principle can *never* provide sufficient warrant for state inter-vention.

Despite Mill's own evident uneasiness about applying his anti-paternalist argument in its full rigour, H. L. A. Hart has complained that 'Mill carries his protests against paternalism to lengths that may now appear to us to be fantastic'. In support, Hart points out that many apparently acceptable features of our present law—he cites as instances restrictions on the supply of drugs and narcotics and the inadmissibility of the consent of the victim as a defence against the charge of assault—can be defended, and best defended, on paternalist grounds.⁵ Hart's complaint is persuasive. There are surely many cases in which the prevention of self-inflicted harm constitutes a good reason for legal intervention; and, at the very least, there seems little merit in excluding such considerations *ab initio* in reaching

³ Ibid., 151–152.
⁴ Ibid., 157–158.
⁵ H. L. A. Hart, *Law, Liberty and Morality* (Oxford University Press, 1963), 31–33.

legislative decisions. For instance, it would seem (to use Hart's word) 'fantastic' to exclude the saving of life as a consideration in the present debate upon the enforced wearing of car seat-belts.

There is then a problem from a liberal standpoint. Mill's 'one very simple principle' is initially attractive since it provides a very clear safe-guard against what could be an abhorrent extension of interference with individual liberty. At the same time, there seem to be instances, there were indeed for Mill instances, in which paternalism does seem to provide sufficient warrant for interference with individual behaviour. Can these two apparently incompatible positions be reconciled? And, if not, can the principle of state paternalism be conceded but its application limited? In an attempt to answer these questions, I shall offer a definition of the principle, explore some implications of this definition, examine some recent attempts at solving these problems and finally put forward a solution which is, at any rate roughly, utilitarian in character.

II

The paternalist principle I take to be one justifying interference with a person's behaviour aimed at preventing that person harming himself, or more strongly making him act for his own welfare.

The definition as stated leaves vague the mode of interference or intervention. The range of possible methods is very wide. We might, for instance, try to prevent a person harming himself by offering advice and information, by offering advice and misinformation, by so manipulating his environment that the self-harming act becomes difficult or impossible to perform, by threatening reprisals if the self-harming act is performed.

In the light of this variety of possible methods of interference, it is difficult to reject the paternalist principle completely. Few, I think, would wish to argue that those aware of the harmful consequences of an action should not inform those unaware and in danger of performing the action. Few, for instance, would oppose the printing of government health warnings on cigarette packets. In this light, Mill himself is committed to the principle of paternalist intervention, for he certainly assumes it to be an obligation on the knowledgeable to guide and inform the ignorant. Further, he accepts that when such guidance is impossible—as is the case with the man about to cross the unsafe bridge or with children and 'barbarians' impervious to reasoned argument—more strenuous forms of intervention become auto-matically legitimate. The debate about paternalism as presented by Mill (and as carried on since) is not directly about the propriety of the principle itself; for who could reject it except those indifferent or even callous towards the sufferings of others? It is rather about which methods of intervention are appropriate in particular circumstances and more specifically what are appropriate forms of state interference. Mill in particular and liberals in general have not questioned the propriety of paternalist interference so long as it is restricted to advice, information and guidance. What has been at issue is whether, and when, other and stronger modes of interference are justified and which of these alternatives are justified forms of intervention.

On this last question, Mill himself gives little guidance since his principle as initially stated refers only in general terms to the exercise of power. Some recent writers have narrowed down the problem to if and when the use of coercion on paternalist grounds is legitimate. Michael Bayles, for example, argues that 'Paternalism may be an acceptable reason for non-criminal legislation . . . But it is not a morally acceptable reason for criminal legislation.'[6] It is difficult to see why this distinction should hold unless it is assumed that coercion is itself a morally unacceptable means of control. States, like persons, may control behaviour through manipulation as well as through threats of reprisal and, if paternalism can justify one means of control, it is not obvious why in principle it cannot justify the other. I might try to safeguard my child against burning by buying a fire-guard or by threatening to smack him if he goes too close to the fire; a political authority might try to cut down pedestrian accidents by putting up pedestrian barriers along streets or by fining jay-walkers. There seem no grounds for arguing that a justification for the first modes of intervention is in principle incapable of providing a justification for the second.

Clearly there might be good reasons for arguing that the first mode of intervention is generally preferable to the second, just as there are good grounds for preferring advising and informing (accurately) to lying, manipulating or coercing. But the major question at issue seems to be when the state may go beyond informing and warning citizens about the danger to themselves of their own actions to actual control of those actions.

III

So the problem (again, I would stress, from a liberal standpoint) is whether or not the state is justified in going beyond informing and guidance on paternalist grounds. If it is not, how can this be reconciled with acceptable cases of apparently paternalist intervention of a stronger kind; and, if it is, are there any limitations on the state's use of manipulative and coercive powers to prevent self-harm?

Two broad lines of argument have emerged in the writings of those who

[6] Michael D. Bayles, 'Criminal Paternalism', *The Limits of Law*, Nomos XV, J. Rowland Pennock and John W. Chapman (eds) (New York: Lieber-Atherton, 1974), 174. Cf. also Joel Feinberg, 'Legal Paternalism', *Canadian Journal of Philosophy* I, No. 1 (September 1971), 105.

have attempted to resolve this liberal dilemma. The first is that paternalist intervention is justified only if it rests on the consent of those whose freedom of action is being restricted. Where such actual or predicted or hypothesized consent can reasonably be asserted, paternalist intervention is legitimate; where it cannot, such intervention is illegitimate. This consent requirement is what allows us, it is claimed, to admit the principle of state paternalism but to restrict its operation. The second broad line of argument is that most of the instances of apparently paternalist interventions by the state which we might wish to defend are not actually instances of paternalist intervention. They are, it is argued, instances of the prevention of persons harming others and so no resort to the paternalist principle is needed to defend them. The first argument recognizes the legitimacy of state restrictions on paternalist grounds, but tries to limit such state interference to areas where it is presently found acceptable. The second argument endorsed Mill's rejection of paternalism as grounds for restrictions on liberty, but claims that the kind of intervention a liberal might be concerned to defend can be defended on grounds other than paternalist.

At first sight, the argument that paternalist intervention is justified only with the consent of those who are restrained seems self-defeating. For, at any rate once interference goes beyond guidance and information, such intervention involves its recipient in being forced by some means to do what he would not otherwise do or to refrain from doing what he would otherwise do. Motor-cyclists are made to wear helmets only because there are at least some who would be unwilling to do so without legal compulsion. Clearly, the consent at issue here must be a subsequent or a hypothesized consent. What has to be argued is that those restricted will or would in certain circumstances agree to the propriety of the restrictions placed upon them.

This points to a distinction that can be made between a strong and a weak version of the argument, the strong version claiming that, for paternalist intervention to be justified, the consent of the recipient must be actually forthcoming, the weak version claiming that the consent would be forthcoming if those coerced or manipulated were rational or fully informed or both (even if there is no expectation of their actually being or becoming so).

The illustration of the strong version that is usually called in play, misleadingly as I think, is the story of Odysseus and the Sirens. Odysseus had himself lashed to the mast and ordered his men not to release him, no matter what his subsequent pleas or orders, since he knew he would be unable to resist the song of the Sirens. This, it is argued, is the classic case of consent, here actual, explicit and precedent, justifying paternalist restrictions, Odysseus's men continuing to restrain him, against his will, to prevent him harming himself. It is just possible to think of political analogues to this story. Rational, self-interested men in a Hobbesian mould

might agree that they (together with all others) need to be coerced into acting in ways which are in their own interests. What is not clear is that
these are instances of paternalist [intervention, rather than self-limitation
of choices to prevent self-harm or to further one's interests. Being tied to
the mast, refusing to allow his men to follow subsequent orders, was
simply the means chosen by Odysseus to prevent his harming himself.
Paternalist intervention seems no more involved here than if I bought
a house far distant from a pub because I feared becoming an alcoholic.

If there is previous agreement to restrictions it is then misleading to
picture those restrictions as paternalist in character. Rather they are self-
imposed constraints decided on by the individual with the object of
avoiding self-harm. The strong version of the consent argument does not
however rely wholly on precedent consent; it sees subsequent consent as
an alternative condition for legitimate paternalist intervention. The
argument has been put most schematically by Rosemary Carter, who
suggests that 'a paternalistic act will be justified only if either:

1. 'prior to the interference the subject explicitly consents to the
   paternalist intervention; or
2. Subsequent to the interference the subject

   (i) explicitly consents to the action; or
   (ii) is disposed to consent either upon request, or upon the receipt
   of a relevant piece of information.'[7]

Condition 1 is a formulation of the Odysseus example; condition 2 (i) is
a statement of the requirement that consent be actually forthcoming for the
paternalist intervention to be justified; and condition 2 (ii) remains within
the strong consent fold if what is being required is that strong empirical
evidence be produced that those subject to intervention have permanent
values and aims consonant with the proposer of the intervention and thus
providing good grounds for a prediction that retrospective agreement will
be forthcoming.[8]

There are some severe difficulties in accepting this strong version of the
consent argument as a solution to the liberal dilemma I have posed. In the
first place, it might exclude from paternalist actions those persons who
could be thought most appropriately subject to them. Whoever else might be
thought proper recipients of paternalist attentions, it is surely right for the
insane or the mentally handicapped to be restricted in their own interests.
By definition interference by way of advice and information would be
inappropriate because ineffective here. Equally, it might in many instances

[7] Rosemary Carter, 'Justifying Paternalism', *Canadian Journal of Philosophy*,
VII, No. 1 (March 1977), 134.

[8] A similar case is put forward by John D. Hodson, 'The Principles of Paternalism', *American Philosophical Quarterly*, **14**, No. 1 (January 1977), 65–68.

be difficult either to demonstrate that the persons restricted have long-term aims and preferences consonant with the objects of the intervention or to predict with any plausibility that agreement to the intervention will be forthcoming.[9] This objection might have still wider application since it could be argued that evidence of permanent incompetence in judging self-interest (even amongst those who are by no means insane or mentally handicapped) constitutes good grounds for paternalist intervention. Hart, for instance, gives as the reason for our now judging Mill's anti-paternalism as 'fantastic', 'a general decline in belief that individuals know their own interests best' and Hart emphatically endorses this scepticism.[10] If Hart is right, then the inability to predict future agreement by no means presents a barrier to paternalist intervention.

Another difficulty about the strong consent argument is that paternalist intervention might in many instances be self-fulfilling in terms of the consent requirement. In other words, a consequence of intervention may well be (and even be intended to be) an alteration of attitudes such that agreement to the intervention *will* be forthcoming. Such an intention is clearly present in much parental control of children. I might force my child to go to school, to do his homework, to practise the piano (instead of or as well as counselling him on the desirability of doing so) partly at least in the hope that the compulsion will produce a taste for what is at present unattractive. In parallel, I suspect we know insufficient about the effects of legal enactments on popular attitudes to discount the possibility that laws breed a disposition to accept their purposes as legitimate. If this is so, then the strong consent argument is circular, for the present intervention is justified by the presumption of future consent, but the intervention may produce a disposition so to consent.

The last objection to the strong consent argument is that, except in the Odysseus case (which in any case I have argued is not an instance of paternalism), the validity of the justification for intervention can only be tested after, and perhaps long after, the event. At bottom, the claim is that a case can be put for paternalist intervention only when it can be firmly predicted that retrospective approval will be given by those subjected to it. The best evidence in support of such a prediction is the degree to which the intervention will have results actually promotive of long-term values held by the subject. In other words, the justificatory argument at the time of intervention rests on the claim that the intervention is in the long-term interests of the subject. This, it is claimed, is a relevant argument only because it underpins a prediction about future consent. At best, any such prediction can only be probabilistic. In addition, is not the justification offered at the moment of intervention sufficient in itself? Would the

[9] Carter does in fact recognize this difficulty; cf. 'Justifying Paternalism', 139.
[10] H. L. A. Hart, op. cit., 34.

justification be invalidated if the subject continued to withhold agreement from the paternalist act (even if it could be demonstrated in some way to have furthered his interests)? If not, the strong consent argument is redundant and the justification for paternalist intervention consists in a demonstration that the intervention actually furthers the interests of the subject, taking this to involve the satisfaction of his permanent values and his leading preferences.

IV

The weak version of the consent argument is that paternalist intervention is justified only when those subject to paternalist intervention would consent were they rational or fully informed or both (even if it cannot be predicted that they ever will be so). As an exponent of this case, I shall take Gerald Dworkin.[11] Dworkin bases his argument on the assertion that the notion of consent is 'the only acceptable way of trying to delimit an area of justifiable paternalism'. Although he distances himself from 'real will' theories about what people would do were they fully rational, he does, I think, end at a position which I here identify as a weak consent argument.

Starting from the Odysseus example, he argues that it would be rational for us, in emulation of Odysseus to take out 'social insurance policies', by way of agreeing to restrictions on ourselves, since we are aware of our own irrational propensitites. What must then be looked for are, he says, 'certain kinds of conditions which make it plausible to suppose that rational men could reach agreement to limit their liberty even when other men's interests are not affected'. Such agreement, Dworkin asserts, could be rationally reached on the protection of those general goods, such as health and education, whose achievement would be universally desired as necessary conditions for the pursuit of particular individual goods. Difficulty arises as Dworkin sees, when these general goods compete amongst themselves or conflict with the particular goods posed by individuals for themselves; Dworkin cites as an example the opposition of Jehovah's Witnesses to blood transfusions on religious grounds. One must then face, he says, the question of persons 'irrationally attaching weights to competing values'. The problem becomes to determine what a rational weighting would be, and paternalist intervention would be justified in so far as it enforced conformity of behaviour with this rational weighting.

This position can be fairly characterized in my terms as a weak consent

[11] Gerald Dworkin, 'Paternalism', in *Philosophy, Politics and Society*, Fifth Series, Peter Laslett and James Fishkin (eds) (Oxford: Basil Blackwell, 1969), 78–96.

argument. For, although Dworkin insists on consent as an essential element in any justification of paternalism, he is not limiting himself to instances where the actual agreement of empirical individuals might plausibly be prophesied, but wishes to extend the consent argument to instances where it could be claimed only that the rational actor would agree. And the rational actor might have, in his view, a different preference—ordering to actual flesh-and-blood persons.

There are two major difficulties in the weak consent argument. The first is to do with the notion of irrational action, and I suspect that there is confusion in the argument between two different understandings of the term. Irrational actions might be actions which are incapable of achieving the ends that the actor has in mind, or, if they do achieve those ends, have foreseeable and harmful consequences which would for the actor outweigh any benefits achievable by the envisaged ends. Irrational decisions of this sort could arise when persons, because of ignorance or mental incapacity, do not appreciate what the consequences of their actions will be or when they are acting in circumstances of emotional stress or under undue psychological influence which prevent them taking full account of the consequences of their actions. Essentially, these are situations in which persons are doing what will not achieve what they want, either immediately or indirectly. Such irrationality might justify paternalist interference of any kind, but it would certainly justify it in the form of advice and provision of information. It is presumably just such situations that Mill had in mind when he used the example of the unsafe bridge; and it is presumably what is in the mind of those who put forward the strong consent argument. Dworkin, however, in talking of 'irrationally attaching weights to values', uses in addition a second and separate understanding of irrationality which acts as a standard of the actual preference ordering established by individuals. It is not at all clear what is implied in claiming that some rational ordering or weighting of preferences can be determined. If it were the case that there are some good or goods—say health or physical well-being—which all persons could agree are fundamental or prior to all other goods, then it would be irrational in the first sense to pursue ends which endanger the fundamental good. But this does not seem to be the case with the Jehovah's Witnesses rejecting blood transfusions on religious grounds, or Sikhs refusing to wear motor-cycle helmets, or climbers tackling difficult rock faces, or those who attempt Everest or try to row the Atlantic, all of whom seem to place physical security if not low at least not highest on their list of priorities. Such people would not recognize the general good of physical health as over-riding all other goods, such as the assurance of salvation or the excitement of risk-taking.

Different issues are raised by these two separate understandings of irrational action. The first does seem to provide a sufficient justification for paternalist interference, but in the main only for weak interference by way of information and warning. It provides a justification for government health warnings on smoking rather than the legal banning of tobacco. Such weak intervention increases the probability of persons acting rationally but leaves the final ordering of preferences to the individual. The justifiable exceptions to this restriction on the mode of intervention would seem to be in situations of urgency, when there is insufficient time to pass on information, or in situations of incorrigibility, where it is clear that there is little hope of persons understanding the consequences of their actions or of acting on such understanding.

Dworkin's alternative understanding of irrational action is, to my mind, unacceptable as an underpinning of strong state intervention. He argues first that there would be general agreement not only that goods such as health and education are goods, but that they are fundamental and over-riding goods. He then dubs as irrational those persons who clearly do not accept these priorities, and holds that intervention is legitimated by their alleged irrationality. The danger is of course that the enforcement of a generally acceptable ordering of ends becomes the object of state intervention. The most that can be claimed is that there are some primary goods, such as physical well-being, which most people would accept as important; and even that for most people such goods would come high on their scale of values. This gives some presumptive evidence that paternalist intervention to protect these primary goods would achieve its end in most cases of preventing persons harming themselves. It gives no warrant for labelling eccentric evaluative judgments as irrational and therefore irrelevant to a justification of intervention.

The second major objection to the weak consent argument—and this parallels an objection I've put to the strong consent version—is that the appeal to consent is redundant. What is being said is that paternalist intervention is legitimized by consent, and consent can be inferred from what the rational actor would agree to. What the rational actor would agree to is what would actually be promotive of his interests, in the sense either of having consequences he desires or of conforming to a rational ordering of preferences. The legitimizing consent necessarily follows from the rationality of the intervention, and the burden of justification for intervention rests on the claim that it will in fact prevent self-harm. It is difficult to see what force the secondary appeal to consent adds to the justification.

V

For these reasons, I am sceptical of the validity of consent arguments in either their strong or weak forms. The strong argument excludes from paternalist concern those who seem most in need of it, and it demands predictions about future attitudes which are either too tentative to be convincing or are self-fulfilling prophecies. The weak argument's appeal to rationality is either supportive only of interference by way of informing and warning, or, in projecting an objective standard against which actual preferences can be judged, postulates a tacit consent that can be assumed whatever the overt wishes of individuals. Both versions of the consent argument, I've also suggested, dilute the consent requirement until all it demands is that those wishing to intervene should demonstrate that the intervention will actually prevent persons harming themselves.

It seems to me nevertheless that these arguments do put forward three points of central importance in the debate. The first and most obvious is that any justification of a paternalist act must start from a clear demonstration that the act will in fact prevent persons harming themselves. Secondly, the strong consent argument goes further in suggesting that we need to refer to the empirical wants of persons and can only justify intervention if the harm whose avoidance is the object of intervention is seen as a harm by those subject to it. In stressing the importance of actual consent, the strong argument does at the least lay stress on the need to link intervention to actually held values and preferences. Lastly, both consent arguments suggest a distinction between witting and unwitting choices, witting choices being those in which the consequences of the proposed action have been fully perceived and taken into account, unwitting choices those in which the consequences have either not been perceived or for some reason not been taken sufficiently into account by the actor. One persuasive implication of the consent arguments is that intervention is only legitimate in unwitting choices. At the least, if the choice is unwitting purely through ignorance, interference by way of advice and information is merited. If the unwittingness of choice arises for other reasons—because the causal links are too complex to be easily understood by the non-expert, because either temporarily or habitually individuals are unable to comprehend knowledge of consequences, because in particular areas persons fail usually to act on readily available and easily understood knowledge—more strenuous forms of intervention might be justified. A further and important implication of this is that paternalist intervention is only legitimate where it is clear that those proposing to intervene are relatively informed and the proposed subjects are relatively ignorant.

VI

I want to look now, more briefly, at the second general approach to the liberal dilemma I've posed. This is that most of the instances of apparently paternalist interventions we might wish to defend are not so, and can be defended without breach of the embargo on paternalist acts. More specifically, the argument is that they are defensible on the grounds that they regulate other-regarding rather than purely self-regarding acts.

One way of pursuing this argument is almost as old as the *Essay on Liberty* itself.[12] It starts from a criticism of the distinction between self- and other-regarding acts, or rather from the claim that the category of self-regarding acts is an empty class. There are, on this argument, no (or certainly very few) particular acts which do not in some way or another affect others (or affect the interests of others, if this is thought to be more restrictive). Even more clearly, from a rule-utilitarian point of view, there are no categories of action which cannot in principle affect others or affect the interests of others. On these grounds, all *prima facie* instances of paternalistic intervention can be alternatively defended in terms of the protection of others. Let me take as an example the present debate on seat belts. The argument would be that, even supposing the non-wearing of seat-belts does not affect others in making more likely injuries to persons other than the agent, nevertheless the greater likelihood of self-inflicted injury does affect others adversely. It may well raise the costs of car insurance to all; it brings about very heavy charges on the National Health Service; it may well deprive the community at large of the social contributions which the injured or the dead could otherwise have made. The compulsory wearing of seat belts need not therefore be defended as a means of preventing self-harm, it can equally well be justified as preventing considerable although indirect injury to others.

From the libertarian standpoint, this is merely a semantic solution to the problem; in reconciling anti-paternalism with instances of apparently paternalist legislation, it leaves the way open to an indefinite extension of state interference in private behaviour. It is moreover a solution which can be undermined by a more strenuous definition of the paternalist principle itself. In fact Mill himself suggests such a tightening of the principle, for he insists that self-regarding acts are those which apply only to the actor 'directly and in the first instance', even if they do produce 'contingent' or 'constructive' injury to others.[13] This redefinition does answer the accusation that the self-regarding category is an empty class, although Mill's exclusion of 'contingent' or 'constructive' injury to others, as well as self-inflicted harm, from the utilitarian calculation is difficult to reconcile with his utilitarian commitments, if this is meant as an absolute exclusion rather than a rule-of-thumb utilitarian guide.

A further objection to this solution of the problem is that many of the costs to others used to justify intervention are, as it were, voluntarily incurred by society. Recently, for instance, a spokesman for the air–sea

---

[12] Cf. J. C. Rees, *Mill and his Early Critics* (Leicester: University College, 1956), 17–20.

[13] John Stuart Mill, op. cit., 137–138.

rescue services asked for further restrictions on single-handed sailings because these are placing a heavy burden on the rescue services. But, of course, there are alternatives. Those who wittingly endanger themselves might be required to bear the costs of rescue; or rescue services might be refused to them. I am not by any means urging such draconian measures. But it does seem to me an insufficient reason for preventing someone taking risks that we might (or even will) be altruistically led to help him if he lands up in difficulties. The costs of altruism should surely be borne by the altruist.

Another line of argument within this second general response to the liberal dilemma is not to diminish the category of self-regarding acts to vanishing point, but to claim only that most if not all of the specific pieces of apparently paternalist legislation a liberal might wish to defend can be justified on other-regarding grounds. Crucial to this argument is the distinction between harm directly inflicted on a person by himself and harm produced by others with his consent. Intervention to prevent or inhibit the first is paternalistic, but legislation designed to prevent the second is not. Thus, the inadmissability of the consent of the victim against a charge of assault, restrictions on the sale of drugs, laws against euthanasia (as distinct from suicide), regulation of licensing laws and so on, all restrict those who are inflicting harm and need no resort to paternalist justification. The fact that the harm is done only with the co-operation of the victim is irrelevant.

This argument seems to me to fail on two counts; it takes an over-narrow view of the modes of state intervention and it ignores the actual intent of such legislation. As I've said, there are a variety of ways in which behaviour can be regulated, of which coercion is just one. The mere fact that a penal law is not directed coercively against particular persons does not mean that the regulation of *their* behaviour is not at issue. Restrictions on the sale of narcotics, for instance, are intended to deter the taking of harmful drugs. The choice between doing this through regulating their sale rather than, say, making their medically unauthorized use illegal is one purely of expediency. The intent of the legislation in either case is to restrict opportunities for people to harm themselves, in the one case by manipulation of their environment, in the other by coercive threats. I agree here with Dworkin, who argues that it would be 'mistaken theoretically and hypocritical in practice' to assert that the first mode of interference involves a different justificatory principle from the second.[14]

Another way of pursuing the argument that much apparently paternalist legislation can be brought under the harm to others principle has been offered by Donald Regan. To put his point briefly, he argues that a person can harm his future self and, since this future self can be regarded as

[14] Dworkin, op. cit., 82.

another person, apparently paternalist intervention can often be defended as preventing harm to others.[15] I do not think that this argument advances the debate at all. Nor do I think it is necessary to discuss the merits of viewing persons in this way. For it is clear that, if the view has any merit, it would simply prompt a reformulation of the anti-paternalist position so that the preventing of harm to future selves, rather than harm to oneself, would become insufficient warrant for intervention.

This second general response to the liberal dilemma, which essentially tries to demonstrate that no dilemma exists, fails to achieve its purpose. At best, it compels some clarification of the anti-paternalist position. But the dilemma remains. The unqualified acceptance of state paternalism could lead to intolerable intrusions on individual liberty. Its unqualified rejection would, however, require the rejection of much legislation that is generally acceptable and to exclude even from consideration in legislative discussion a factor—self-inflicted harm—which it seems perfectly proper to take into account.

VII

The justification for paternalist intervention must be broadly utilitarian, the prevention of harm. The dilemma I've posed requires some principle by which to limit such utilitarian intervention, a principle which many recent writers have found in consent arguments. What I wish to suggest as an alternative is that the constraints upon paternalism might be inherent in utilitarianism itself, that there might be good utilitarian arguments for restricting, although not for eschewing altogether, paternalist interventions.

The first question to be considered though is whether or not there is a utilitarian case for excluding all legislative intervention in self-regarding conduct. I've said that, on the face of it, it is difficult to see why self-inflicted harm should be excluded from a utilitarian calculus. Rolf E. Sartorius has recently tried to explicate further Mill's case for exclusion.[16] Sartorius argues that, if there is a class of actions in which most actions are wrong but some are right on utility grounds and if it is difficult to distinguish correctly the right from the wrong actions, a utilitarian would be justified in prohibiting all actions of that class. Mill's position is, Sartorius claims, that legislative interventions in self-regarding behaviour constitutes just such a class of actions, and so an absolute ban on these interventions

[15] Donald H. Regan, 'Justifications for Paternalism', *The Limits of Law*, Nomos XV, J. Rowland Pennock and John W. Chapman (eds) (New York: Lieber-Atherton, 1974), 201–206.

[16] Rolf E. Sartorius, *Individual Conduct and Social Norms* (Belmont: Dickenson, 1975), Ch. 8, Sect. 3.

is legitimate. If this is a correct characterization of Mill's position, his conclusion is, as Sartorius recognizes, challengeable on utilitarian grounds. If it were clearly the case that it is impossible to identify reliably those cases of paternalist intervention justifiable on utility grounds, then obviously there could be no utilitarian route out of the liberal dilemma. It may not, however, be impossible, as Mill on this account thought, to distinguish right from wrong acts of paternalist intervention, at least to the extent of tracing the limits in utility terms of justifiable intervention.

Some constraints are inherent in any sort of utilitarian intervention, paternalist or otherwise, and are I think fairly obvious. In the first place, the intervention must actually achieve its object; for it to be justified, it must inhibit actions which would actually, or in all likelihood, cause the harm in question. If government is to prohibit smoking, or even to restrict the advertising of tobacco or to insist on health warnings on cigarette packets, it must be able to demonstrate a clear link between smoking and lung cancer or other physical ills. Secondly, any utilitarian intervention must achieve a favourable utility balance. At the least the costs of intervention must not outweigh the benefits gained, the harm prevented. Clearly relevant to any such calculation in cases of paternalist intervention is the likelihood of particular acts having the harmful consequences claimed, the degree of risk taken by the actor. Equally, consideration of the costs of intervention might give good reasons for generally preferring advice to manipulation and coercion as modes of interference, and perhaps also manipulation to coercion.

These general utility constraints do, I suspect, cover much that is urged by consent theorists. Certainly, so far as consent arguments do rest on the claim that consent can be inferred from a demonstration of what is in a person's overall long-term interests, then simple utility requirements restrict intervention as much, or to the same degree, as the consent requirement.

I would like to go further than this, and suggest that there are utility constraints on intervention which apply peculiarly to paternalist intervention. Broadly, my argument will be that in some respects an individual is more likely to know what is in his interests, than others, not because he will necessarily be better informed about the consequences of his actions, but because he will better know what his wants and preference orderings are.

To pursue this argument, let me begin by appealing to Mill. He puts forward in defence of his anti-paternalist stance, arguments that throw doubt on the effectiveness, in utility terms, of much paternalist intervention.

He is the person most interested in his own well-being: the interest which any other person, except in cases of strong personal attachment, can have in it, is trifling compared with that which he himself has; the interest which society has in him individually (except as to his conduct to others) is fractional, and altogether indirect; while with respect to his own feelings and circumstances, the most ordinary man or woman has means of knowledge immeasureably surpassing those that can be possessed by anyone else. The interference of society to overrule his judgment and purposes in what only regards himself must be grounded on general presumptions; which may be altogether wrong.[17]

Two different claims are packed into this quotation. The first is that a person is likely to be more concerned about his own interests than others, and certainly than society at large. If this is true, and given that altruism is the first condition of paternalist action, persons can be best entrusted with preventing harm to themselves, and entrusting others (including governments) with this task might invite the misuse of power.

The second claim is that persons are more knowledgable about what is in their interests than anyone else. Clearly if this were wholly true, many people would be out of a job—doctors, solicitors, surveyors, insurance brokers—all those whose advice we seek on what it is in our interests to do. Equally, paternalist interference, even by way of advice and in those limited cases of which Mill approves, would be illegitimate because necessarily ill-informed. But it is clear that persons can perform what I have called unwitting actions, can through ignorance or misjudgment or fecklessness or derangement do things whose consequences they do not wish. To this extent, others might be in a better position to judge what is in a person's interests; and it is this very possibility that justifies paternalist intervention. However, Mill talks of purposes as well as judgment and here, I believe, he is on firmer ground. Because a person knows better than others his own wants and preferences, he is in a better position to assess his own interests. And, if his ignorance or misjudgment about the consequences of his actions might justify intervention, the relative ignorance of others about his purposes prompts, in utility terms, restrictions on intervention.

In saying this, I am making some assumptions about the nature of persons' interests which are contestable, and which I have no space here to defend adequately. I am assuming that what is in a person's interests has some reference to the satisfaction of the actual wants and preferences of that person, and that in consequence what is in a person's interests cannot be defined in ignorance of his actual pattern of wants and preferences. Brian Barry contests these assumptions by identifying what is in a person's interests with what will increase his opportunities to get what he wants, whatever it is he may want. Because, he argues, there are a number of generalized resources, with wealth as the paradigm, which will increase

[17] John Stuart Mill, op. cit., 133.

such opportunities, it is possible to define what is in a person's interests without reference to his actual wants.[18] There are, briefly, three major objections to this position. Firstly, it suggests that it is never in a person's interests to expend resources, never in his interests to satisfy wants, since this would decrease his future opportunities to get where he wants. Secondly, it is not the case that generalized resources such as health, education, wealth or power will always and necessarily increase a person's opportunities of getting what he wants, whatever he may want. Some goals a person might set himself could, for example, require vows of poverty and obedience. Thirdly, increasing opportunities to get what one wants might require the translation of generalized resources into particular resources. If I want to be a violinist, it might be more in my interests to have a good violin than to have money in the bank. What particular resources a person might need cannot be decided in ignorance of his goals and preferences.

In this sense, although perhaps only in this sense, Mill is right in claiming that 'the most ordinary man or woman has means of knowledge immeasurably surpassing those that can be possessed by anyone else'. For, if others might be better informed about what the consequences of particular actions will be, the individual is likely to be better informed about what is to count for him as harmful. This particularity of interests is what justifies the confinement of paternalist intervention to unwitting actions. Or rather, if a person's interests are in some sense self-defined, paternalist intervention in fully witting actions is contradictory. If a person is fully aware and taking account of the consequences of his actions, then he cannot be acting against his interests and intervention cannot be justified on the grounds that it prevents him harming himself.

Such considerations must, it would seem, create doubts in the mind of the utilitarian about the efficacy and legitimacy of state paternalism. The state must remain in ignorance of individual interests. If it necessarily has to act largely through general rules, it must, to act paternalistically, assume a uniformity in individual preference orderings which is very unlikely to exist. It is this, I take it, that Mill has in mind when he says that '(t)he interference of society to overrule his judgment and purposes in what only regards himself must be grounded on general presumptions; which may be altogether wrong'. Mill's argument seems then to be that, because paternalist legislation must assume a common scale of values and because no such common scale exists, no paternalist interference is legitimate.

I would argue, on the contrary, that, despite particularity of interests, there is still a utility case for intervention. In saying this, I do not want to blink at the implications. Given the notion of interests I've put forward,

[18] B. M. Barry, *Political Argument* (London: Routledge and Kegan Paul, 1965), 176–186.

state paternalist intervention may for some persons not only fail in its objective of preventing self-injury, but make them act in a way that is positively harmful to their interests as they conceive them. And I do not want to excuse this by predicting future consent or hypothesizing rational consent. There may still be a justification for intervention based on the balance of advantage. To take the case of car seat belts, there may be some drivers for whom the risk of injury to themselves is a major part of the major pleasure of driving, and who therefore take the witting decision not to wear belts. It may also be, however, that most motorists who fail to wear belts do so because of ignorance, or forgetfulness or a habitual disregard of the possible consequences of their actions. In this situation the utilitarian legislator could legitimately rule that the prevention of harm to the unwitting non-wearers might outweigh the damage to the witting non-wearers and the inconveniences attendant upon enforcement to habitual wearers. Nevertheless, it is of importance that the intent of the legislation would not be to over-ride witting decisions; indeed doing so would be on the debit side of the utilitarian account. It would be to over-ride unwitting decisions.

There may then be reasonably clear instances when paternalist intervention is justifiable on utility grounds, even acknowledging the variety of human ends and preferences. But the requirements of justification are nevertheless fairly severe. Those in favour of intervention must give evidence that the good endangered by the action which it is proposed to restrict is a good not only accepted as a good by most persons, but is a good whose achievement would be valued by most potential performers of the action over any possible good achievable by the performance of the action. No doubt such cases would not be susceptible to exact measurement or conclusive proof, but in this they do not differ from utilitarian cases for legislative intervention to prevent harm to others.

Two other restrictions on state paternalism are suggested by what I have called the particularity of interests. The first is that, if it is at all effective, interference by way of advice and information is preferable to interference by manipulation or coercion. For, by definition, information and advice can affect only unwitting choices, and state intervention of this sort cannot over-ride or even influence witting actions. Since the over-ruling of witting choices is harmful in utility terms, this mode of interference is to be preferred. Secondly, the particularity of interests suggests the desirability, where possible, of allowing 'conscientious objection' to paternalist legislation. The kind of instance I have in mind here is the Sikhs and motor-cycle helmets. Here was an identifiable group who were, it would seem, making a witting choice of risking injury rather than abandoning turbans. In this case, the exemption of Sikhs from the requirements of the law is desirable on utility grounds, since for them the law, if enforced on them, would not be preventing self-harm.

VIII

The objective and the justification of paternalism must be utilitarian, the prevention of harm. What I've suggested is that utility considerations also suggest severe restrictions on the extent to which state paternalism should penetrate into individual life. Let me conclude by setting out these restrictions schematically.

1. The linkage between the action to be inhibited or required and the harmful consequences claimed should be very clearly demonstrated. Where there is no necessary causal connection, the risks of harm following from the action should be high.
2. The intervention should have overall beneficial utility consequences. This is to say not just that the costs of enforcement should not outweigh the harm prevented, but that the inhibition of the action should not have consequences for individuals as harmful as the consequences for them of the performance of the action.
3. The harm whose avoidance is in question should be accepted as a harm, and even as a primary harm, by most of those affected by the intervention. In other words, the actions claimed to harmful must be unwittingly chosen by most who will be affected.
4. Where possible, the state should act through information and advice rather than manipulation and coercion. This is desirable on utility grounds since in most circumstances the utility costs of supplying information will be less than those of legal enforcements; and also because interference through advising does not affect witting choices.
5. Where possible, legal paternalist intervention should allow for conscientious objection, at the least for those groups or persons who can reasonably show that they value ends circumscribed by the prohibition more than the harm avoided by it.

Rights, Consequences, and Mill on Liberty[1]

D. A. LLOYD THOMAS

Mill says that the object of his essay *On Liberty* is to defend a certain principle, which I will call the 'liberty principle', and will take to say the following: 'It is permissible, in principle, for the state (through law) or society (through social pressure) to control the actions of individuals "only in respect to those actions of each, which concern the interest of other people" '.[2] The liberty principle is a prescription of intermediate generality. Mill intends it to support more specific political prescriptions, such as liberty of conscience, of expressing and publishing opinions, of framing a plan of life to suit our own character, and of combination for any purpose not involving harm to others (p. 75). The liberty principle is more general than these prescriptions but less general than its possible moral foundations, such as utilitarianism. My concern will be with attempts to defend the liberty principle by showing it to be supported by an acceptable moral position.

It is not my intention to offer a defence of a reading of the liberty principle in terms of 'interests', although I believe this is the most plausible construal of the text taking into account all of the formulations Mill offers. However, such a reading does call for an account of the term 'interests'. A distinction will be made between 'desire-based' interests and 'rights-based' interests. It will be argued that Mill must have intended 'interests' to be taken as 'rights-based interests'.

To explain the notion of desire-based interests, let us suppose that each person has some set of non-instrumental desires: things desired not, or not only, as a means to something else. Let us further suppose that each can say which of his own set seem to him to be of greater significance. The

---

[1] This is a revised version of a lecture given in the Royal Institute of Philosophy series, Feburary 1981, and at the Political Thought Conference, New College, Oxford, January 1981, under the title 'Mill's Kantian Liberalism'. My thanks are due to those present on both occasions, and to Jerry Cohen, John Gray, John Halliday, John Kelly and Anne Lloyd Thomas for their helpful and encouraging comments.

[2] J. S. Mill, *On Liberty* (Everyman Edition), *Utilitarianism, Liberty and Representative Government*, 74. All page references in the text are to this edition of *On Liberty*. For a similar reading of Mill's principle, see J. Rees, 'A Re-reading of Mill on Liberty', in *Limits of Liberty*, Peter Radcliff (ed.) (California: Wadsworth, 1966), 100.

most significant sets of non-instrumental desires may be expected to cluster around a person's more important activities, such as work (if not regarded merely as a means to other things) and various kinds of association with others. Such clusters of desires may be called a person's non-instrumental interests. Though based on desires, this account of interests allows for a distinction between a person's interests and his 'mere' likings, such as the desire to eat chocolate mousse, which may not be part of a cluster of non-instrumental desires a person regards as significant. And some of the things one is interested in (the career of Kiri te Kanawa) may not be part of one's interests, or something one has an interest (i.e. a stake) in. An account of desire-based interests must also include the notion of 'instrumental' interests: those things which, though they may not be desired as such, or even at all, are needed to secure a person's non-instrumental interests. Perhaps some instrumental interests are common to all people, such as health, while others vary from person to person according to what happen to be a person's non-instrumental interests. It is doubtful whether a person can be mistaken about his non-instrumental interests, but he can be mistaken about his instrumental interests: about what is in his interests.

Desire-based interests do not serve well for a reading of Mill's liberty principle. On this account actions concerning the interests of others would be those which impinge on another, either by way of affecting the pursuit of his non-instrumental goals, or by way of affecting his instrumental interests. Now whereas it is perhaps an exaggeration to say that any action would concern the interests of (some) others, some liberties Mill insists upon certainly would not be justified if we accepted this reading of 'interests'. Many exercises of the liberty to express and publish opinions (e.g. those by Ralph Nader) concern the desire-based interests of others. As this reading of 'interests' leaves little of significance that may not be controlled by the state or society it is to be rejected, for it is clear that Mill intends his liberty principle to leave much of significance.

An alternative conception of interests is based, not on desires, but on rights. We think of persons as having rights to control themselves and (if we believe in private property) segments of the material world external to their bodies. A person has the right to decide who has access to his body, and no one else has this right, except with his consent. On the rights-based conception of interests, a person's interests are all those things over which he has rights of control. On this view every person has a sphere protected by rights in which choices about how things are to be in that sphere are reserved for that person.

The question 'Does this action concern your interests?' may receive different answers depending upon which conception of interests is being used. Whether your rich aunt will strike you out of her will is a matter that concerns your desire-based interests (unless you are already wealthy enough). But her decision does not concern your rights-based interests, for it is your aunt, not you, who has rights of control over her assets. In striking you out of her will she does nothing that concerns your rights-based interests, for by so doing she does not invade your protected sphere. If you steal a trifle from your aunt you do something that concerns her rights-based interests, but stealing so little may have no effect on her desire-based interests.

Reading 'interests' as 'rights-based interests', i.e. as those things over which one has rights of control, makes better sense of the liberty principle, because then it will rule out, in principle, external control of many significant actions. It is also a reading that fits several passages in the essay.

> there is no parity between the feeling of a person for his own opinion, and the feeling of another who is offended at his holding it; no more than between the desire of a thief to take a purse, and the desire of the right owner to keep it (p. 140).

Holding an opinion is like owning something: you have rights of control over your opinions. That their existence is an annoyance (or worse) to me, and hence, possibly, in conflict with my desire-based interests, is of no more significance, so far as the rights of the situation go, than the fact that your owning a Gaugin I want has dashed one of my ambitions as a collector. One of a number of other passages which fit this construal of 'interests' is the following.

> The only part of the conduct of anyone, for which he is amenable to society, is that which concerns others. In the part which merely concerns himself, his independence is, *of right*, absolute. Over himself, over his own body and mind, the individual is sovereign.[3]

If the term 'interests' in the liberty principle is to be read as 'rights-based interests' the next question is 'What is the source of this account of rights?' In at least one passage Mill appears to draw his account of rights from what are recognized as such in a particular society:

> This conduct consists . . . in not injuring the interests of one another; or rather certain interests, which, either by express legal provision or by tacit understanding, ought to be considered as rights (p. 132).

But it is not clear that this passage *must* be read as having relativistic implications. For there are two ways in which it may be taken:

(i) Express legal provision or tacit understanding is what *makes* certain considerations into rights-based interests for the purposes of the liberty principle.

(ii) Certain considerations *are* interests, and their being so is not

---

[3] p. 73, emphasis added. Other passages favouring an interpretation in terms of rights-based interests are to be found on pp. 120, 121, 132, 136 and 137.

dependent on express legal provision or tacit understanding. These interests ought to be recognized for what they are—people's rights—either through legal recognition or tacit understanding.

The second way of taking the passage does not have relativistic implications.[4]

In any case, it is difficult to believe that Mill's considered position could be a relativistic one. For if it were it would follow that the significance of the liberty principle, in its applications, would vary from one jurisdiction (and set of social customs) to another. But Mill's stated objective is precisely to find a principle avoiding such variations.

> . . . the practical question, where to place the limit—how to make the fitting adjustment between individual independence and social control—is a subject on which nearly everything remains to be done . . . Some rules of conduct . . . must be imposed . . . What these rules should be is the principal question in human affairs; but if we except a few of the most obvious cases, it is one of those which least progress has been made in resolving. No two ages, and scarcely any two countries, have decided it alike; and the decision of one age or country is a wonder to another (pp. 68–69).

There follows an attack on deciding the matter by reference to the influence of custom. Further, those rights-based interests recognized in some jurisdictions (even in England) would not allow Mill to draw from the liberty principle the more specific liberties he wants, for example, the liberty to utter words offensive to Christianity (p. 90). But clearly Mill thinks that his liberty principle requires liberty of expressing and publishing opinions under any jurisdiction, anyway under any in a society not in a 'backward state' (p. 73).

Rights drawn from law or convention traditionally have been contrasted with natural rights. It would appear, however, that natural rights cannot be Mill's basis for an account of rights-based interests, for he says:

> I forgo any advantage which could be derived to my argument from the idea of abstract right, as a thing independent of utility (p. 74).

This passage is, I believe, incompatible with *one* account of natural rights. That account is to be found in places in Locke (though it is not his only

---

[4] On the other hand Mill says at p. 132 that the conduct each is bound to observe includes 'bearing his share (to be fixed on some equitable principle) of the labours and sacrifices incurred for defending the society or its members from injury and molestation'. This suggests that there is a choice of acceptable 'equitable principles'. So perhaps Mill's view is that some of the interests he refers to in his formulations of the liberty principle are constant for any of its applications, while others are partly a matter of which of a permissible set of options a particular society chooses to take up.

account of natural rights), and also, more recently, in Nozick. On one Lockean view there is some characteristic(s) of each person such that possession of that characteristic implies each person's having a certain natural right. For example, that someone exists implies that he has a property in his own person. For this view of natural rights the label 'perceived' may be used, as it is thought that any rational person will be able to 'see' the connection between possession of the characteristic(s) and possession of the right.

This view of natural rights cannot be reconciled with the passage just quoted from Mill, nor with the more general consideration that Mill's ethical theory is consequentialist. A 'perceived' natural right requires no appeal to the consequences of its recognition as part of its justification, and therefore must be 'a thing independent of utility'. But there is another conception of rights, with a good claim to the title 'natural' (in that it too may be contrasted with rights conceived as deriving from positive law or convention) which is compatible with Mill's position. Natural rights may be seen as related to justifiable practices. The requirements of a practice supply the connection between the characteristic(s) possessed by a person, and the claim that he has a certain right. The justification of the practice requires a comparison of the consequences there would be if that practice existed with the consequences if alternative practices existed, the comparison to be made in terms of some end(s), such as aggregate utility. (This way of justifying rights will be referred to as 'practice consequentialism'.) On this view the connection between characteristics possessed by persons and rights must be made through a practice consequentially justified, whereas the justification of perceived natural rights does not require any reference to practices and their consequences.

We can use the term 'assigned' for natural rights justified in the practice consequentialist way. Persons are thought of as in an initial condition of 'rightslessness', and are then assigned rights on the basis of justified practices. A reluctance to allow that assigned natural rights really are natural rights is due perhaps to the belief that natural rights must be 'natural' in both of two ways. They should be 'natural' rather than 'artificial' where 'artificial' indicates a construction of positive law or social convention. They also must be 'natural' rather than 'artificial' where 'artificial' indicates that no 'contrived' processes of reasoning are necessary for their attribution: they are simply properties people have. Assigned natural rights are 'natural' in the first way, but not in the second.

As Mill does not forgo making use of the notion of abstract right, but only of abstract right 'as a thing independent of utility', he could make use of a conception of natural rights assigned on the basis of the consequences of practices assessed in terms of utility. The rights-based interests made use of in the liberty principle therefore may be those things over which a person ought to have rights of control by reference to the best assignment of rights from the point of view of the principle of utility. We may call such interests 'utilitarian rights-based interests'. It should be noticed that there need be no connection between prescriptions justified by reference to utilitarian rights-based interests and prescriptions justified by the direct application of the principle of utility to desire-based interests. If the rule 'Whenever one person's desire-based interests are in conflict with another's, decide what is due to each by reference to what would maximize utility', then no one would have any rights and, ergo, no utilitarian rights-based interests. Direct applications of the principle of utility to desire-based interests would leave few, if any, classes of action not in principle controllable by the state or society.

Should the term 'interests' in Mill's liberty principle be understood as 'utilitarian rights-based interests'? Not if by 'utilitarian' is meant 'desire-satisfaction utilitarian', i.e. the view that a certain psychological state, satisfied desire, is the only intrinsically good thing, and that the goodness of anything other than satisfied desire is wholly dependent upon its relationship to satisfied desire, either by way of 'producing' it, being a precondition for it, etc.[5]

The reason why a conception of rights-based interests for use in the liberty principle cannot be grounded in desire-satisfaction utilitarianism is apparent if we consider, as an example, Mill's claim that we ought to have the liberty of 'framing the plan of our life to suit our own character' (p. 75). It follows from the formulation of desire-satisfaction utilitarianism that the consequential justification of a practice securing this liberty must be based solely on how granting or withholding it would affect the satisfaction of the desires of all concerned. The position over-all of granting or withholding that liberty may be regarded as the sum of how granting or withholding it would impinge upon each of the individuals concerned. So let us consider the case of one person, P, in isolation.

P's desires may be divided into two categories. Firstly, there is P's desire (or lack of it) to enjoy this liberty for its own sake, apart from the effect its possession may have on the satisfaction of P's other desires. Secondly, there is the incidence this liberty will have on the rest of P's desires (i.e. those other than the desire to enjoy this liberty as such). If it is likely that P's choice of a plan of life will be better (from the point of view of maximizing the satisfaction of P's desires) than someone else's choice on P's behalf, then there is a *prima facie* utilitarian case for P having this liberty. Thus a utilitarian defence of P's having this liberty will depend upon (a) how much P desires to frame her own plan of life, and (b) how well P can be

[5] The argument to follow would not be affected if we adopted the more plausible position that 'satisfied desire' covers a set of distinguishable psychological states. 'Desire-satisfaction utilitarianism' also could be adopted as a label for the different view that what is intrinsically good is the world coming to conform to how we desire it to be, whether or not this gives us 'satisfaction'.

expected to frame her own plan of life from the point of view of satisfying the rest of her desires.

Now clearly people differ in how much they desire this liberty and, if they have it, in how likely they are to frame a plan of life that will maximize the satisfaction of their desires. For some it is plausible that possession of this liberty will be for their utilitarian good, for they have a significant desire to enjoy it and can be expected to plan their lives better (from the point of view of satisfying desires) than anybody else could do it for them. Others, however, appear to have no strong desire to enjoy this liberty, nor much capacity to frame a plan suitable for maximizing desire-satisfaction. (They may prefer life in some clear institutional structure.) From a utilitarian point of view it would seem reasonable, therefore, to say that this liberty should be enjoyed by some but withheld from, or granted in only a qualified form to, others. But Mill believes that the liberty principle requires that this particular liberty should be enjoyed by all, at least in societies no longer in a backward state.

It may be objected to this argument that we think not only in terms of matching people's liberties to the desires they already have, but also of instituting a liberty in order to encourage a desire for it which does not as yet exist. If everyone is assigned the liberty to frame her own plan of life, then even if at present such an assignment is best only for some (perhaps a minority) it may encourage a desire for the liberty in many who do not as yet have it.

This objection fails, however, because the fact that a desire for such a liberty may be encouraged in this way can be of no significance for a desire-satisfaction utilitarian. To suppose that there is reason to encourage a desire that does not already exist is to assume that some objective value is placed on having that desire: a value not itself wholly desire-dependent.

To this it may be replied that there are cases where a utilitarian could advocate the encouragement of a desire in those who do not already have it, without assuming that some objective value is to be placed on having that desire. One example is the encouragement of a desire of a kind reasonably supposed to hold out particularly good possibilities of intense desire-satisfaction. This consideration does not, however, affect the present argument. While those deprived of liberty can desire it intensely, in general it would be implausible to encourage the desire for liberty as such on the ground that it held out particularly good possibilities of intense desire-satisfaction.

There is another case where a desire-satisfaction utilitarian can justify a policy not in keeping with the existing distribution of desires, but do this without assuming that an objective value is to be placed on the satisfaction of some desires. Suppose most people desire to be dependent upon an addictive and debilitating drug. In the short run a policy of discouraging dependence is not optimal in utilitarian terms, as it does not provide people with what they want. However, a utilitarian may argue that if the dependence persists future aggregates of satisfied desire will diminish, and hence that there is a utilitarian case for the policy.

This objection also fails. The example of drug dependence differs from encouraging a desire to frame one's own plan of life in that the former calls for no discrimination between the objective value of satisfying various desires: if most are drug dependent the satisfaction of desires of whatever character can be expected to reduce to zero, including desires related to drug dependence. No similar consideration applies in the case of fostering a desire for liberty to frame one's own plan of life: the reason for encouraging that desire is a non-desire-dependent preference for it over more passive inclinations.

Mill recognizes that the value of framing one's own plan of life is not wholly desire dependent:

> He who lets the world . . . choose his plan of life for him, has no need of any other faculty than the ape-like one of imitation. He who chooses his plan for himself, employs all his faculties . . . And these qualities he requires and exercises exactly in proportion as the part of his conduct which he determines according to his own judgment and feelings is a large one. It is possible that he might be guided in some good path, and kept out of harm's way, without any of these things. But what will be his comparative worth as a human being? (p. 117).

Mill's utilitarianism is not, or not only, desire-satisfaction utilitarianism, and later it will be argued that the most interesting support Mill lends to his liberty principle does not derive from that form of utilitarianism. But it must be allowed that Mill sometimes places more emphasis on his Benthamite origins, as in this passage:

> Such are the differences among human beings in their sources of pleasure, their susceptibilities of pain, and the operation on them of different physical and moral agencies, that unless there is a corresponding diversity in their modes of life, they neither obtain their fair share of happiness, nor grow up to the mental, moral, and aesthetic stature of which their nature is capable (p. 125).

Such a justification of the liberty to frame one's own plan of life is weak. At best it is only a *prima facie* case, and over-all the case against allowing persons the liberty to lead new or unusual ways of life may be stronger. The gain for a few in being able to better match their particular desires and dispositions to an appropriate way of life easily could be outweighed by the distaste felt by many at people living lives like that. Such gains also might be outweighed by the anxiety produced in many about the worth of their own more conventional ways of life.

An account of rights-based interests suitable for Mill's liberty principle is not to be found in desire-satisfaction utilitarianism. But it may be suggested that a more satisfactory account is to be found in a more complicated form of practice consequentialism. The consequences of the practices on which certain rights are based could be assessed by reference to certain supposed objective and intrinsic goods, such as individual autonomy, as well as by their tendency to maximize desire satisfaction. (To regard individual autonomy, say, as an objective good is to take account of it when estimating consequences in a way not wholly determined by its relationship to satisfying desire.) This amendment may repair the faults revealed in a justification based on desire satisfaction alone. For example, if individual autonomy is an objective and intrinsic good, it may be reasonable to assign a right to everyone to frame her own plan of life, not just those for whom it would be best in desire satisfaction terms.

But if this approach is taken some reason needs to be given why individual autonomy (say) should be regarded as an objective good—a reason not requiring Mill to seek support outside a consequentialist ethic. It will be argued that a suitable form of consequentialism ('experimental consequentialism') is to be found in Mill alongside the more familiar elements of desire-satisfaction utilitarianism. Experimental consequentialism does not give us precisely the conclusion that individual autonomy is an objective good, but it does provide reason for taking account of autonomy in a way not wholly dependent upon its effect on satisfying desires.

Experimental consequentialism may be introduced by way of noting an objection to desire-satisfaction utilitarianism. The claim that things other than desire satisfaction are of value only in so far as they are related to satisfied desire is plausible in some cases. The nicotine addict may allow that there is nothing good about his smoking other than that it satisfies one of his desires. If the desire to smoke were to cease he may then see nothing good about smoking. This is not, however, the way we view all objects of desire. With many we would not suppose that they ceased to be of value if our desires for them happened to cease. We separate the desirability of an object from its capacity to satisfy our desires. In some cases the occurrence of desire may be taken as a discovery of the value of the object of desire.

Experimental consequentialism is based on regarding the significance of some desires in this light. There well may be things other than the experience of satisfied desire which are intrinsically good. We come to believe that some things are intrinsically good by way of their capacity to arouse and to satisfy desire. The capacity to do this for some particular person is not, however, conclusive evidence that the object of desire is intrinsically good. Sometimes we revise our beliefs about the value of the object of desire, at first thinking that the object itself is of value, but later finding that its value lies only in its capacity to satisfy our desires. The extent to which people who have experienced the object of desire regard it as intrinsically good is an indication, though no conclusive indication, that it is so.

Experimental consequentialism differs from desire-satisfaction utilitarianism in its attitude towards certainty and evaluative knowledge. The latter assumes that we know what is intrinsically good. Such room as there is for new evaluative knowledge will be about the kind of thing which can give rise to satisfied desire. We may come to desire new kinds of thing, or come to recognize new sources of satisfaction of the desires we already have, but in all this we make no discovery about that which is intrinsically good. By contrast, experimental consequentialism, though an objectivist position, makes no claims to certain evaluative knowledge: the attitude towards whether this or that has intrinsic value is provisional.

Experimental consequentialism contrasts with desire-satisfaction utilitarianism in one further way. If desiring something is a possible indication of the intrinsic goodness of that which is desired, then although it is through your desires that you come to realize this, its goodness is not dependent on its happening to be your desires, in particular, that are aroused or satisfied. There are objects of possible desire desirable as such, though we may remain uncertain about what they are. For a desire-satisfaction utilitarian, however, all statements about the desirability of things (other than desire-satisfaction itself) are implicitly person-relative.

Mill appears to adopt experimental consequentialism in some places in his ethical writings. J. L. Mackie bases his account of the 'proof' of the principle of utility on a similar interpretation of Mill.[6] There is further evidence that Mill took this view in the first two chapters of *Utilitarianism* and, especially, in the last chapter of *A System of Logic*. It is inappropriate to attempt to argue the case for attribution here. It is not claimed that this is Mill's only ethical position: frequently he appears to be defending desire-satisfaction utilitarianism.

The connection between experimental consequentialism and Mill's liberalism may be traced through these steps:

1. Possible objects of human desire may be divided into those whose existence is not dependent on human activity, and those created, partly or wholly, by human activity. Obviously most objects of human desire fall within the latter group, including what Mill calls 'a pattern of human existence' or a 'mode of life' (p. 125).

2. From experimental consequentialism we have the claim that the only way of recognizing that which is objectively good is through its becoming for us an object of desire. Though preferences may be expressed between 'modes of life' known to us only through abstract characterizations or

---

[6] J. L. Mackie, *Ethics—Inventing Right and Wrong* (Harmondsworth: Penguin Books, 1977), 142.

hearsay, such preferences are of little significance for a determination of their desirability.

3. The best indication, though still a fallible one, that a 'mode of existence' is intrinsically good (or contains elements that are so) is that many who are well acquainted with it come to desire it.

4. The foregoing considerations indicate two political desiderata:

(a) People should be free to participate in the creation of as great a variety of 'modes of existence' as possible.

> There is no reason that all human existence should be constructed on some one or some small number of patterns (p. 125).

(b) People should be free to experience as many 'modes of existence' as possible.

> As it is useful that while mankind are imperfect there should be different opinions, so it is that there should be different experiments of living; that free scope should be given to varieties of character, short of injury to others, and that the worth of different modes of life should be proved practically, when anyone thinks fit to try them (p. 115).

5. Thus, if a state or a society takes a constricted view of desirable 'modes of existence', making it difficult for anyone to live in other than one of a few acceptable ways, members of that society will be prevented from experiencing new 'modes of existence'; ones which may have contained something of worth. This could be a reason why Mill is, if anything, more concerned about freedom from social pressure than from illegality: a 'mode of existence' can survive illegality in a tolerant social environment, but it is difficult for it to last in a hostile one, even if it is not threatened by illegality.

Two further assumptions must be added to arrive at Mill's political position: his commitment to specifically *individual* liberty, and his belief in progress.

The reason for Mill's preoccupation with the liberty of individuals becomes clearer in the light of the ethical theory attributed to him. In the chapter 'Of Individuality', Mill several times affirms that initiatives for experiments in new 'modes of existence' come from individuals. For example:

> ... there are but few persons, in comparison with the whole of mankind, whose experiments, if adopted by others, would be likely to be any improvement on established practice. But these few are the salt of the earth; without them, human life would become a stagnant pool (p. 122; see also pp. 124 and 128).

Belief in progress is the remaining component in the relation between Mill's experimental consequentialism and his liberalism. For a desire-satisfaction utilitarian progress would *be* a process of reforming social and political institutions so as to make possible ever larger aggregates of desire satisfaction. His *belief* in progress would be a matter of supposing that scope for such improvement exists and is likely to be realized. But his commitment to maximizing desire satisfaction remains viable even with pessimism: his principle provides a basis for social choice even if it is believed that the best option available now is worse than the best option available in the past, and that future prospects will become worse still. By contrast, belief in progress is essential to Mill's position. He supposes that a process of individuals creating and choosing between new modes of existence under circumstances of freedom will have a direction. It will tend to throw up a wider variety of more significant modes of existence, and they will become available to a greater proportion of the population.

Belief that such progress *will* occur under circumstances of freedom is indispensable to Mill's position. If it were thought that choice under such circumstances would lead to the adoption of ever more insignificant modes of existence, this case for individual liberty would collapse: it then would be more reasonable to preserve such significant modes of life as already existed. A belief in progress *given* circumstances of freedom is essential to Mill's position, but a belief that there will be progress *towards* those circumstances is not, as is evidenced by his remarks on Chinese civilization (p. 129).

This defence of liberalism meets two conditions indicated earlier. It *is* consequentialist: persons ought to be free from control by the state and society because this is necessary for progress towards more significant modes of existence. Mill is not represented as regarding individual freedom as an end in itself. But although the defence is consequentialist, the importance of individual autonomy is not dependent on the consequences of protecting it in terms of desire satisfaction. Indeed the argument given for individual autonomy does not depend upon adherence to any particular conception of what is good, but on a view of the method by which we discover what is good.

There is a problem, however, about using this approach to defend Mill's liberty principle. What has been justified is a presumption favourable to experimentation with new modes of existence. The liberty principle is both more general and more specific than that. It is more general in that it allows liberty to persons and groups even if it is unlikely that they will participate in any experimentation. The liberty principle is also more specific. It says that people should be free from constraint in any activity not concerning the rights-based interests of others: it proposes specific freedoms and absences of freedom, thus indicating what experiments in modes of existence are permissible. Any particular system of rights-based interests definies and protects certain modes of existence and the values exemplified in them. The cost of this protection is that people may not pursue modes of existence incompatible with that system. For example, the conception of rights-based interests currently accepted in the West is incompatible with the pursuit of most private ways of life involving violence and its associated values. Mill recognizes that any given mode of existence requires restraint as well as freedom.

> All that makes existence valuable to any one, depends on the enforcement of restraints upon the actions of other people. Some rules of conduct, therefore, must be imposed, by law in the first place, and by opinion on many things which are not fit subjects for the operation of law (p. 69).

The assignment of any specific set of rights-based interests presupposes a definite view of what modes of existence are more, and what are less, worthwhile. It is implausible that all of those modes of existence made difficult or impossible to pursue because of our current conception of rights-based interests are ones in which there is simply nothing of value to be discerned. The attempt to formulate a liberty principle, however, supposes that there is a fixed framework of rights-based interests and that people should be free to choose their own plans of life provided they respect that framework. This supposition is consistent with a Lockean natural rights view, and it perhaps also could be justified by a form of consequentialism which assumed that we know that certain ends, other than desire satisfaction, have value. But if our consequentialism takes an experimental attitude towards what is intrinsically good, the supposed fixed framework of rights-based interests dissolves. There is no definitive knowledge of values by reference to which a fixed conception of rights-based interests can be assigned.

If experimental consequentialism is incompatible with a determinate conception of rights-based interests, and hence with even the project of formulating a liberty principle of the kind Mill sought to defend, what can liberalism amount to? One option would be to take as a starting point the set of rights-based interests implicit in the law and morality of a particular society. To be a liberal would be to take a certain attitude to that received conception: an awareness not only of the modes of existence protected by the existing assignment of rights, but also of the cost of that protection: the difficulties the present assignment of rights puts in the way of experiments in some new modes of existence. This way of formulating liberalism gives it one feature in common with conservatism: both are attitudes towards an existing social and legal structure rather than a definitive body of principles.

This characterization of liberalism cannot be formulated in 'one very simple principle' allowing us to read off stances on practical issues. Any modification to the existing conception of rights-based interests probably will involve costs for some modes of existence as well as possible gains for others. Nevertheless, one concession to the wish for principles can be made, though it is a principle quite distinct from, and less ambitious than, Mill's liberty principle. Sometimes the existing conception of rights-based interests is unnecessarily restrictive, in that a more permissive one would protect present modes of existence just as well, while allowing people to follow new ones if they wished. Perhaps a conception of rights-based interests permitting only heterosexual forms of sexual activity would be an instance. If it is possible to change current conceptions of rights-based interests so that the position for the present modes of existence is not significantly worsened, and experiments in new ones are made possible, such a change is warranted. That these changes may result in new modes of existence offensive to others (though they do not threaten their modes of existence) would be no reason against the change. But admittedly this is a limited outcome, and much more has to be done to explain the permanent significance of the traditional liberal freedoms from the approach of an experimental ethic.

Freedom and Custom

ROGER SCRUTON

1. There is a certain attitude which makes freedom the main business of political thought and civil liberty the aim of government. I shall use the word 'liberalism' to refer to this attitude, in the hope that established usage will condone my description. And I shall explore and criticize two aspects of liberal thought: first, the concept of freedom in which it is based; secondly, the attack upon what Mill (liberalism's most eloquent exponent) called the 'despotism of custom'. My conclusions will be tentative; but I should like to suggest that, properly understood, freedom and custom may require each other. Moreover to describe them as *opposites* is to make it impossible to see how either could be valued by a rational being, or why any politician should concern himself with their support or propagation.

2. I will not consider any particular liberal thinker in detail, partly because liberal thinkers tend to be rather difficult to pin down on the issue which concerns me, that of their underlying assumptions about human nature. My method will be to start from a very simplified version of the liberal idea of freedom, and then impose upon it the kind of complexity which alone can endow it with value. In the course of this the definition of freedom will be seen to move precisely towards, and not away from, a conception of customary usage. For the strategy to be at all persuasive I must begin from an idea of freedom that is stripped of all the qualifications that liberal thinkers normally provide for it. Those qualifications usually smuggle in the unexamined beliefs about human nature that I wish to question.

3. Here, then, is the simplified idea of freedom: a man is free to the extent that he is able to obtain what he desires. This is intended not as an exposition of the metaphysical idea of 'free will', but as a definition of political freedom, or rather, of that kind of freedom which can be thought to be advanced or hindered by political arrangements. According to this idea, freedom is measurable. If we assume from the start that it is also valuable (perhaps, even, that it is the sole value that can be politically *pursued*), then we are likely to define the ideal state in liberal terms, as the system of constraints necessary to maximize freedom. Since the nineteenth century the dominant concept used to define those constraints has been that of 'harm'. I do not think that this concept can be made to do the work that liberal thinkers require from it: it stands in need of a theory of human nature which will describe as fully as possible the peculiar ways in which

men can be harmed. (For men are a very special kind of thing.) To some extent, however, such a theory is implied in the doctrine—variously expounded by Mill, Sidgwick and Hart—that 'harm' is an interference with 'interests', and that the only interests that can be taken into consideration in the political sphere are those founded in 'rights'. The concept of a 'right' can be assumed to be prior to that of political liberty only by assuming one of the standard doctrines of liberal thought: that there are 'natural' rights. and in that doctrine a whole theory of human nature is contained. Until it is fully expressed and defended, however, it would be wrong to think that we have given a serious justification either for constraint or for its opposite.

Notice that the above way of justifying political constraint is very different from, although it might eventually support, the constitutionalist theories inspired by Montesquieu. These tend to show why and how the *powers* of institutions and of individuals might be politically limited. This procedure seems at first sight to lay less emphasis on the concept of liberty. It merely assumes that every man has reason to be protected against power. It might be true, however, that this reason cannot be expounded without recourse to an ideal of political freedom, together with the theory of human nature which gives support to it.

Rather than criticize either of those over-arching political theories I shall concentrate, instead, on the original idea of freedom, since it seems to me that the principal defects of liberal theories of the state are already contained in that idea.

4. First, I should like to make some distinctions among desires. Desires may be fleeting or enduring: and I take it that there is a sense in which a merely fleeting desire is less involved in the personality of the agent than an enduring desire, so that the agent normally suffers less through its frustration.

There is also a distinction between a serious desire and a mere velleity. This is related to, but not identical with, the first distinction. A velleity is a desire which persists only until obstructed: that is, it has minimal motivating power, enough only to overcome the general friction of agency, and not enough to set itself against a resistant world.

It seems to me that a political arrangement that sought to encourage and satisfy fleeting desires and mere velleities, but which did this by creating conditions that hindered the fulfilment of genuine agency, would be an arrangement that deprived us of something that could reasonably be called our 'freedom'. Extremes of pamperedness, where no desire transgresses the limits of the fleeting, and all desires are fulfilled, are not states of freedom. Or if they are, then it becomes puzzling that anyone should think freedom to be a value.

5. Let us consider then only enduring and serious desires. There are still

many important distinctions to be drawn. For example, we can distinguish the mild from the intense (a distinction of motivating power), the calm from the urgent (a distinction of a less quantitative kind, concerning the ability of a desire as it were to conceal itself until its time has come), the shallow from the profound. The last difference is not truly quantitative at all, and it may be thought, therefore, by those liberal theories that depend upon the measurement of one desire against another, that it does not exist, or is reducible to some other distinction which fits more readily into the liberal picture. (The same thought is common also to those who describe human and political matters in terms of preference theory, the theory of games, and other intriguing simplifications.) But I shall argue that it is a real distinction, and an important one, since it concerns the relation of the desire to the self of the agent. An example might make the distinction clearer: a desire to seduce someone with whom I have become casually acquainted may be intense, urgent, and also calculating. Suppose the desire is not fulfilled, and on the next day is either forgotten or cast over with a veil or irony. This I should call a shallow desire. By contrast, I may wish to seduce, or rather, unite myself with, someone whom I have long known and respected. This desire is not urgent, nor is it intense in the sense of determining my action against all normal opposition. And yet it persists, I return to it, and as the years pass and I see it unfulfilled, I feel part of myself dwindling away in sadness or incoherence. This I should call a profound desire. It is possible that some people do not have profound desires; it is extremely unlikely that there are people whose desires are not sometimes intense, urgent or domineering.

The distinction is related to two others: that between the spasmodic and the persistent, and that between the long term and the short term. The latter distinction (commented on by Kenny, and in another way by Nagel) deserves some mention here. I can desire to do this, here, now. Or I can desire something for my future without wanting it now. It is plausible to suggest that certain beings—notably those with no concept of the future—can respond to the promptings of the first kind of desire while remaining forever unacquainted with the second.

6. Two of those distinctions interest me in the context of the present discussion: that between the profound and the shallow, and that between the long term and the short term. In neither case, it must be said, is the distinction to be elucidated in terms of the concept of intention, although of course an account of human agency that failed to consider the idea of intention is unlikely to generate a theory of political freedom. I can imagine a theory which said that an urgent desire is distinguished by the fact that it is (or, according to your theory of intention, is accompanied by or realized in) a present intention, the calm desire by the like presence of an intention for the future. But in neither case, it seems to me, need there be

any intention at all. I may, out of moral or religious scruples, intend not to satisfy a desire, however urgent. Similarly, while it is natural to associate long-term desires with planning, deliberation, and so again with intention, this reference to intention is neither sufficient nor necessary to distinguish the long-term from the short-term desire. I may, for example, have a long-term desire one day to redeem my wasted life by a noble gesture; and yet self-knowledge might at the same time remind me of the impossibility of achieving this, and so (by a well-known law) remove the possibility of intending it.

7. Nevertheless, the introduction of the concept of intention makes it possible to make a first serious attack on the primitive notion of freedom from which I began. Among all the many desires that circulate within me, there are some which correspond to intentions and some which do not. The first carry a peculiar personal endorsement, the nature of which it is part of our business to discern. A political order which obstructs only those desires which a man has no intention to fulfil clearly removes less of his freedom than one which obstructs his intentions while leaving other desires to fulfil themselves at will. Indeed, it is hard to see how the agent *himself* can see the first state as interfering in his freedom in any way whatever. (Here we see the beginning of a complication, long familiar to Marxists and their forebears: that between the first and third person view of freedom. Are we aiming at a state in which people cannot *feel* the constraint on their freedom, or a state in which the constraint is not there? Is it more desirable to be really free although perpetually deluded into thinking oneself in bondage, or really in bondage and deluded into thinking oneself free? To put it in Leibnizian terms: would it matter if freedom were no more than a 'well-founded phenomenon'? I return to this question below.)

Given such considerations, it seems odd to think that the concept of desire will be sufficient alone to generate an idea of political freedom.

8. A second difficulty for our original definition derives from the fact that we can distinguish desires, not merely in terms of their motivational character, but in terms of their satisfaction. It is a necessary truth that desire seeks its own satisfaction. But it is not a necessary truth that the state which constitutes that satisfaction be desired under the description that would be applied to it by someone who is in it. For example, I may desire to drink, but not to be in the state of having drunk, a bottle of wine. As my knowledge of myself and the world increases, this disparity between my desires to have and my desires to hold becomes steadily greater.

The disparity to which I refer is no easy matter to understand. It has at least the following aspects, or 'moments'. (The Hegelian term suggests itself, since in an important sense each stands to the next as anticipation and as necessary condition, while the full complexity of the tendency which they exhibit can be understood only from the final, 'realized' stage.)

(a) I may desire to have something and find that I desire not to keep it when obtained, an experience from which I may or may not learn. (Learning here involves acquiring practical knowledge, specifically, that disposition of character known as temperance.)

(b) I may desire to have something and find that the satisfaction of that desire leaves me restless and unhappy. Here we see the divergence between the idea of the satisfaction of a desire and that of the satisfaction of the person who experiences it.

(c) I may desire to have something which I discover to be undesirable, not just in the sense of wanting to be rid of it, but in the sense of ascribing to it a negative value. By an almost inevitable transition, the idea of value has entered my reflections on the object of desire. It is difficult to see how this long-term view of things, which involves comparison between past desire and present satisfaction, could long forbear the thought that some states of being are more worthwhile than others.

(d) I may desire something while *at the same time* realizing that it leads to my personal dissatisfaction, and thinking it to be undesirable. I may again learn to overcome such desires, and the disposition involved in this is wisdom.

Reflecting on such features we may notice the following: first, self-consciousness has a central role in the make-up of the desire to *hold* what I have obtained. Secondly, the concept of value is inseparable from some of the thoughts upon which such a desire depends. Thirdly, there is the beginnings of a distinction, made from the agent's point of view, between satisfaction of desire and satisfaction of self. I cannot argue the point here, but it seems to me that these three phenomena come and go together.

9. The distinction between desire and intention (see section 6) is integral to the notion of a self-conscious being. And it is the freedom of the self-conscious being that concerns us, since only such a being is a *zōon politikon*. Drawing on the conclusions implicit in the last section, we find ourselves obliged to consider how we would describe the freedom of a being who has, not only desires and intentions, but also a conception of his own satisfaction, and a conception of the desirable (of the value of the object of desire). It then becomes increasingly difficult to confine ourselves within a definition that refers freedom to the satisfaction of desire alone. Consider the following two political arrangements:

In the first human beings are given every opportunity to satisfy each desire as it arises, whatever its profundity, and whatever the state that results from it. Yet the members of the community live in such circumstances that none of their desires leads to personal satisfaction or to a sense of the value of holding what they need struggle so little to have (cf. Huxley's *Brave New World*).

In the second many desires are impossible to fulfil. But all those fields in which the expression and development of human energy is permitted involve desires for things considered desirable by those who are motivated by them, and which bring the satisfaction of the person in addition to the satisfaction of desire.

If you said that the first of these is a state of political freedom, the second a state of enslavement, then you would find it impossible to say why men should value freedom and not servitude, and your political philosophy (if you are a liberal) would be at an end. But of course there is something absurd about calling the first state described above a state of freedom, since it is one in which all true decision-making is eroded. There is no room now for deliberation, and a man might as well give himself up to the vagaries of every impulse. Intentions wither, and so too does the sense of oneself as an agent.

10. That last idea is one that I should like to try to clarify. For we now find ourselves at the point where the true challenge to liberalism must be offered, and the idea of agency is integral to that challenge. All kinds of beings have desires and satisfactions, but not all of them have intentions or values or self-consciousness. Yet our sense of ourselves as agents is intimately connected with those three features. How, then, can we specify the conditions of our freedom and not take them into consideration? So our final amendment to the first idea of freedom will have to read like this: political freedom consists in the absence of obstacles to those desires which are profound, long term, satisfying to the self, consonant with personal values and able to issue in consistent intentional activity, together with any 'lesser' desires which can be shown not to conflict with them. Some such view was once expressed by D. H. Lawrence:

> All that matters is that men and women should do what they really want to do. Though here [i.e. in questions of sex and marriage] we must remember that man has a double set of desires, the shallow and the profound, the personal, superficial, temporary desires, and the inner, impersonal, great desires that are fulfilled in long periods of time. The desires of the moment are easy to recognize, but the others, the deeper ones, are difficult. It is the business of our chief thinkers to tell us of our deeper desires, not to keep shrilling our little desires into our ears (A propos *of Lady Chatterly's Lover* (London, 1931), 52–53).

It is natural that this kind of challenge to the original liberal position should be raised by the problem of sexual relations, and I shall mention the problem again. But I should like to remove from Lawrence's remark the element of atavism: the distinction we are pursuing is not that between the personal and the impersonal. On the contrary: if we represent it in that way then we shall lose what I shall argue to be essential to any account of political values—the first person viewpoint of the agent. The distinctions towards which I have gestured indicate that some desires belong more deeply to the agent than others; but it is those that belong, and not those which pass him by, that are significant. Those—the profound, long term, self-satisfying, and so on—I shall call collectively the 'primary' desires of the agent. It is the constraints on primary desires that will hurt, and which the agent will seek to overthrow; and it is in terms of such desires that the true 'harm' of a self-conscious being should be defined.

But now we have a far deeper question than that of the acceptability of the definition of freedom. Suppose we accept it, or some modified version of it. It would still seem impossible really to understand the conditions of political freedom if we do not also understand the conditions which generate or permit the formation of primary desires. It could be (for all that Mill and his progeny have said) that the uninstructed political agent, acting out of liberal impulses, and armed with some 'experiment in living' which he seeks to protect from the opprobrium of the multitude, will, in furthering the cause of liberty, bring about the conditions which make primary desires impossible. It could be, as Bradley once argued, that the ethic of tolerance voids the world of all sense of a distinction between what is desirable and what is not. It could also be that, from a third-person point of view, liberal society is, as some Marxists say it is, simply a congeries of fetishistic impulse, allowing satisfaction to every desire only because every desire is an artificial product of its own remorseless negation of true human nature.

11. Both those speculations are intemperate, and as much in need of philosophical support as the practices which they disfavour. But whichever way we now turn, it is clear that we can no longer avoid the question of 'true human nature'. In particular, we must say something about its relation to the three features of 'primary' desires that I emphasized: self-consciousness, self-satisfaction, and the sense of the desirable. In due course, I shall consider one small part of the vast issue concerning the real distinction (if there is one) between beast and man. I shall reflect on a central feature of self-consciousness, which I shall call the 'sense of my identity through time', and it is worth anticipating later discussion by indicating already why I should single out such a feature for consideration.

The sense of identity through time is necessary for the formation of long-term desires: I must believe that I shall exist in the future if such desires are to be possible. It is also necessary for the formation of intentions, as is obvious. It is required for the existence of profound desires, since such desires arise out of, and also go to constitute, the image of myself as having

13

a 'life' in which I may be fulfilled or frustrated. It is—if Kant's argument in the 'Transcendental Deduction' has force—a necessary ingredient in self-consciousness as such. Finally, it is integral to our idea of the desirable, since we must see the desirable as that which we shall be pleased to keep, and not just as that which we wish to obtain; such a thought is impossible wihout the sense of identity through time.

Notice that I have spoken of a 'sense'. In fact the logical relations to which I have referred argue only that certain states of mind involved in agency require the *belief* in my continuity through time. Nevertheless, I do not think that it is a mere phenomenological luxury to describe this belief as a kind of 'sense'. This is not merely because of the ineliminable indexical component in the belief. It is also because the belief so transforms my motivation as to be active in all that I perceive, suffer and do. It would be impossible to remove it and to think that anything of my experience would remain unaltered. In this respect, if in no other, Kant was surely right to speak of time as the 'form' of inner sense.

12. The mention of Kant leads me to consider a deep metaphysical stratagem which is available to the liberal, and which we must explore as a preliminary to considering the sense of identity through time. This stratagem was adopted by Kant in giving expression to the particular political liberalism which appealed to him, and versions of it reappear in modern liberal writings—notably in the work of Rawls.

I have introduced a distinction between desire and intention, together with certain conceptions that have some intimate connection with the concept of the self. Kant, in his moral philosophy, and in that small part of his philosophy which could be described as political, fastened on to those intuitive conceptions, and the distinction associated with them, and distilled from them, as it were, a metaphysical essence. The picture is this: when a man is motivated by the desire to do something, we often find it plausible to say that he is acted on by the desire, as though the desire were some force of which he is the (perhaps entirely passive) victim. It is most plausible to say this in the case of those desires which are intense, urgent, and have some animal component (by which I mean a component which it would make sense to attribute to a creature without self-consciousness). We might even speak of a man being *overcome* by a desire; this expression suggests that the agency of a man lies elsewhere than in his desires, since we can describe his desires as though they were external forces which he may fail to combat.

By contrast it never makes sense to say that a man is overcome by an intention, or even that intentions act on or through him, in the manner of desires. On the contrary, he *himself* acts through his intentions. They are the manifestation of his agency, and when, for example, someone intends to do what he desires not to do, or desires to do what he does not intend, we do not think of him as a kind of battlefield, in which warring forces gather—intention on the one side, and desire on the other. We think of *him* as standing in opposition to his desires. In other words, we regard the person (or self) as governed by a principle of agency which is intrinsic to it, and not reducible to any 'motivating force'.

If we take those intuitive observations and exaggerate them to the point of near implausibility, and if we combine our exaggeration with the intuition that a central feature of self-consciousness is the sense of identity through time, then we arrive at the following picture. The self is a temporally extended autonomous agent, acting on the world through intention (or 'will'). This will aims at the satisfaction, not of desire, but of the self, and its guiding principle is value. But, being autonomous—that is, motivated by nothing outside itself—it must itself be the originator of that principle. The will creates, out of its sovereign autonomy, the values which direct it. By contrast desires act on the self externally, and belong to another part, what Kant called the 'pathological' part, of man. They neither create values nor enact them. They are forces which constrain the will much as the will is constrained by any other aspect of nature.

From this picture we now derive a new sophisticated version of the liberal theory. Freedom is freedom not of desire but of the will. Political freedom consists in the absence of constraint upon our 'autonomy'. A society is free to the extent that it is possible for an individual to be self-commanded in the peculiar manner of the rational agent. If we combine this with the view of Kant, that the autonomous will envisages and (where possible) creates that Kingdom of Ends in which all wills act in harmony, it follows that nothing further need be said about the constraints which will maximize political freedom.

13. Kant claimed that the autonomous self will bind itself by a universal law. This law claims to be, and, in the event of full autonomy, actually is, universally valid, since it is recommended on the basis of reason alone. Take away that idea of objectivity and the result is not far from the existentialist concept of authenticity: I exist as an agent to the extent that I determine my actions; self-determination requires me to free myself from the arbitrary sway of all laws and impulses that are not self-imposed. But what I will for myself is unique to me. It is indeed my individuality (the point of view which is uniquely mine), so that I cannot be bound by a universal law without ceasing to be myself.

This gives rise to the most metaphysical of all expressions of the liberal theory of freedom. But since the background metaphysics is founded in a real sense that human freedom is different in kind from the freedom of an animal, it is ultimately of greater philosophical interest than the theories offered by Mill. It provides, I think, the master-thought of many recent liberal philosophies.

I have day-to-day desires and predilections, and these demand satisfaction. But they have value to me only if I see them as arising in harmony
with what I 'choose to be'. What I choose to be is a thing with a 'life' of its
own, and with a 'style' of life that realizes its autonomy. True political
freedom is, primarily, the freedom for existential choice, and only second-
arily the freedom to satisfy desire. (If you like, it is freedom to satisfy those
desires which express the autonomy of the agent.) It is essential to Rawls'
theory of justice, for example, that his 'model-conception' of the individual
in the original position is that of a Kantian moral agent. But Rawls'
Kantian agent is concerned to protect his capacity for 'authentic' choice,
and recognizes the possibility that his values may in the end be divergent
from those of the community that surrounds him.

The following picture may now emerge as a possible liberal doctrine: I
have desires which, however urgent, may go unfulfilled without any sense
of injury to myself, ranging from the desire for a beer while driving across
a lonely moor, to the urgent desire to make love to someone who rejects
me. I have other desires which are so deeply connected with my sense of
myself that I must inevitably regard their violation as a violation of right.
It is a violation of right because it is a trespass upon my existence. Consider
an interdiction which prevents, for no reason connected with the interest
of the parties, marriage between two people who wish to marry. Or an
interdiction which prevents me, for no reason connected with my interest,
from pursuing the career which I have chosen, and for which I am suited,
and for which I have prepared myself. Or the edict which arbitrarily
transports me from my homeland to some inhospitable place, and scatters
my children abroad. The indignities which are genuinely resented in those
countries described as totalitarian seem to have this character, of radical
and arbitrary interference with a man's desire to be what he really is. The
doctrine might then go on to define political freedom as the political ability
to satisfy that desire.

14. But without the metaphysical doctrine of the autonomous, self-creating
and self-commanding will, all this can only be a metaphor and, if we are
persuaded by it, this must be because we guess at some way of rewriting the
doctrine that will remove its well-known and intolerable conclusion—the
commitment to a transcendental self that acts in a world to which it is
metaphysically impeded from belonging. The best way to re-write the
doctrine is in terms of the distinction among desires that I earlier referred
to. In the course of that re-writing we will find that the notion of political
freedom leads us to look with some favour upon customary constraint.

First let us reject, what I think modern philosophers have given us many
good reasons to reject, the Kantian idea that the will can be wholly
separated from desire and assigned to a different subject from the subject
of desire. My desires are as much *mine* as are my intentions, and while it is

true that I can sometimes speak of them as though they were forces *acting* on me, this is possible only sometimes and for special reasons. If I thought of *all* my desires in that way then I should be incapable of deliberation, and my capacity to form intentions would vanish.

If we reject the absolute Kantian view of the distinction between desire and intention then we reject much. In particular, we reject the possibility of forming in any coherent way the existentialist doctrine of man as self-created. But we can still reconstruct another distinction that might provide the grounds for a definition of freedom. This is the distinction (now a matter of degree) between desires which belong to the self and desires which do not.

15. This reconstruction will depend on our being clear about the methodological significance of the first person case. Much of the attraction of liberalism lies in the fact that it intends to describe a state of political freedom which can be seen to be such by the individual agent. Anti-liberal theories sometimes begin from a doctrine of the 'real interests' of the subject, while adopting a wholly third-personal stance towards the social world—the stance not of participant but of observer. It may then seem quite arbitrary whether the 'real interests' of the subject should also be recognized by him as desirable. A doctrine of political freedom which said that a state is free provided men could pursue only their real interests within it, if combined with a theory of human nature which makes a man's 'real interests' things which he does not, or perhaps even cannot, value, is clearly not a doctrine of freedom. Suppose it were argued that his own death is always the 'real interest' of a Jew (as it is now sometimes argued that death is the 'real interest' of the deformed foetus); or suppose it were argued that the renunciation of all rights of ownership, all claims of personal and local allegiance, all self-aggrandizement and personal pride, were the 'real interest' of every man. Both those doctrines have been used to perpetuate tyranny, and the second is often preached in England. Their repellent aspect derives from the fact that the real interest of the victim is described in such a way that, from his own point of view, he cannot (in normal circumstances) desire it.

It might be thought that what is wrong with that tyrannical account of 'freedom' is the assertion that political freedom should make possible *only* the pursuit of real interests. But it seems to me that, if you have the conception of a real interest, you cannot think that you give people true freedom by allowing equal expression to those desires which do, and those which do not satisfy it, unless you also think that there could not possibly be a conflict between the two kinds of desire. The real interest of something is that which is in accordance with its nature, and which fulfils it according to that nature. (It is a 'need'.) A thing which deviates from its real interest deviates from its nature and hence from itself. And it would be impossible to see why we should value freedom if it meant *simply* the indefinite licence to diverge from our nature.

The real problem is not with the idea of a 'real interest', but with the conception of human nature with which it was conjoined. It is an essential feature of human nature that we have a first person perspective on our actions. It is part of our 'real interest' that we should be able to do that which, from our own point of view, we can see to be desirable. The idea that, if you oppose liberalism, you must do so in the name of tyranny, seems to me almost always to be founded on the mistaken view that liberalism alone can give a first-person perspective on political freedom—that is, that liberalism alone can show why the *agent* should desire to be free.

16. At the heart of our first person perspective on the world there is, I have suggested, a peculiar sense of our continuity through time. This sense is most vividly manifest in our ability to have long-term desires and ambitions for ourselves, and to separate in our deliberations those desires which, when gratified, gratify only themselves, from those desires which contribute to our fulfilment. It is in terms of this sense of our continuity through time that the Kantian doctrine of autonomy can be reconstructed, and with it the thought that underlies the original definition of freedom. But we find that, as this reconstruction proceeds, the liberal ideal of freedom ceases to be persuasive. For it seeks to derive the constraints that are licensed by freedom from the idea of the autonomous agent, without recognizing that there must be constraints which make the autonomous agent possible. These constraints must be understood independently. It seems to me that there are such constraints. There are disciplines which foster the first-person view of action, together with the primary desires which constitute our true autonomy. These are not things which we *choose* from a state of autonomy, but things which generate our autonomy precisely because they are not chosen. In normal circumstances custom is one of them.

I have supposed that our reconstruction of the Kantion autonomy will be in terms of primary desires. It is those which we can think of as being definitive of what we are, rather than of what happens to us. To reach the state from which the desirability of freedom can be perceived, a being must acquire primary desires. It is often said that the world of the autonomous being (the being with primary desires) is a different world from the world of the animal. And yet the transition from animal to free being does not involve any change in the world, only a change in intentionality (in how the world is seen). This change comes about when a being begins to see his extension in time from the present to the final moment and to envisage what it would be like then to *have* been the person that he now is. All the primary desires that I mentioned earlier are bound up with the pressure to see ourselves in that way. Our autonomous being is therefore constrained by whatever is necessary to bring about such a picture of one's life.

The first thing that is necessary is the capacity to envisage the future, and to envisage oneself as part of that future. The 'free' being must also contemplate his place in the future in such a way as to incorporate it into present deliberations, both under the aspect of value and under that of desire. There are many ways in which this might be done, and I cannot see that we can give an *a priori* argument for the superiority of one way over another. But I should like to emphasize the fact that all the obvious ways in which this moral education is acquired involve reference precisely to the kind of constraint that custom introduces into our lives. The agent who surveys the future in the light of present values must have some sense that his mode of action towards the world in the future, and the world itself, will still be comprehensible to him. If it were the case that custom were mere repetition, blindly and mechanically performed, then it would of course be absurd to suggest that custom could play a part in developing that sense. But custom is an intentional activity; a customary act contains within itself the reason for its performance; it looks backwards to how things have been and forwards to how things will be, while representing the present as consonant with past and future. It is against the background of custom that primary desires acquire their force and vitality.

18. As I say, I can give no conclusive *a priori* argument in favour of that position. But I believe that it suffices to shift the onus of proof. The habitual liberal assumption is that the onus lies always on the other side: that the liberal defence of freedom is sufficiently complete in itself to challenge all-comers to refute it. On the contrary, I have argued that the liberal conception of freedom *presupposes* an idea of autonomy. And it is simply a natural assumption to make, that an autonomous being does not leap into existence like Athena from the head of Zeus. On the contrary, he may be the product of an elaborate education which already contains and imposes the constraints which the liberal wished to use his concept of freedom to test. In other words the liberal definition of political freedom presupposes a theory of human nature, one consequence of which may be that constraint on human conduct can be justified without referring to that definition. The concept of freedom cannot, then, be the single master concept in political thought, nor the aim of freedom the single constituent of political practice.

But let me add a few points which will shift the onus further, by removing what I take to be the prevailing prejudices against custom. These prejudices seem generally to exemplify three things: a confusion between custom and habit, a failure to understand tradition and its place in human conduct, and an inaccurate perception of the nature of social institutions.

19. *The confusion between custom and habit.* A habit is an activity that is repeated, but which embodies within itself no reason for its repetition that is accessible to the agent. It is something one does without knowing why. (Of course it may be that there are reasons for acquiring habits, and it may also be true that without habits the development of primary desires is impeded.) If habit seems like a form of bondage it is because its value is usually apparent only from the third person point of view. Thus, in the theory of evolution, or functionalist theories of social behaviour, the habits of animals and people are shown to be useful to them, even when they connote no gratification, or none beyond that involved in instinct, or appetite. Even though customs are not themselves chosen, to act out of custom is to act intentionally, and in such a way as to create a link between oneself and others. The customary action is the one for which the answer to the question 'Why are you doing that?' is 'It is what is done'. In that answer many things are embodied: the thought of a community of rational agents who act alike; the thought that their acting alike is reasonable; an indifference to time, and a consequent sense of what it would be like to act likewise at any other time. In this way customary activity effects two important results in the consciousness of the rational being. It reassures him of the existence of a public world, in which the validity of certain forms of action is recognized or at least recognizable. And it enables him to project his activities forward into the future, by laying hold of the continuity through which to experience that future as safe. (Consider here the customs of common courtesy.) It is hardly surprising that there is a peculiar pleasure in the customary act, or that people are genuinely attached to customs. One can regret a habit, and try unsuccessfully to break with it. But one cannot try to break with a custom unless one is being *forced* to comply.

Now there are people who imagine that custom has an inevitable 'despotic' power—people like Mill, or the Shelley of *The Revolt of Islam*. But is it not more plausible to suppose that a sense of the public validity of action, and a sense of the safety of the future (of the future as a place where one exists still knowing what to do) are normal preconditions for the development of primary desires? If so, then custom can be seen as a normal step on the way to autonomy.

Custom is often associated (notably, of course, by Yeats) with ceremony. This is perhaps for the following reason. Ceremony takes a particular occasion of personal significance—a birthday, a feast day, a marriage, a death—and represents it as an instance of a universal. The ceremony contains a significance that transcends the present moment, and an intimation of values that are shared. But this value in ceremony is a value for the participant: it consists in the temporary saturation of his first person perspective with a sense of the permanence of the social world. That is a very special case of custom providing the facilities for our primary desires.

It is surely no accident that these desires (in particular, those involving erotic love) require ceremonial enactment.

20. *The misconception of tradition.* Tradition provides one of the ways in which men acquire the sense of their continuity. Custom is the simplest case of tradition, but tradition is habitually misrepresented by liberal thinkers, probably on account of the mistaken argument that to belong to a tradition is to be unthinkingly subservient to the authority of the past. This view neglects the role of consciousness in the exercise of traditional forms of behaviour. Consider marriage. The reason for marrying lies in the past: not just the past relations of the couple involved, but the past history of sexual union. This is the way in which the bond between the sexes has been cemented; it is familiar, accepted, and associated with settled expectations. It enables the participants to envisage what they are doing in becoming attached to each other. By enacting this tradition the agent sees a greater significance in his act than the desire that propelled him towards it. His future becomes present to him, and he knows himself as part of that future. In this way the marriage bond clarifies the agent's responsibility towards the world. There is a *prima facie* case for thinking that the existence of such traditions and the enormous constraints implicit in them is precisely what is required for the full development and exercise of primary desires.

It is of the essence of a tradition that it is alive, that it grows, develops and declines, in obedience to the inner determination of its nature. A tradition exploits the freedom of its participants: they grow into it, but adapt it through their participation. A model for this kind of development is provided by the tradition of common law, which is neither a habit, nor merely a custom, and still less a body of rules. It is a developing way of seeing the social world, and redefines the place of the individual in that world by responding to and influencing his own self-image.

21. *The inaccurate perception of social institutions.* If we consider that, because men are free by nature, their freedom does not need to be acquired, then not only do we commit an evident logical fallacy; we naturally begin to think of institutions in a single, highly distorted way. They become not the precondition but the outcome of human freedom. (Or, it they are not the outcome of freedom, they are then dismissed as local tyrannies.) It is characteristic of liberal thought to see all institutions on the model of what lawyers call 'voluntary associations'—even the institutions which constitute the state. (Hence the connection of liberal ideas of freedom with the politics of the 'social contract' and 'tacit consent'.) But the legal reality of most serious institutions cannot be accommodated by the idea of a voluntary association, as has been recognized since Roman times. In a similar way the moral reality of those institutions which are involved in the formation of the autonomous being cannot be considered as derived from

autonomous choice. An institution which forms the character of the autonomous being must also have a soul or character of its own. Consider the university: the institution provides us with the reasons we have for remaining in it. We could hardly have understood those reasons had the institution not arisen (in the long and mysterious way in which such institutions arise). There is a deep question of political philosophy as to how such non-contractual associations can be considered legitimate. But they exist, and are a natural offshoot of the requirement of formative experiences in the history of the autonomous agent. These facts are evident to reflection.

All institutions require custom if they are to endure. Were custom to be constantly broken down, then it is reasonable to suppose that no non-contractual institution could even be *formed*. The state is such an institution. If we concede that *any* political constraint is required for the creation of an autonomous being, then the state is necessary. So custom is necessary too.

22. I have given a few, partly empirical, partly *a priori*, reasons for thinking that custom and its associated forms of conduct are necessary for the formation of the 'primary' desires which form the basis of our autonomy. It is only such desires that political freedom should be concerned to foster, since it is only then that freedom can be considered to be a value. Custom is not, then, the enemy of freedom, but its necessary precondition. The business of government is not the generation of abstract civil liberty, but the founding of the institutions which make liberty possible. Without a background of customary usage the activity of government would be impossible.

Of course a sophisticated liberal, armed with a philosophical theory of human nature, might very well accept what I have said. But the theory of human nature is certainly not there in Mill. Had it been there then it may have awoken him to the fact that freedom is not the only political value. If we look back on the liberal attack on custom we can see a reason why it avoided the theoretical commitment which would have given it cogency. In attacking custom the liberal was attacking the freedom of the majority, by tearing down the institutions through which their self-identity is formed. If people react now to the self-assertiveness—indeed the self-righteousness —of *On Liberty*, it is partly because they feel the aggression that underlies Mill's simplification of the human world. But could a liberal of Mill's persuasion really tolerate the political void which the acceptance of his doctrine generates? I doubt it, for, just as his idea of freedom is parasitic on deeper assumptions about human nature that he prefers not to explore, so is his life-style parasitic on a social order which he fails (such is the self-involvement of his nature) to support or condone.

Freedom as a Skill

K. R. MINOGUE

I

The *word* 'freedom' leads a double life. As a rallying cry in the mouths of politicians and publicists, it features in speech acts which inspire men to brave endeavours. Freedom or death are the proffered alternatives, and they are generally linked with fatiguing dispositions such as vigilance. As a philosophical *concept*, on the other hand, freedom is a territory in which battles are fought about such issues as positivity and negativity, virtue, determinism and the character of the will. There is remarkably little connection between these two lives. Philosophers do not seem to take much interest in courage, and politicians do not tarry to specify whether it is negative or positive liberty they are talking about.

My aim in the argument that follows is to sketch a view of freedom which covers the preoccupations both of philosophers and of politicians. I propose to do this by beginning with one of the most important roles played by the idea of freedom: namely, that of self-definition. We in Britain, like the peoples of most European countries, believe that we live in a condition of freedom, and we admire this condition so much that we have attempted to export it to the peoples of those countries whom we formerly ruled as colonies. This aspect of our export trade has had about the same measure of success as most other British exports in the period after 1945. We have boxed up constitutional materials—freedom kits— and shipped them off to our ex-colonies, only to find that this equipment has often rapidly rusted, and been replaced by unfree, foreign models. In this field there is much to be gained, I believe, from making a brutal simplicity our starting point: and the brutal simplicity from which I propose to start is the assertion that we know how to be free, and that other people do not. We have, in other words, a skill they do not have. This explains my title, but it requires a little more elucidation before we can begin.

To say that we live in a free society can be glossed in many ways, but what I mean by it is that we sustain a life of public discussion—in Parliament, 'pubs and the press—which very largely determines how the state is governed. The contrast at the other end of the scale would be the kind of oriental despotism in which no one could participate in public life, for there was none, and in which all decisions were taken by the despot. The Chinese are a useful example of people who have always been governed in this way, because they are evidently a great civilization, and all manner of subtle discriminations have come into existence there which owe nothing to what we call freedom. I mention this point because I would like to treat the condition freedom simply as one condition of living among others. It happens to be the one that we prefer, but it would be absurd to set it up as the one true way in which all human beings should live. The societies called totalitarian are evidently not free in my sense, and the complexities of current politics may be accommodated here by observing that the Czechs in 1968, and perhaps—perhaps—the Poles in 1980—were trying to bring to birth some of the conditions of freedom under difficult circumstances. In the modern world at least, most people think that they want freedom, and they may fail either because of brutal intervention from outside, or perhaps—as I shall suggest—because they simply lack the skill to sustain a free life. As in all political matters, luck also plays a part.

As against my view, however, it is often suggested by politicians, and sometimes by philosophers, that all human beings seek freedom as naturally as they breathe, and hence that only external betrayal and oppression prevents the entire human race from enjoying this condition we admire so much. It is this assertion we may take as our starting point.

II

We begin, then, from a situation slightly less desperate than that of Jean Jacques Rousseau who thought that *everyone* was in chains. We start by assuming merely that *most* people are in chains. Indeed, given my modest ambitions, we ought to dispense entirely with foolish Western rhetoric about chains, and observe simply that most people in the world do not live in a condition of freedom. We thus leave open the question of whether this results from choice, or merely from the misfortune of succumbing to oppressive rulers. The problem we face is: what sense can we give to the view that all men love freedom?

Part of the answer to this question can generate a variety of familiar paradoxes. It consists in observing that freedom is like money: we delight in spending it. We contract marriages, enter into contracts, pledge our service, get jobs and make arrangements. Our favourite use of freedom, it would seem, is to get rid of it. Seen in these terms, freedom must be an instrumental virtue. It provides us with the opportunity to achieve the things we really care about. But if so, we might imagine a situation in which some expert, who knew perfectly what we needed, might well dispose of our lives much more satisfactorily than we could do ourselves, since we often suffer disappointment because the obligations we contract provide us with less satisfaction than we expected. In the case of children, there actually *is* such an expert, who is called a parent. But then, we do not think of children as free until they attain adult status. And then we think that the freedom adults enjoy is valuable, not simply as an instrument of pursuing satisfactions, but rather as intrinsically valuable, because it allows them to exercise free choice. For such is the way we construe a human being.

If that is the answer to our question, it is obvious that many human beings do not, in fact, value freedom. Many of them prefer a life of service, in which their lives are fairly closely circumscribed within such institutions as families, firms, churches and unions. Many of them have no serious interest in public affairs; often, indeed, they are not interested even in the running of the institution to which they belong. This is a truth well known in the experience of all university men, though one often forgotten in the pronouncements upon freedom by academic inquirers. It is evident, in fact, that freedom is a taste, and a taste not much less circumscribed than that for oysters.

If we pay attention to these facts of human behaviour, then the proposition that all men seek freedom is simply false. How then can we account for the great popularity of this view? The answer is quite simple. It is not that all men love freedom, but that all men hate frustration. Prison walls are the very image of frustration because they take away from us our *power* to go where we choose. Slaves are at the beck and call of their masters, children often frustrated by the commands of their parents. Slaves, children and convicts make up, of course, a very heterogeneous list, and we must recognize (with Aristotle) thay they are unfree in very different ways. But it is these differences which tend to be obliterated when we convert the true statement that all men hate frustration into the false statement that all men love freedom.

Let us call this confusion by an appropriately abusive name: the infantile concept of freedom. The name is appropriate because it is peculiarly the character of children to resent a check to their desires *solely* on the ground that it frustrates them; and weeping at frustration is our image of infantile behaviour. Such a view is often assumed when we criticize political dictatorships not because of arbitrariness or the lack of a public life, but because a supposedly coherent thing called 'the will of the people' is being frustrated. Some of the best statements of this idea may be found in the literature of irony. Consider, for example, the reflections of Good Soldier Schweik on being consigned briefly to a lunatic asylum:

I'm blowed if I can make out why lunatics kick up such a fuss about being kept there. They can crawl about stark naked on the floor, or caterwaul like jackals, or rave and bite. If you was to do anything like that in the open street, it'd make people stare, but in the asylum it's just taken as a matter of course. Why the amount of liberty there is something that even the socialists never dreamed of . . . Everybody can say what he likes there, the first thing that comes into his head, just like in parliament . . . Nobody comes up to you and says: 'You mustn't do this, you mustn't do that, you ought to be ashamed of yourself, call yourself civilized?'[1]

Here then is the distilled essence of the infantile idea of freedom: a paradise where frustration does not exist. And yet, as David Hume reminds us, it is generally thought that madmen have no liberty. And the reason in the case of lunatics is that there is nobody home, no one who could be the agent or bearer of that freedom. Nothing but a succession of impulses, rather than a coherent organization of desires responding to the public world of reality.

The infantile concept of freedom is the underlying postulate of every misunderstanding of the condition of freedom available to us. It leads to the assumption that the beginning of freedom is the moment when the slaves rise up and overthrow the masters: what we may suitably call the Spartacus legend. It is in part built into the myth of liberation as it fascinates our time: the pervasive idea that a thousand spectral dominations warp our lives, and that the business of life is to unmask and destroy them. And in all cases, it rests upon the confusion of questions of freedom with questions of power.

For example, the way in which the child emerges from the unfreedom of childhood is not by overthrowing the domination of parents. It lies in the development of an adult character such that the unfreedoms necessarily attendant upon tutelage are no longer necessary. If our only image of unfreedom is that of slavery, then we shall detect only the one polarity of freedom and domination, and all dominations are, virtually by definition, bad. If we include at least also the image of the child, we shall at least make the small advance of recognizing the further polarity of freedom and tutelage: and the conditions for release from the unfreedom of tutelage are very different from the conditions for release from the condition of domination. As it happens, analytic remarks upon the polarity of freedom and tutelage gain support from the fact that they correspond pretty closely to the way in which, historically, the Greeks conceived *eleutheria* and the Romans conceived *libertas*.

These considerations are enough, I think, to allow us to analyse what is inadequate in the contemporary theory of liberation. Such a theory covers all the great modern revolutions (which have mostly failed), to colonial uprisings, and to the oppression from which many classes in modern society have imagined themselves to suffer. In all of these cases, the unfreedom includes at least two elements: there is, firstly, the external or

[1] *The Good Soldier Schweik*, trans. Paul Selva (Harmondsworth: Penguin, 1951), Ch. 3, 37–38.

physical fact that one set of people dominates and oppresses another class of people. And secondly, there is the initial internal fact that the positive habits and characteristics of the supposedly enslaved population are unsuitable for freedom. This lack of the skill of freedom has often been identified as a condition for which tutelage was appropriate: many people in nineteenth-century Russia, or India, thought that the people ought to be taught the usages of freedom. But here we need to be wary, for it is obviously a deficient and negative judgment to say of a whole people that they *lack* such and such a quality. The question is rather: what are in fact their positive characteristics? And, pursuing this line of thought, we shall be able to avoid the trap of imagining that whoever does not possess the skill of freedom is thereby deficient. It may be that there are some peoples who have attained some particular sort of skill at associating such that the question of freedom may not, and need not, arise, at least in anything like its inherited form. One might imagine, for example, that the Japanese are exponents of such a skill; and we might call it, merely for having the convenience of a name, community. It is a condition of more or less spontaneous social harmony, and if it has any reality at all, it will allow us to set up at least three conditions which contrast with freedom: namely, domination, tutelage and community. And to each of these conditions, of course, there corresponds a different sense of freedom.

III

This particular notion of 'community' is one in which the frustrations of the individual are construed entirely as a form of *inability* to achieve what is necessary for the good of the group, as that good is expressed in the dictates of custom. And for this reason, it is a diversion from this first stage of the argument, in which freedom is understood entirely in terms of a release from frustration. The issue of power and freedom has long been a matter of enormous fascination in our culture, and I suppose that the passage on lordship and bondage in Hegel's *Phenomenology of Mind* is one of the classical discussions of the theme. The argument of that discussion is the essential instability of the master–slave relation, which eventually issues in the achievement of freedom by transcendence of the terms in which the problem is posed. Given the profundity of his treatment, it is clear that Hegel is using the idea of freedom in a strictly limited sense when he argues (in the *Philosophy of History*) that in an oriental despotism, *one* only is free. The despot is free because he never suffers the frustration of prohibition: no gate is locked against him, no woman refuses him and all attend upon his every whim. He gives commands, but receives none himself. But then, as Plato pointed out in Book 9 of the *Republic*, a ruler of this kind is in fact the most unfortunate of men, since he is the slave of the passions. He lacks both friendship and rationality.

Dissolving the concepts of strong and weak, master and slave, has long been one of the great preoccupations of literature. What we generally find is a rather facile reversal, in which the weak turn out to be strong and vice versa. There are, indeed, treatments of the theme in which this polarity is transcended, but they are usually cases where the real focus of attention is elsewhere. A splendid example is P. G. Wodehouse's account of the relation between Jeeves and Bertie Wooster, in which the master–slave dialectic is marvellously transcended, though Wodehouse would no doubt have been very surprised to hear it.

Our problem, then, lies in the fact that the commonest understanding of freedom, in terms of the master–slave relation, is not really a treatment of freedom at all, but rather a treatment of power. And both in theory and in practice—as Plato and Hegel both show us in their different ways—there seems to be no way in which this axis can generate a stable freedom, or, more precisely, a stable balance of power which might plausibly be mistaken for freedom.

We must seek, then, for a way of understanding freedom which transcends this sterile polarity.

IV

What I have called the infantile view of freedom amounts to a demand that the world should conform to our desires. Such a view must lead to perpetual frustration. If this is our view of freedom, then we must not be surprised that after thousands of years of endeavour, mankind still feels unfree. How then is it possible, thinking along these lines, to achieve freedom? One obvious answer consists in turning the infantile view of freedom upside down: freedom consists in making our desires conform to the world. This is the basis of what might be called the Stoic view of freedom.[2] We become free by the exercise of our faculty of rational understanding, and thus understand whatever happens to us as necessary. As expressed brilliantly by Epictetus, it consists in the argument that freedom, like happiness, is a quality of the soul, and that whatever concerns the soul is within the power of our will. It follows that, by an appropriate disposition of the will we may achieve an inner freedom which arises from a cultivated indifference to the trials and tribulations of this world.

It will be evident that this Stoic version of freedom has very little to do with the condition of freedom which I set out to investigate. In a free society, men are free by virtue of the society in which they live, whereas Stoic freedom is in no way a social condition. It must arise, no doubt, from

[2] It is discussed as 'The retreat to the inner citadel' in Section iii of Isaiah Berlin's essay on 'Two Concepts of Liberty', in *Four Essays on Liberty* (Oxford: Oxford University Press, 1969), 135.

a tradition of thought (in which the Socrates of the *Gorgias* and the *Phaedo* played an important part) but it recommends a view of the world in which each individual's freedom depends upon himself. It is remarkably indifferent to social conditions. Epictetus believed that there was no real difference in freedom between a slave and his master; and Epictetus spoke from experience, since he had himself been a slave. The attitude is exemplified at its most remarkably extreme in a story which Celsus told in his controversy with Origen. Illustrating pagan fortitude, he said that Epictetus's master one day began tormenting Epictetus for amusement by twisting the slave's leg. Epictetus said—not warned, but said, which, as we say these days, has a different illocutionary force—'If you go on, you will break my leg'. The master persisted, and the leg was broken, and Epictetus only said, with unruffled serenity: 'Did I not tell you that you would break my leg?'[3]

It clearly takes great nobility of mind to sustain an unruffled demeanour such as is illustrated in this kind of hagiography. A similar attitude and nobility of mind is found in the self-reliance of dissident groups who have kept some freedom alive in modern totalitarian states. Here is a recourse which will always be available to some men in preserving freedom and humanity even in the midst of the most horrible barbarity. Perhaps, indeed, it is one of the seeds from which the condition of freedom must itself grow.[4] Nevertheless, for all its nobility, this is a doctrine primarily concerned with the axis of power and frustration, and it is thus the mirror image of the infantile view of freedom. It is, indeed, transcendence of a kind, but transcendence which simply leaves the problem of freedom behind, and transposes it into another key.

V

Our problem remains, then, that of getting beyond a treatment of freedom which remains trapped within the polarity of dominance. The way out, I suggest, lies in concentrating upon the distinction between a command, which frustrates a desire, and a rule or law, which may or may not do so. When, for example, a parent sees a child sliding down the domestic banisters and cries out: 'Stop that!' he or she issues a command. It frustrates an intention of the child and is felt as a restriction upon his freedom to exercise his own powers. But what happens if the parent proceeds to to turn this into a rule: 'Sliding down the banisters is forbidden under penalty of being fined a day's pocket money'?

[3] *The Teachings of Epictetus*, translated and introduced by T. W. Rolleston, (London: Walter Scott, n.d.), xxxvi.

[4] I shall later emphasize the ludic quality of the condition of freedom; and it is notable that the Stoics were great exponents of the game of freedom.

What has happened? On one view, the command has merely solidified, and now operates even when there is no commander in the hall ready to issue it. Every time Junior arrives at the head of the stairs and succumbs to an ilinxic[5] impulse, he is subject to the frustration of this command ossified into a rule.

And it would indeed be consistent with the infantile view of freedom to interpret the matter thus. There is, however, an alternative interpretation of what has happened. Our youth, discovering in himself this bent for ilinxic pleasures, accepts the rule in a law-abiding spirit, but sets himself to satisfy it in ways not covered by the rule. He begins to haunt adventure playgrounds, goes often on Big Dippers and Merry-go-rounds, and takes up skiing, rock-climbing and aviation when he grows up. In doing so he would, I think, be illustrating in a rather nice way, a point buried deep in the idea of the Stoic view of freedom: namely, that it has more to do with imagination and inventiveness than it has to do with reason.

I am arguing, then, that the practical form of the transcendence of the master–slave relation lies above all in the move from command to law. And in case this sounds unnecessarily abstract, let me point out that it corresponds to the historical development of European ideas of freedom. When Voltaire came to England in the 1720s and investigated what Continental writers have since recognized as the special Anglo-Saxon vocation for freedom, he was impressed above all by the ubiquity of law in England, by contrast with important areas where a Frenchman of low degree was at that time subject to the arbitrary caprice of king or aristocrat. Let us return, then, to the distinction between law and command.

A command may be distinguished by the fact that it is personal; that it is spatio-temporally specific, that it relates to known concrete circumstances, and that it may directly frustrate an impulse. There is a personal element to commands, and it is precisely that which makes them unusual and unsuitable ordering devices in the modern condition of freedom. Children and soldiers these days are those who typically experience commands, the one from tutelage, the other from contract of engagement and the necessities of vocation; but otherwise, commands are relatively little used, even in employee–employer relationships. The modern world works on spontaneity, and rules: the network of abstract understandings, of varying degrees of authority, through which decisions are mediated. To analyse the different kinds of rule, role and convention relevant here is impossible in a short time. I must, therefore, identify the central point I must make,

---

[5] *Ilinxic* is an adjective taken over from the French of Roger Caillois's work, *Les Jeux at les hommes* (Paris: Gallimard, 1958), 57, in which it describes his fourth class of types of games, which is where '*on joue a provoquer en soi, par un mouvement rapide, de rotation ou de chute, un état organique de confusion et de désarroi*'.

and hope that a few remarks will sustain its plausibility sufficiently to carry me through to the next stage of the argument.

The central point is that a command, strictly considered, is personal and detailed, while a law, at the other extreme, is impersonal and abstract. RSM Brittain,[6] for example, who had, reputedly, the loudest voice in the British Army, intervened directly in a specific moment of the lives of those he commanded. Similarly, custom in customary societies is a kind of rule whose mode of implementation is given detailed form by those who enforce it: parents, for example, arranging the marriages of their children. One must accommodate to custom, and obey commands; but one follows rules, and 'subscribes to'[7] laws. The movement in each case is towards the less detailed and more abstract. The notion of a rule, much discussed in modern philosophy, covers a great variety of cases, many of them fairly specifically geared to some collective end or purpose: the rules of a game, or a Church, or an enterprise, for example. A law may here be distinguished as a peculiarly broad kind of rule, authoritatively stated, and relevant to a collection of people who may well have nothing else in common than membership of the same state.

It is true, of course, that there are occasions when a rule may directly frustrate a desire, and this possibility often tends to be seen as the essence of a law. If this view is taken, then a law becomes a kind of solidified command. The temptation to take this view of the matter lies in the fact that it helps to solve the problem of authority, since a law is a rule commanded by a sovereign authority; and the most obvious way of finding a relation between a sovereign and a law is by way of taking the rule as commanded. There are points at which Hobbes comes close to this view, which was later to be elaborated by John Austin. Thus Hobbes writes:

> But as men, for the attaining of peace, and conservation of themselves thereby, have made an artificial man, which we call a commonwealth; so also have they made artificial chains, called *civil laws*, which they themselves, by mutual convenants, have fastened at one end, to the lips of that man, or assembly, to whom they have given the sovereign power; and at the other end to their own ears. These bonds, in their own nature but weak, may nevertheless be made to hold, by the danger, though not by the difficulty of breaking them.[8]

A law, however, while it may be an impediment to some desire or other that we entertain, is a standing and calculable impediment, and in that respect, rather like a fact of nature. It is thus a standing invitation to our

---

[6] See obituary and correspondence in *The Times*, January 1981.

[7] I borrow this form of words from the second essay in *On Human Conduct* by Michael Oakeshott (Oxford: Oxford University Press, 1975).

[8] *Leviathan*, II, Ch. 21, Michael Oakshott (ed.) (Oxford: Blackwell, n.d.), 138.

ingenuity to discover forms of satisfaction in places or circumstances not covered by the rule; and this kind of activity is entirely legitimate. A pure command, by contrast, incorporates us within the purpose of another will, and though each command, being couched in abstract language, may leave us free in various respects to choose the manner of our obedience, the kind of subordination involved in a direct command means that further commands may be issued so as to make us conform more closely to the will of the commander. I conclude that the command theory of law, which solves some problems in the field of jurisprudence, creates others nearly as serious.

The more the form of order we create in our social life approaches this law-governed condition (by contrast with forms of order in which we are subject to custom, command, and purposive rule) the freer we become to think unthinkabilities, to create new satisfactions of our desires, and in general to explore the potentialities of our human situation. A common way of putting this point is to say that we become subject to law rather than will. It is often further said that we are free only if these rules issue from some general or rational will in which the subject himself participates. This view no doubt points to important features of modern versions of free states. But it is a view which is difficult to develop without the temptation of falling back into the infantile concept of freedom, and concluding that laws ought not to frustrate the wills of those subject to them. Avoidance of this conclusion leads to the alternative fork by which it may be said that we can be 'forced to be free'. Here again, we approach questions so complex and wide-ranging that we are once more in danger of losing the thread of the argument, and the best I can do is to observe that whatever its deficiencies, Hobbes's remorselessly formal way of stating the matter saves us many problems.

For Hobbes is clear that any external impediment to the way a man chooses to use his own powers is a qualification of his freedom; and hence he argues, in a famous phrase, that liberty is the silence of the law. It is clear that he had a certain impatience with the idea of liberty, as being the obvious recourse of mischievous and ambitious men, for, as he says in the dedicatory letter to *Leviathan*, 'in a way beset with those that contend, on one side for too great liberty, and on the other side for too much authority, 'tis hard to pass between the points of both unwounded'. And when at the end of the book, Hobbes delivers a brief eulogy of his friend Sidney Godolphin, 'who hating no man, nor hated of any, was unfortunately slain in the beginning of the late civil war . . . by an undiscerned and an undiscerning hand', he attributes to him two interesting, juxtaposed qualities: 'a courage for the war, and a fear for the laws'. But it is clear from other remarks he makes that this 'fear for the laws' is, precisely, not a *fear* but a sentiment of obedience arising from honour. And when he is not concerned with the issue of the sovereign authority of laws, his remarks accord with the argument I am presenting. Consider what he says in Chapter 30:

> For the use of laws, which are but rules authorized, is not to bind the people from all voluntary actions; but to direct and keep them in such a motion, as not to hurt themselves by their own impetuous desires, rashness or indiscretion; as hedges are set, not to stop travellers, but to keep them in their way.'⁹

These remarks appear, incidentally, in a context where Hobbes is saying that sovereigns should restrict themselves to those few laws that are necessary for good order, which suggests a problem in our time on a scale such as Hobbes could barely have comprehended: is it the case that beyond a certain point, the sheer number of laws intended to promote freedom and order may come to destroy it altogether, rather as (it has been plausibly suggested) beyond a certain size in numbers, schools become unmanageable. Is there perhaps a science which might fix the critical quantity of law, showing us the point at which the fabric of freedom and order begins to break down? We have, it is true, so far lived happily enough within the framework of the immense number of laws of Britain which have piled up in the law books, and most of us go about our business, or did until recently, without any very evident sense of strain. But as the quantity of laws grows, and above all perhaps, as they change their character, new problems will arise; indeed, have arisen.

But again, we are in danger of losing our path. Let me simply observe that the self-defeating dialectic of dominance found in the master–slave relation is transcended when a cacophony of wills becomes an arrangement of laws; and that the exploration of the concept of freedom is inextricably bound up with the elucidation of the set of concepts I have so briefly alluded to in this section. Our next task must be to sketch out some of the concrete conditions of the actual emergence of this kind of legal sophistication.

VI

My argument is that the skill of freedom is the skill of constructing a social order out of laws which leave people free, in a significant sense, to make their own decisions. And before looking more closely at how we might specify this skill, I want to ask how it came into existence in the first place. Again, the subject is a huge one, and we can only focus it for our purposes if we put it this way: domination in all its forms—winning, commanding, having one's way, even tormenting and playing with people—is clearly

---

⁹ *Leviathan*, op. cit., 227.

a delightful pleasure for most people most of the time. How then, did human beings ever manage to transcend the axis of dominance and submission?

The first materials for an answer to this question must consist in the observation that freedom is evidently a good class of condition, one fundamentally enjoyed by the best people. It is in fact, of course, that feature of a human society which has always been the special charge of warriors. Freedom unmistakably begins in blood, and is first enjoyed by tough young men who stand shoulder to shoulder and are prepared to hack their way through the enemy without being too squeamish about blood. This is in fact what lies behind the rhetoric of courage, and it is worth putting it in such a dramatic way because we have long forgotten a world in which the aristocracy, and later soldiers, enjoyed a peculiar respect because, primarily, they were the ones who put their lives on the line whenever some rapacious collection of invading nomads appeared on the horizon. Inevitably, this respect (and its attendant benefits) made many of them arrogant, oppressive and intolerable. They ruled by right of conquest.

There are many possible outcomes of this basic situation, but in the West, the common outcome was that over many generations, conquest turned into custom (as it always must) and, especially, the set of more or less equal warriors who had to deal with the public business of an area evolved constitutional procedures in which ruling became essentially disconnected from inequality. Aristotle distinguishes a polis as one which is ruled, in turns, by people who are essentially equal to each other. In medieval Europe, the story is even more fascinating, and correspondingly complicated, and revolves around that age of chivalry whose obituary Burke wrote in 1790. Partly it is a story of greater numbers of people achieving the set of rights pioneered by such barons as those who brought King John to signing the Great Charter in 1215. And partly, it is a story typical of one of the great comedies of the human condition, in which those who begin by being superior in power attempt to translate that superiority into moral terms, and then become trapped by their own moral conceptions. European freedom rests very largely upon a sense of honour. This is by no means a ubiquitous sentiment—none of the sentiments upon which freedom depends are ubiquitous—but it has proved strong enough to dominate the public rhetoric of European countries. The convention of cowboy films by which the hero does not shoot the villain in the back appears in Hobbes as:

> That which gives to human actions the relish of justice, is a certain nobleness or gallantness of courage, rarely found, by which a man scorns to be beholden for the contentment of his life, to fraud, or breach of promise.[10]

[10] *Leviathan*, Ch. 15, op. cit., 97.

Hobbes also refers to:

a glory, or pride in appearing not to need to break [one's word]. This latter is a generosity too rarely found to be presumed on, especially in the pursuers of wealth, command, or sensual pleasure; which are the greatest part of mankind.[11]

The problem is how we may state this without simply invoking a virtue. There are various options available, and I shall opt for the simplest: what emerges from the primitive situation of conquest is a set of usages which depend upon life being construed as a kind of game. Mostly, no doubt, life is a matter of getting and spending, late and soon. We move from purpose to purpose seeking satisfactions. But in a wider context, the achievement of purposes is seen as being significantly qualified by the kinds of means we have used in attaining them. To win a game by cheating is not really to win the game, and to achieve our purposes by fraud, deception or breaking the rules brings, in some characters, a significant form of dissatisfaction in its own right. Or, to put the matter in another way, our actions are influenced by the fact that the manner of our actions reveals something about what we are: and questions of self-definition of this kind are far more complex and insistent for those who live in what I have called the condition of freedom than they are in societies where customary relations are merely dependent upon shame. The condition of freedom, then, begins to appear when the spirit of the warrior begins to turn into the ethos of the game. And in seeking for evidence for this view, I do not even think it entirely irrelevant to notice that the English, generally thought to be those in the modern world most adept at the practices of freedom, have also been among the most fertile inventors of games.

It follows from this that one presupposition of the condition of freedom is equality. The condition of freedom is always found in conjunction with social and political usages which emphasize equality, usually that between citizens. The classical Greeks and the Romans of the Republic detested prostration, or indeed any form of the idea that their rulers were, in any significant sense, different from themselves. Manners amongst us are saturated in small and subtle indications of equality even amidst the inevitable inequalities of economic, social and intellectual life. This equality has come down to us primarily in the religious form of a belief that all are equal in the sight of God, but in essence, it seems to me to be the kind of equality necessary to games players; for the more unequal the players, the less interesting the game.

It is evident that the point of a game is not to win (though the human passion for domination is such that everybody does indeed love to win) but to draw out remarkable performances from oneself. One always plays, as it

---

[11] *Leviathan*, Ch. 14, *op. cit.*, 12.

were, against oneself. And this is the characteristic way in which great performances are elicited in a free society, by contrast with the communal or domination structures by which they are elicited in other types of civilization. It will be noticed that one implication of my argument at this point is that the term 'competitive' is interestingly ambiguous in modern self-understanding. Its vulgar usage is a passion for domination, for doing the other man down, and in this sense it often features in contemporary attacks upon modern conceptions of freedom. It is from this usage that the contemporary practice of understanding an individualist to be a selfish and aggressive person has developed. But in terms of the argument I have advanced, 'competitive' may well refer to a propensity to regard problems as if they were elements in a game.

If I am right about the ludic character of the modern condition of freedom, then we have stumbled upon another of the paradoxes that infest this subject. For it will be obvious that freedom depends upon men for whom certain sorts of behaviour (shooting a man in the back, cheating on tax returns) are, in an important sense, unthinkable. The free man accepts a set of limitations upon the conduct of his life which are additional to the ordinary limitations of life, and which cannot, furthermore, be easily defended as being rational. Indeed, in the sense that they may often impede his attaining of his objects (in the crude sense of merely getting what he wants, rather than the way in which he wants to get what he wants), they would have to be classed as actually being irrational. Freedom thus resembles art in being one of the finer flowers of self-limitation.

It is, however, the very strength of these unthinkabilities that they make the condition of freedom essentially social and co-operative. The Greek city states used the phalanx to great effect, and its strength in warfare depended upon the fact that each citizen could concentrate his energies on one side in confidence that his fellow would be protecting the other side. Roman public life depended upon an ethic of *fides* by which oaths and agreements could be relied upon. It used to be said that an Englishman's word was his bond. Now we need not doubt that some Greeks were cowards and fled, and that some Romans were crooks, and that there were some Englishmen whom only a simpleton would have trusted. What matters is the dominance of an ethic of this kind, and an ethic which depended in large measure, not on fear of the sovereign or the gods, but upon some such internal considerations as honour. And given the prevalence of such an ethic (which was, of course, powerfully conveyed by the English public schools) then men in a condition of freedom will, and must, take the risk of relying upon one another. It is only when such an ethic begins to break down that men come to be tempted by the Stoic conception of freedom in which a man hitches his spirit not to the life going on around him, but rather to some shadowy rock he may find in his own soul. This is not to say that religion may not play a large part in sustaining the condition of freedom: it always has. But it is to say that freedom depends upon the possibility of taking the risk of depending upon one's fellow citizens.

What I am arguing here can best be grasped if I make it clear that I am rejecting the alternative view in which freedom is located in the indomitable scepticism and resilience found in such figures as Sir John Falstaff. Bernard Levin, for example, has very recently sung the praises of *The Good Soldier Schweik* from which I have earlier quoted, and I have no trouble in agreeing with his admiration for Jaroslav Hasek's splendid book. Schweik, it will be remembered, is a sceptical survivor who finds himself in many a fix from falling foul of authority. For forty years, says Levin, 'I have loved him, for the spirit of liberty that drives him on'.[12] And there is indeed something splendid about the ingenuity of Schweik's responses, the determination to think his own thoughts and see through to a certain reality in things, and above all in the way in which his spirit never succumbs to the constant pressure of domination in the world he experiences. But there is something desperate in this world which makes it merely the comic version of the Stoic sense of freedom we have earlier discussed. A similar kind of indomitability is expressed in the films of figures like Charlie Chaplin and Woody Allen. All of these people are rather desperate free spirits living in a world which has, they think, lost its freedom. When Falstaff says that the word honour, for which many a knight has got himself killed, is but a bit of breath, he is letting a little realism into the public rhetoric of the aristocratic world. But his freedom depends not upon himself, but merely upon the space that more courageous men are prepared to allow him.

What this reveals is that there is a high and a low version of freedom. The one is bound up with courage and honour, the other with scepticism and resilience. Western civilization has always found room for both conceptions of freedom, as Hegel's irritable remarks about psychological valetism testify. Perhaps the best we can do for a synthesis is to say that both of these conceptions, or modes of action, are necessary to what I have called the condition of freedom: the idealism of the one is saved from falling into priggishness and pomposity by the raillery of a low realism; while the realism of the Schweiks of this world is saved from total extinction by the freedom and justice that could only be sustained by a public rhetoric of honour.

VII

Like all skills, freedom depends upon the character and tastes of those

[12] *The Times*, 10 February 1981.

who practise it. Only a set of people with a taste for the pleasures of speed, for example, would have invented the various forms of racing. Just as some skills depend upon natural dexterities, so others depend upon natural psychological characteristics which, from another point of view, would be regarded as virtues. Skill in football depends upon courage in tackling, and and many skills require great qualities of endurance. Skills may thus be seen as growing in a soil of dispositions, tastes and virtues. What is the soil in which freedom can grow?

It follows from the argument that we have been presenting that a central component of freedom must be a taste for dealing with other people as equals. It is perhaps a little odd to construe this as being a matter of taste; and yet there can be little doubt that there are some people who take pleasure in the subordination of others; while others find it displeasing. Some people are stimulated by disagreement, others find it irritating. Some people take pleasure in the variety of dispositions cultivated among human beings, while others find human beings essentially irrational and unmanageable. These tastes, as I have described them, are evidently found in individual character, and to some extent, freedom does depend upon the predominance of one character rather than another. For, as Socrates remarks in the *Republic*, of what can constitutions be made? Only out of the the characters of the people who live in them. But what is no less important here is the public rhetoric to which this disposition gives rise: to an admiration for independence of mind and the courage to follow through one's own convictions. It is the combined strength of a public rhetoric and a predominance of character which constitutes the soil of freedom.

The second taste which is important in freedom is that for making one's own decisions. Aristotle defined man as a rational animal, and thought that making rational choices was the quintessence of a properly human life. In a Christian civilization, particularly, choosing is the expression of one's individual character. We purport to admire people who make up their own minds and 'think for themselves' and, idiotic as these familiar idioms may be if one takes them literally, they represent a powerful strand of moral opinion among us. On the other hand, to act is to be responsible, and to come to conclusions of which others disapprove is to suffer the weight of collective disapproval. It took some courage to say in Berlin in 1938 'Some of my best friends are Jews'. But even in relatively tolerant Anglo-Saxon countries, there are strong feelings of disapproval directed against those who hold views contrary to what others have tried to establish as an orthodoxy. Until very recently, the conclusions of such psychologists as Jensen and Eysenck on differential racial differences in performance at IQ tests provoked violence and intemperate abuse; and even in our own pretty liberal times, speakers in universities have been shouted down from the rostrum and occasionally subject to physical assault. These relatively trivial events give us some notion of what the religious passions of earlier centuries must have been like. I adduce these considerations in order to make a little more vivid the familiar proposition that freedom depends upon making up one's mind, and this is a taste which some people have and some people do not.

Hence the virtue on which the skill of freedom depends is generally thought to be that of courage. And this is, I think, a plausible view, since among us, the condition of *un*freedom is that one or other among the tendencies towards dominance of opinion or action should arrive at an ascendancy intimidating to those not in natural sympathy with it. Under such circumstances—and situations resembling these circumstances have arisen in universities in many countries within living memory—it is clearly upon the courage, above all, of the members of an institution that its freedom would depend. There are circumstances, perhaps, in which the disappearance of freedom might be the appearance merely of some new and charming form of communal harmony such as is perhaps enjoyed by people in some other civilizations. Yet it can hardly be said that Westerners, who are free, are also more courageous than other peoples, since courage is, I presume, reasonably widely distributed over the human race; whereas freedom, I have argued, is not at all so distributed. Hence, while I am convinced by the argument that freedom depends upon courage, I am also convinced that there must be some particular specification of courage which is relevant to freedom itself. But I lack the courage to push on with this difficult question, and plead time's winged chariot as my excuse for pressing on, at last, to giving you some direct indication of what I think the skill of freedom actually is.

VIII

We may define the condition of freedom as: the skill of generating, sustaining and keeping in repair appropriate rules for the game of life. Like most philosophical definitions, it is severely formal, and every phrase needs to be glossed.

What, in the first place, is meant by the 'game of life'? I have already sketched out an argument connecting freedom with a ludic view of life,[13] and here I need merely point to the centrality of this attitude in sustaining our institutions. Modern politics came into existence between the seventeenth and the nineteenth centuries as the result of a process in which political rivalry ceased to be dominated by a deadly purposiveness, and turned into the game of government and opposition. A criminal trial is a kind of game played out according to fixed rules which attempt to balance the claims of the prosecution and the defence. Much entrepreneurship in the field of production is seen in competitive terms. In the culture in which we live, as among the Stoics, life is frequently grasped in terms of the

---

[13] Cf. *Homo Ludous* by J. Huizinga.

metaphor of games. Now in all these cases the emergence of a gaming structure may be seen as a response to a felt uncertainty. We can never be *certain* that such and such a political policy is the right one; and hence we turn the process of selecting policies into a game. We can never be sure of the guilt of an accused, and hence we give him the chance of a fair trial: the accused does not even have to score himself in order to win: he merely has to prevent his opponent from scoring. What is being institutionalized in the emergence of the game of life is a range of dispositions which characterize the civilization we have developed: a sceptical view about what we believe, and a taste for spirited behaviour.

Next, let us consider what is meant by the three activities with which my formula began: generating, sustaining and keeping in repair. By *generating*, I mean being able to bring a condition of freedom into existence in the first place; and although this in itself is not entirely necessary (since the condition of freedom may be learned from an imperial power) it is much easier to sustain freedom if men have the initial capacity to generate it. The colonists in the American states are here an object lesson in freedom, since, if we exclude a number of hiccups arising from passions relating to such matters as witchcraft and anarchism, Americans have always been self-conscious and creative exponents of what I have called the condition of freedom. And this example helps me to explain what is meant by *sustaining*. The most obvious kind of failure to sustain a condition of freedom is a civil war, in which the game is abandoned in favour of a desperate scramble for objects of policy. There are also the sorts of occasion which historians have recently been calling 'great fears' (such as the episode of Titus Oates in seventeenth-century England) in which the game of life is obliterated by the passionate certainties of dominant groups. Sustaining the game of life depends in the first place on a recognition that we have inherited something valuable; and hence it is usually threatened by intellectual fashions which denigrate our culture and civilization as a whole. Nor is it merely recognition of what freedom entails that is at stake. Freedom evidently depends upon people being prepared to make sacrifices for it, and John Hampden's rejection of Ship Money is enshrined in English legend as an example of such desirable commitment. And this example further reminds us that the sustaining of freedom depends not upon the motives of the defender (which are usually obscure) but upon the issue, and the principle, to which he appeals.

The notion that these rules must not only be sustained but also *kept in good repair* may at first seem like an unnecessary qualification. But it is impossible to begin considering this question without becoming aware of how much and how continuous is the preoccupation, especially of lawyers, with this very question. A good example is the recent anxiety, especially among lawyers, about the way in which the press treatment of the arrest of a suspect in connection with the case of the 'Yorkshire Ripper' might be construed as prejudicing the possibility of a fair trial. (The possibility of the release of such a suspect on purely technical grounds does open up a fascinating moral abyss.) Another example is the provision, in the new Transport Bill before Parliament, by which officers are excluded from demanding a specimen of breath from drivers whom they suspect of having drunk too much alcohol 'while the constable is a trespasser in a place from which that person is entitled to exclude him'. The Chief Constable of Warwick has protested (in *The Times* of 14 January 1981) that such a rule excessively, and perhaps dangerously, favours the drunken driver.

It should be noted that the activity of keeping these rules in repair depends upon the presumption of a fundamentally patriotic population which understands what freedom is. One of the problems of civil liberties arises from the fact that fundamentally subversive people (such as terrorists) whose inclination is to destroy the game altogether will, when weak and defensive, appeal to the rules of the condition of freedom not because they care a fig for freedom, but because it gains them a temporary advantage. Thus both left-wing and right-wing subversives have recently been using the appeal of civil liberties, and the skill of liberty under these difficult conditions requires very delicate judgments about how far the rules can be adjusted without the game being destroyed entirely.

The question of what rules are *appropriate* is something of which very little can be said in a philosophical treatment of the subject. What one may say under this heading, however, is that different parts of the comunity have different roles to play in sustaining the rules of the game of life. As we have seen in our examples, lawyers and judges are clearly important, and politicians obviously vital. There is even some plausibility to the usually self-serving remarks made about the responsibility of the fourth estate; and similarly, sustaining academic freedom keeps alive a ludic attitude to ideas which facilitates the condition of freedom. But the more general point is that freedom depends upon certain quite widely distributed propensities among an élite of people in the community, and as long as these attitudes can be sustained, the more specialized requirements will follow. Most people, most of the time neither need, value, nor are particularly aware of living within a condition of freedom. They certainly benefit from it, but in irregular and intermittent ways.

Here, then, is a sketch of what I mean by freedom as a skill. Its philosophical interest, if it has any, lies in the attempt to integrate philosophical and popular accounts of freedom. It will be obvious that I have tried to transpose our understanding of freedom into a positive key; and I can only hope that I have managed to avoid the imputation, often made against some versions of the positive view of liberty, that it is in any way totalitarian.

Property, Liberty and *On Liberty*

ALAN RYAN

There are at least three tolerably distinct views about the connections between liberty and property; two of these I shall discuss fairly briefly in order to get on to Mill's central claims about the relationship between property rights and freedom, but in conclusion I shall return to them to show how they bear on what Mill has to say.

I

The first view is what I call the republican view. The claim is that the preferred system of property rights is essential to preserve political liberty. On the republican view *liberty* just is what republics possess, and republicans must espouse the system of property rights which best secures liberty. The thesis is as much sociological as philosophical, but it rests on some debatable conceptual foundations, the nature of which can be brought out by a little name dropping. Essentially, the sort of liberty in question requires us to deny Hobbes's famous claim that: 'There is written on the Turrets of the city of Luca in great characters at this day, the word Libertas; yet no man can thence inferre, that a particular man has more Libertie, or Immunitie from the service of the Commonwealth there, than in Constantinople. Whether a Commonwealth be Monarchicall or Popular, the Freedome is still the same.'[1]

Hobbes's claim is denied by all republican writers. Popular government is free government, and various sorts of constitutional republic are free governments, but tyranny is a great deal more than monarchy misliked.[2] In Machiavelli's *Discorsi*, which are the locus classicus of reflections on the maintenance of republican freedom, property and liberty are linked through an argument both moral and sociological in intent. A free state is doubly autonomous; it is governed by its own laws, and those laws are imposed upon themselves by those who are subject to them. Freedom is, in this context, a status word. The crucial status is that of being a person whose word can bind himself for the future. It is not only a matter of not being subject to the will of another, important though that is; it is a matter of having the positive capacity to bind oneself. The slave is paradigmatically unfree, since he cannot bind himself by his own words and

---

[1] Thomas Hobbes, *Leviathan* (London: Dent, 1914), 113.
[2] Hobbes, *Leviathan*, 97.

acts—I mean, of course, in theory and at the narrowest ideological level; in Roman practice there were even slaves who owned slaves.

On this view Hobbes's observation that there may be more immunity from the service of the commonwealth in a monarchy than in a popular republic is true but beside the point. Citizens can bind themselves very stringently, but they do not thereby lose their status as free men, seeing that their obligations are ones they have freely imposed upon themselves.[3] There are, however, many things which will damage the freedom aimed at in a free polity. From our present point of view, the most important of these are those social and economic developments which encourage people to prefer their own economic self-interest to the exercise of the duties which free men are called on to fulfil, those conditions (much the same, as it happens) which encourage the wrong sort of class conflict and internal dissension, and those conditions (again much the same) which make some men the servants of others and therefore not independent citizens. Machiavelli and after him Rousseau tell us to aim at no greater prosperity than the limited amount necessary to provide men with the leisure to contemplate public issues.[4] We do not want *abject* poverty, for no great things can be achieved by men whose whole life is a struggle for survival; but we ought to keep our economic activities at the level which energetic men would achieve in difficult but not hopeless conditions—for this provides a training in the frugality, self-discipline and forethought necessary to free governments.[5]

We should discourage conspicuous consumption, since it is simply intended to irritate others by flaunting the signs of superior fortune. It is not that class conflict is necessarily ruinous; Machiavelli approves of class conflict up to a point, on the grounds that only those who stand up for themselves *whenever* their rights are challenged will be able to maintain the state against subversion from within and without, as well as on the grounds that the balance of forces necessary if the state is to be constitutional rather than tyrannical requires the different social classes to stand up for their interests.[6] What Machiavelli anyway was attacking was the behaviour of those he calls 'gentiluomini'—the petty nobility whose behaviour displays a standing intention to reduce the state to their own plaything. It isn't on for a Florentine gentleman to build a castle in the countryside and fill it with his retainers, since that is not a case of doing as he pleases with his own, so much as equipping himself to do down everyone else. The point extends

---

[3] Jean-Jacques Rousseau, *The Social Contract and Discourses* (London: Dent, 1973), 178.

[4] Niccolo Machiavelli, *The Discourses* (Harmondsworth: Penguin Books 1970). 102–104.

[5] Machiavelli, *Discourses*, 104.

[6] Machiavelli, *Discourses*, 113.

beyond the obvious cases where what is being purchased is a private army, to any expenditure with the same subversive effects.

This line of thought denies that there is a sacrifice of *liberty* if some sorts of economic activity are forbidden for the sake of republican virtue. We cannot infer from the fact that something is a man's property that he is therefore at liberty to do what he likes with it, and read arguments about stopping him doing what he likes as arguments about the terms on which *his* liberty is to be traded against other values. That is certainly the standard modern view, but it is not the republican view. Nor, however, can we say that on the republican view property is not a matter of liberty *at all*— which is, in effect, Bentham's view. On the republican view, a man has to have property to be a free man at all; if he is dependent on another for his bread and butter he will be dependent on him in politics too. This is not a view which only appears in Machiavelli and in Rousseau's avowedly nostalgic and Machiavellian reflections on the loss of republican liberty. It occurs in Kant's argument for distinguishing between what he terms 'active' and 'passive' citizens, those who ought and those who ought not to have the vote.[7]

Indeed, Kant's exploitation of some antique as well as some decidedly modern worries about the connection between liberty and property is worth noticing in a little more detail. This provides a transition to the second conception of liberty I am concerned with; it also suggests that Hobbes exaggerated in claiming that the republicans' arguments came from reading Aristotle and Cicero and getting muddled about what 'liberty' *means*. Kant also provides a distinctively liberal view of the connection between property and political liberty which challenges Professor Dworkin's recent attempt to dissociate them in his little essay on 'Liberalism'.[8] For Kant tries to show that the existence of property is essential to reconcile the legitimacy of coercive positive law with our inalienable moral liberty and to provide the basis of civil liberty within a republican constitution.

We are conceived to belong to a civil association in accordance with an ideal social contract which allows each of us to coerce others from coercing us, on condition that our inner moral freedom is not a possible object of coercion.[9] To implement such a contract, possession of things and actions 'as external' is essential. The way in which a promise binds me to performance but not to the adoption of any particular attitude towards the performance illustrates the point. If I promise to read a paper to a meeting, what others get is a right to the paper, but they can have no right that I

[7] H. Reiss (ed.), *Kant's Political Writings* (Cambridge University Press, 1970), 139–140.
[8] Ronald Dworkin, 'Liberalism' in *Public and Private Morality* Stuart Hampshire (ed.) (Cambridge University Press, 1978), 113–143.
[9] Reiss, *Kant's Political Writings*, 132–134.

should enjoy giving it, or that I give it out of a sense of duty or whatever. Indeed, to demand that I not merely do it, but like doing it, is what Kant calls the worst form of tyranny, that of wanting other people to be happy in accordance with *our* conception of their happiness. To demand anything of the sort is to treat others as means to our ends, and to violate their independence.[10]

Property is simply the general name for handling rights to external things in a way that preserves order without violating moral freedom. To put the point in a way that challenges Professor Dworkin's separation of property and liberty rather more directly, Kant's claim is that it is only by locating control over things in independent individual sources (and by establishing a distinction between the internal and the external which allows some behaviour and some characteristics to become 'thing-like') that equal liberty for each person can be maintained within a juridical framework. This characteristically Kantian claim is closely related to Dworkin's insistence that the liberal state is obliged to give every lifeplan equal respect, but it denies his belief that the granting of equal respect can be divorced from the defence of the rights of private property. (I ought to say that I do not mean that Kant's argument is an obviously and incontrovertibly valid argument for private property as ordinarily understood, but it is certainly tenderer to contractual agreements and less tender to equal outcomes than Professor Dworkin's essay appears to be.) Negatively, too, Kant's argument is a *prima facie* case against the collective allocation of resources, though in saying this it is well to acknowledge that Kant is far from denying that the state may create public bodies with limited proprietorial rights of their own;[11] what is quite clear, however, is that Kant lets in collective ownership only as a means to fostering the values of individual choice and mutual independence, and therefore only interstitially.

The Kantian twist to the familiar republican argument about the need for some property of one's own to secure one's political liberty is now evident. Morally, arm's length dealing between persons related through their property allows co-ordination without subordination; politically, the man who can live off his own resources is practised in making up his own mind and binding himself for the future through present agreements; he has in addition a place or vantage point from which to see the political system and from which to contribute his conception of what the public good demands. Being able to do that is what is needed for citizenship or political liberty. Kant's complaints against feudalism and its restrictions on the ready sale of land are an argument about freedom rather than prosperity. He does not argue that opportunities for welfare go begging, but that with fewer owners the state contains fewer citizens. I shall soon suggest that

[10] Reiss, *Kant's Political Writings*, 79–80.
[11] Reiss, *Kant's Political Writings*, 148.

Mill's discussion of liberty and property mostly sticks within something like the utilitarian framework offered in Bentham's *Constitutional Code*, but I think it is worth recalling already that one ground in Mill's defence of co-operation against both state socialism and conventional capitalism is the claim that self-government is a central element of liberty and that producer co-operatives are, evidently, self-governing.[12]

II

However, it is time to turn to our second conception of liberty, commonly associated with Hegel, and perhaps best described as self-development—or self-determination, with the overtly political aspects of self-determination played down somewhat. On this view, the connection between liberty and property seems to be this: freedom is self-determination; determination by something external is a matter of restriction and limitation, but self-determination is a matter of filling out and making explicit what we already implicitly are. So, granted Hegel's initial claim that the essence of humanity is freedom, and that only rational beings can be both free and determinate—that is, that they are not merely unfinished and incomplete, but ready to become rational and human—the question is, what does this imply for the existence of rights to private property. The first thing to see is that it evidently does not generate what Honoré terms the 'liberal conception' of individual ownership.[13] That it does not is evident thrice over; Hegel himself disavows the intention to derive it when he denounces the extreme liberty of testamentary disposition permitted by English law—a man may disappoint his family and give everything to a dogs' home, behaviour which Hegel treats as mere arbitrariness rather than the exercise of freedom. Aside from Hegel's own employment of the argument, Marx seems not to have misunderstood Hegel when he took over Hegel's premises about the importance of externally expressing our freedom in the control and use of mere things in order to show that the existence of private property was inconsistent with that goal rather than being the essential means to achieving it.[14] Lastly, it is anyway a matter of some dispute to what extent Hegel's argument covers property rights in particular. For our purposes this does not matter; the important contrast is between Hegel's view that owning things is an element in freedom as self-expression and the republican view that property rights preserve political liberty on the one side

[12] J. S. Mill, *Principles of Political Economy* (Harmondsworth: Penguin Books, 1970), 133–140.
[13] A. M. Honoré, 'Ownership' in *Oxford Essays in Jurisprudence*, A. G. Guest (ed.) (Oxford University Press, 1961), 108ff.
[14] Karl Marx, *Early Writings* (Harmondsworth: Penguin Books, 1975), 324.

and the modern view that the essential argument is between liberty, construed as liberty-to-do-as-you-like-with-your-own, and equality on the other.

On Hegel's view, claiming to own something is calling on other persons to recognize a relationship between yourself and an external thing, where it is your will and your purposes which endow the external thing with its 'soul' and its value. (These are Hegel's terms.) The thought seems to be this. Freedom involves choice, choice involves making the world come to be this way rather than that, and this involves sovereignty over mere things. There is no real question whether we *may* own things; the only questions are what might defeat our claim of ownership and how far our sovereignty over things extends. This, incidentally, seems to be the right way to deal with the odd questions which Nozick raises in his discussion of the Lockean theory of appropriation. The reason why 'mixing our labour' does not work on the analogy of the tiny drops of radioactive tomato soup dispersed throughout the Atlantic is that the theory of appropriation is properly about control and not contamination. Even Locke refers to God's command to *subdue* the earth, and Hegel's account is even more straight-forwardly one which is geared to showing how we get legitimate authority over mere things. Things themselves cannot acknowledge our authority, but authority requires acknowledgment so we have a non-consented authority over things agreed to by other persons.[15]

Hegel turns the question of how we get rights over things inside out. The question is not so much how can I make a thing *mine*, as if it failed to be mine unless I make out a specially good claim to it, but, *given* that I claim it as mine, what defeats that claim? The onus lies on those who would stop me treating it as mine, for, given that I am a person and therefore capable of subduing something to my ownership at all, the fact that I treat an otherwise unowned thing as mine is no more contestable than the fact that when I raise my arm I beg the question whether I have the right to raise my arm. Of course, much *can* defeat the claim—the proximity of your nose may be exactly what defeats my right to swing my arm; *I* may be disqualified from making a successful claim, either because of my age or status or because I have contracted away my rights in advance; the *extent* of the right I get may be questioned, especially if I may be able to take advantage of a monopoly or some such things; and, crucially, ownership depends on my being a member of a juridical community which can recognize my intentions and see them as requiring respect. The point to insist on is that Hegel's is a doctrine about the relation between my free will and inert stuff on the one hand, and about the relation between the free wills of all of us on the other. To show that any precise conclusions about

[15] G. W. F. Hegel, *The Philosophy of Right* (Oxford University Press, 1942), 45.

particular institutional forms can be got from such general considerations seems an appallingly difficult task.[16]

I want to extract three small implications from the argument. The first is that ownership and freedom are mutually implicated; what Hegel's argument does is pick up Roman law conceptions of ownership and legal personality and detach them from such unlovely Roman ideas as that of the *patria potestas*, and such unlovely institutions as that of slavery. Hegel's doctrine is essentially modern in insisting that everyone can be a person, and it is modern in separating out relations between, say, husband and wife or employee and employer from proprietorial relations. But it hangs on to the claim that being the locus of control of external things, an important element of which is ownership in the usual sense, is an indispensable part of being free.

Secondly, the credibility of some of this is not much assisted by the way in which the conception of ownership involved is allowed to be so flexible; at the point where, say, freedom of testamentary disposition is at issue, it is extremely hard to see whether we are being told that one's rights as an owner are being restricted, or whether we are being told that there is no restriction involved in not having one's caprices pandered to by the legal system, and that what a cruder view would think of as restriction a maturer view would see as something more like the provision of an appropriate framework for people who want to be parents in a wholehearted fashion.

Thirdly, one can see why Marx's rage against the entire argument is so intense. Hegel deduces the rights of owners from the idea that law must be understood as the rules which free agents employ to guide their lives together; but Marx thinks that the capitalist economy is necessarily one in which they are neither free nor rational, because the way property is employed is dictated by the market, not by associated individuals at all. A utilitarian sympathetic to Marx would cheerfully misread him and think that the problem was one about co-ordination and the provision of public goods; but Marx was a good Hegelian, and he thought it was a problem about liberty. Hegel offered to show how the right to own property made persons persons, and how the institutions of private ownership expressed the control of mind over matter, of reason over irrational stuff. The offer was fraudulent, for under private property persons were treated as things, and sacrificed to things, and controlled by things. *Le mort saisit le vif* is what Marx says about capitalism, which is not a remark that any utilitarian is likely to make, but is one which someone attached to this self-expressive conception of freedom is likely to make.[17]

[16] Hegel, *Philosophy of Right*, 146–152.
[17] Karl Marx, *Grundrisse* (Harmondsworth: Penguin Books, 1973), 461.

III

Finally, then, to what I call the standard modern view and Mill's awkward relationship to it. The standard view is that if there is property, either in oneself or in external things, a conflict can be expected between liberty and equality for the following reason. To own something must involve, among other things, being free to dispose of it as one chooses; the person who is for the sake of equality made to dispose of what is his in some fashion that he does not choose is the victim of coercion, and has suffered a loss of liberty. Mill, I think, would have had nothing to say against that claim; although his relationship to Bentham on the analysis of rights is extremely complicated, it is evident that *one* aspect of a right is that the possessor of the right may employ his natural abilities as he chooses in a way nobody else may. (That is, if I own a piece of land, I can do to it those things I am naturally able to do, like digging it or walking on it, whereas other people may not do so.) Commonly, writers who insist that there will be a conflict between liberty and equality in the sense suggested think this is a matter of a simple loss of liberty on the one hand and a gain in (say) equality or welfare or whatever on the other. I do not think Mill would have thought this, but I will first make out the case for supposing he should have.

Suppose I am ill and you own the drug that can cure me; you will not sell it to me at a price I can pay. Your loss in welfare from being made to part with the drug will be less than my gain from receiving it, so there is a *prima facie* argument from welfare for your being made to part with it; it is also evident that our fates are made more nearly equal in welfare terms by the enforced transfer. We don't seem inclined to think that my *liberty* is limited by your ownership of the drug, even if my welfare is threatened by it, or at any rate is less than it might otherwise be. There are two ways at least of glossing the thought that my liberty is not affected; in the first place I am *at liberty* to find a seller at a lower price if I can do so, I am *not forbidden* to find a seller at a lower price as I would be if there was a law against my doing so, or you had threatened me with dire penalties for doing so; in the second place, I am *not disqualified* from buying it at the going rate —it is not like my trying to make a valid marriage while still firmly married already, and it is not like the pre-revolutionary bourgeois unable to purchase land without a patent of nobility. Since I have every right to obtain the drug if I can, my liberty is untouched. This does not settle the question of whether you should be made to sell; but it does seem to explain why people should think that the conflict is evidently between liberty on the one side and some other value on the other.

But this really only serves to begin the argument. For we can ask whether it is so clear that your property right is no infringement of my liberty; and an answer which would have clearly commended itself to Mill and which has been recently popularized by G. A. Cohen is that your property rights certainly are a curtailment of my liberty.[18] This reply in turn raises another question, and that is, whether there is some set of rights over things which creates as much liberty as possible. To see how Mill answers that question involves a detour through *On Liberty*, but the answer seems to be that there is some reason to suppose that Mill's more-or-less socialist leanings rest on two claims, one that property rights are not defensible as dictates of liberty in the context of the arguments against coercion except in self-defence (which is one branch of the discussion of liberty in *On Liberty*), the other that the choice-enlarging, rationality-increasing and individuality-promoting arguments (which form the other branch of the discussion of liberty in *On Liberty*) very much bear on the question of what property rights to recognize.

The proposition that A's ownership of x limits the liberty of everyone else rests on the simple observation that if A has rights over x, everyone else has duties of forbearance in respect of x. On Bentham's account of it, indeed, the implication runs the other way; what it is for A to own x is explained in terms of the prohibitions addressed to everyone other than A. Everyone else must ask A's permission before using x as he or she otherwise would be able to; that is, other people are not free to act in the ways A is. If the drug had come into the world unowned and there for the taking, I should have been free to take it; the difference made by your ownership is precisely that I am not. The point is impossible to resist; certainly Sidgwick, for one, treated the legitimacy of property as a question about the grounds for allowing the appropriations or would-be appropriations of the first occupier to limit the freedom of everyone else, and it is evident that this is how Mill treats the case too.[19]

The only way in which Mill would have understood the claim that the non-recognition of property in something was an infringement of someone's liberty is as the claim that each person could acquire a *natural property right* in what he appropriated; that there was no such right he took for granted. What one might argue, purely on the basis of the doctrine of *On Liberty*, would be a thinner case on behalf of the first occupier. *If* someone uses an object or a piece of ground or whatever it is, we may not stop him or her doing so unless their doing so harms us. The claim made in *On Liberty* that the sole ground on which we are warranted in interfering with the liberty of one of our number is self-defence gives us a reason for not disturbing the harmless enjoyments of others. This, however, does not in Mill's eyes amount to recognizing property rights, for it does not amount to conferring on the occupier the conventional powers of disposal and the like which are central to property in the usual sense. That is, if you,

---

[18] G. A. Cohen, 'Robert Nozick and Wilt Chamberlain: How Patterns Preserve Liberty', *Erkenntnis* **11** (1977), 5–23.

[19] H. Sidgwick, *The Elements of Politics* (London: Macmillan, 1891), 66–70.

occupying a piece of land harmlessly to others, admit someone else to share it with you, what licenses your so doing is not that it is *your* land, but only that what you and they agree together is agreed voluntarily and harms no one else. If the situation changes, as it might from entirely natural reasons, you have no property rights to put into the scale against our arguments from self-defence. If you build a dam and cut off our water supply, we can demolish it in self-defence; harmless occupation is all you can argue for and if your occupation is now harmful, that is the end of it.

There is a thought, on which Nozick trades, to the effect that the argument I ascribed to Mill, Sidgwick and Cohen runs foul of the fact that if it were not for the existence of property rights much of what we are forbidden to use without the owner's permission would simply not exist at all. We therefore should not compare the situation in which x exists and I am not free to use it with that in which x exists and I am free, but with that in which but for the existence of rules of ownership x would not be there at all. Mill himself uses a version of this argument to back up his view that the only rights of ownership which come close to being sacrosanct are the rights of workers to the fruits of their labour—without their labour the fruits would not exist, so it seems proper that the creators should determine how they are used.[20] In fact, it is not an impressive consideration; it is what Bentham termed a grandmother egg-sucking instruction. Any forward-looking, utilitarian account of why we should *invent* property rights is bound to rely very heavily on precisely this argument. The utilitarian sets out to explain why we should restrict some freedom of action, in order to preserve other freedoms and create affluence and security. The argument lends no support to the idea that there is property by natural right.

One temptation to think that there must be seems to stem from the idea that if things, and especially people's abilities, bodies and the rest, do not belong to them, they must belong to somebody or everybody else. Nozick, again, seems to rely on this to make us accept that either Wilt Chamberlain owns Wilt Chamberlain and his abilities, and owns them outright, or else other people have partial ownership of him and have him as a partial slave. One can see why this seems plausible: the person who decides what Wilt Chamberlain does is he himself; the actions he performs are *his* actions, the abilities he uses are *his* abilities. The reply to this, though, is familiar enough. The sense in which his actions are his has nothing to do with ownership; it is the sense in which his headaches are his, and there is no compelling reason for assimilating this to proprietorship.[21]

This does not mean that *making* Wilt Chamberlain play basketball other than in ways he chooses is not forced labour; since he has *de facto* control

[20] Mill, *Principles of Political Economy*, 359.
[21] J. P. Day, 'Locke on Property', *Philosophical Quarterly*, **16** (1966), 207–221.

over his own body, what we don't achieve by way of inducement and bamboozlement we shall have to achieve by force. It does not follow that letting him play for whom he likes and then taxing the proceeds is also forced labour, even though it is true enough that the taxes he pays are an enforced contribution to the social order.[22] All that Mill-like considerations about non-coercion imply is that we may not stop him playing basketball; the terms on which society establishes a currency, enforces contracts and the rest are matters for utilitarian calculation. Nor do we have to assert property rights in him and his actions to justify taxing his earnings. Of course, if you begin with an essentially proprietorial view, as Nozick does, and make the only legitimate route from freehold in ourselves to obligations to others a contractual route, then it is true that if we have claims at all they must rest on partial proprietorship—due acknowledgment then being made for whatever moral analogies exist to the distinctions made by lawyers between contract- and property-based claims. But, it is unnecessary to start from self-ownership to defeat the horrors that Nozick threatens us with if we should succumb to utilitarianism; that the terms of social co-operation should exclude such practices as sacrificing people in order to use their organs in transplant surgery seems more readily explicable in terms of how we feel about life and death, accidents and deliberate killing, our bodies and things other than our bodies. That it is my *kidneys* you are requisitioning is more to the point than that they are *my*, not your, kidneys.

Having suggested that Mill's response to the thought that people have a natural right in their property would have been to deny that they had any such thing, and that his 'non-coercion' principle would generate only limited rights based on *de facto* control and possession, I will end by raising the question of whether there is some further way in which property rights and freedom are connected. It seems plausible to suppose that there must be, and that one might even try to show that some more egalitarian system of 'rights to use' at any rate would increase liberty. I begin with recent attempts to show this, but then I recur to Mill, partly because I think that unless we have a fairly elaborate account of liberty-as-self-government such as he offers the attempt fizzles out rather boringly.

Starting where Cohen starts, with Wilt Chamberlain, it seems that if we agree that Wilt Chamberlain's rights over the use of his abilities restrict our freedom to use those abilities, we must also agree that it is an open question whether some other system of rights than that which gives him absolute control over his actions would result in an increase in freedom on the whole. But to do anything exact with the thought is hard for the following reason. We need, but do not have, a measure of how much freedom a given allocation of rights restricts. Suppose we agree that giving *me* the right to

[22] Robert Nozick, *Anarchy, State and Utopia* (Oxford: Basil Blackwell, 1974), 161–164.

decide who gets to use my kidneys leaves me free to allocate them as I like, but means that no one else is thus free. Suppose, again, that one of you very much needs the kidney I can donate without killing myself, and that since it is life and death for you, but only some discomfort for me, your gain from my parting with it will be very much greater than my loss. We may say that before the transfer the allocation of kidneys is sub-optimal; but would there have been more freedom if you had had a *right* to one of my kidneys in virtue of your needs?

It seems to me intuitively implausible to say so, unless we follow Professor Feinberg in analysing freedom in terms of obstacles to getting/doing what we want.[23] If we do that, then the kidney being ungettatably in my body is a negative external restraint on your getting what you want. But that seems to me to be more nearly an argument against Feinberg's way of analysing freedom than an argument for the desired conclusion. For, aside from anything else, it comes very close to collapsing questions of liberty into questions of subjective welfare, and to making maximal want-satisfaction the very same thing as maximal liberty.

Yet, there certainly are cases where we seem tolerably clear that we can compare two distributions of property rights and say that one offered more freedom than the other. The simple case is that of the enclosure of common land. Before the common is enclosed everyone is free, that is at liberty, to pasture his cattle on the common, collect wood and so on; this includes the man who is the sole owner now. All were formerly not free to enter into individual contracts to sell any part of it including the whole. Now the commoners have ceased to be free to do the things they were formerly free to do; they have certainly lost a freedom or a set of freedoms, and they have gained no freedoms in exchange. The new sole owner has one freedom that nobody had before, the freedom to sell the property and to create lesser interests in it.[24] That is what it is to turn the common into private property. I incline, though hesitantly, to say that here there has been a net loss of liberty—lots of people face new prohibitions, and one person is either exempt from one old prohibition or has got a new power. I say this hesitantly, since I am not sure how one would defend this claim against someone who said that the gains and losses were incommensurable, or against someone who held that for whatever reason there could not be a net increase or decrease in liberty. Someone who insisted on decomposing the prohibitions might argue that in the old days the combined peasantry were free to graze 200 cows on the common, and so is the new owner, so that the number of unprohibited actions remains the same.

[23] Joel Feinberg, *Social Philosophy* (Englewood Cliffs: Prentice-Hall, 1973), 12–13.

[24] Cheyney C. Ryan, 'Yours, Mine, and Ours: Property Rights and Individual Liberty', *Ethics* **87** (1977), 126–141.

The feeling that the creation of private property rights can reduce liberty has affected even Nozick; this emerges in his discussion of Fourier's claim that the landless deserved compensation for their lost freedom to hunt and gather over the territory which had subsequently been turned into farmland.[25] Nozick explains, uncharacteristically, that the landless cannot really complain since they are much better off than they would have been if hunting and gathering had continued. This will not do, though, for it relies on essentially utilitarian considerations—exactly the ones that Bentham appealed to. What Nozick is officially committed to showing is that there is no freedom which has been lost by the appropriations of our forebears, or, rather that there is no right which the landless have which their predecessors' behaviour has violated. What he actually shows is that they have been given compensation for their lost liberty, not that there isn't a (real) liberty that has been lost.

Thus far I have deliberately left the notion of liberty employed here as undefined as possible, partly because it seems evidently true that questions about the extent to which a system of property rights maximizes liberty depend very heavily on what conception of liberty we want to work with. This is one reason why I did not try very hard to see how far we could get with the notion of liberty as 'unobstructedness' which Cohen and Feinberg rely on. Another is that I want to sketch Mill's treatment of the issue, which does rest on a particular conception of liberty.

I have already said that non-coercion is relevant in providing a basis for, among other things, a right to harmless occupancy and the right to act as one chooses subject to not damaging the interests of others. But *On Liberty* and Mill's economic writings employ a richer notion of liberty than that. In particular, they rely on such ideas as that a man is not free unless his way of life is one he has chosen for himself in some consciousness of competing alternatives, and that a man is not free unless he has the sort of character which allows him to pursue plans even in the face of distraction and temptation. If this is a doctrine of positive liberty, Mill is a positive libertarian. Now, given this, we can see that although the existence of property rights is not a direct deduction from natural right, freedom is relevant to the question of whether a system of property rights is a good one. It is no infringement of liberty for a society to set up whatever system of property rights seems good to it, but it would be a mistake to stop the argument there. The whole point of *On Liberty* is to argue that a properly understood utilitarianism will make liberty in a sense which is not exhausted by non-coercion the central test of policy.

Thus read, Mill's main complaints against capitalism are libertarian ones. The relationship between employer and employee is objectionable because it deprives the employee of the chance of self-government and

[25] Nozick, *Anarchy, State and Utopia*, 178n.

teaches him none of the virtues of self-discipline, far-sightedness and loyalty which free men need. The question of profit and exploitation is incidental to this argument, but the question of how a firm is managed is not; Mill contrived to get things as wrong as he ever did in predicting that with the growth of self-government generally the working class would soon refuse to work for employers who did not associate them in the management of the enterprise and only the worst class of workman would be found in traditionally managed and owned firms.[26] Mill does not go into details about the sort of property rights which would best encourage the growth of co-operatives; on all such issues he professes a sort of virtuous agnosticism: since the workers themselves have the greatest interest in how things are to be run, we can wait for them to decide. All the same, the argument is predicated on a thorough anti-paternalism and a view of liberty which has obvious affinities with both what I called the republican view and what I called the self-determination or self-development view.

This being so, I will try to tie up two loose ends and finish. It is, of course, true that if there were to be a change in the law, people would be compelled to do things with their property that they would not otherwise choose to do—like placing it in a trust or whatever. Mill does not think that this raises a serious question of liberty; since the existing right is the gift of society, society may withdraw the gift. What is at issue, if liberty is not, is justice; although it may be true that an existing set of legal rights ought not to exist, the current holders of those rights are not to be blamed for their existence and ought not to suffer loss—a point Mill makes in the most obvious context of all, that of the owners of slaves. Slavery is plainly an offence against liberty, but existing slaveowners did not invent the institution and if they lose their property they ought to be paid off for the loss. There are more and less strenuous ways of changing institutions, and in that sense liberty may be less injured by one way of altering them than by another, but since property rights do not rest on the general prohibition against coercion save for the sake of self-defence, they cannot be defended by reference to it.

This settles, too, a familiar problem. Mill seems to some commentators to break his own rules against paternalism by insisting that society should not enforce unbreakable contracts—in particular that society should not help somebody to sell himself into slavery. However, we can see that the would-be slave is free to exercise his natural ability to do whatever the person he nominates as his 'master' tells him to; so long as he does not harm anyone else by behaving in a slave-like fashion, we have no right to stop him doing so, even though we are encouraged by Mill to exhort and entreat him to do something different. But, for him to be a real slave there would have to be a system of property rights which allowed people to own other

[26] Mill, *Principles of Political Economy*, 129.

people, or which treated them as the owners of themselves and allowed them to sell themselves to another owner. There is no obligation on us to set up such a system, and plenty of reasons why we should not do so. The broad utilitarian reasons which justify setting up systems of legal rights which allow people to expand their range of choices are decisive against setting up slavery. What we do is decline to enforce facilities enabling him to limit his freedom with no hope of regaining it, and this is not paternalism. Indeed, it is just the sort of case which shows the subtlety of Mill's position, and which makes it necessary to approach his account of the connections between property and liberty in the rather roundabout fashion I have adopted.

Selective Index

Bantock, G. H., 112
Bereiter, C., 115n.
Berlin, I., 79, 131, 137

Carter, Rosemary, 152–153

Dearden, R. F., 126n.
Devlin, Lord, 11ff., 129
Dworkin, G., 110, 123, 154–156, 159, 220

Feinberg, J., 228
Flew, A. G. N., 61ff.

Galbraith, J. K., 47
Gibbs, B., 46ff.
Gierke, Otto von, 91ff., 97
Gentile, G., 131

Hart, H. L. A., 11, 148
Hegel, G. W. F., 201–202, 221–223
Hobbes, T., 3ff., 19, 114, 205–208, 217–218
Humboldt, W. von, 117–118
Hume, David, 58–59, 200
Huxley, Aldous, 45, 186

Johnson, Samuel, 131, 136

Kant, I., 188–189, 191–192, 196, 219–221

Lawrence, D. H., 186
Lenin, V. I., 46n.
Locke, J., 55n., 70, 112, 114, 222

Machiavelli, G., 218
Marx, K., 2ff., 132, 221–222
Mill, J. S., 5ff., 24, 27, 29, 31ff., 46, 102–103, 110–111, 117ff., 147ff., 158, 162–163, 167ff., 224ff., 229ff.

Neil, A. S., 128
Nietzsche, F. von, 140–141
Nozick, R., 227, 229

Peters, R. S., 127n.
Plato, 1ff.

Rousseau, J. J., 1, 115–116, 128, 198
Russell, B., 115

Sartorius, R. E., 160–161
Sartre, J. P., 144
Spencer, H., 114, 120
Spinoza, B. de, 17
Stephen, J. F., 12, 21
Stevenson, C. L., 45

Trotsky, L., 49n.
Taylor, C., 8off., 112, 134n.

White, J. P., 123–125

DATE LOAN